FIRE OVER THE WATERS

Fire Over The Waters

RENEWAL AMONG BAPTISTS AND OTHERS
FROM THE 1960S TO THE 1990S

Douglas McBain

DARTON · LONGMAN + TODD

First published in 1997 by
Darton, Longman and Todd Ltd
1 Spencer Court
140–142 Wandsworth High Street
London SW18 4JJ

ISBN 0–232–52192–1

A catalogue record for this book is available
from the British Library

Phototypeset by Intype London Ltd
Printed and bound in Great Britain by
Redwood Books, Trowbridge, Wiltshire

With grateful thanks
for
EUNICE LOIS CHAPPLE
8 JULY 1897–27 JUNE 1989
'For this reason I remind you to fan into the flame the gift of God that is in you.' (2 Timothy 1:6)

Contents

Preface

The story of the emergence of an unlikely looking renewal movement making progress among a denomination that was only reluctantly involved, with unexpected benefit to both, is the theme that I attempt to pursue in the following pages. As I do so, it becomes increasingly clear that all the blessings the renewal has brought have been of mixed worth, as I indicate in one special section. It is a mistake of the first magnitude to imagine otherwise. Yet for all the faults, the exaggerations, the follies, and the sinful distortions of the Gospel that have from time to time become a main characteristic of the renewal message, I stand by my own conviction that the Spirit of God is stirring in these activities in a renewing way for our common good.

There are good reasons for choosing the Baptists as a case history for the wider Church, apart from the fact that it is here that my own ministry has been exercised. We are strongly evangelical in our theology and are probably most at home among the more theologically conservative. We are characterised by our commitment to the study of the Scriptures and the promotion of biblical convictions. Since evangelicalism is the growth point in the wider Church, Baptists provide a good working model for the progress of renewal in this kind of churchmanship.

At the same time we have been active participants in the great contemporary adventure of ecumenical relationships. Hence, we represent an open-minded form of evangelicalism that is not afraid of a certain breadth of viewpoint in our own midst and in our wider relationships.

In Britain today we are also well aware of the development of many new Church streams. Baptists too belong to the same independent tradition that regards the essential nature of the Church as a fellowship of believers. Of all the mainstream denominations, the Baptists are most likely to understand where many of the new groups come from and where they want to go, since much of our own history is so similar. Hence, what has happened among the Baptists immediately reflects or anticipates similar developments in many other sections of the whole Church.

Since completing this text, I have come across Andrew Walker's latest work entitled *Telling the Story: Gospel Mission and Culture* (SPCK, London, 1996). Not only did I enjoy this book but I found that, quite independently, I had been led by a different route to the need for a renewal in our liturgy to accompany every other form of renewal for which I argue in my last chapter. We need to harness the power of what C.S. Lewis described as the baptised imagination, to meet the challenges posed by the post-modernism of which Walker writes so helpfully. As my readers will see, I believe that in most of its current expressions the renewal we know is small compared with the renewal we need.

I pay glad tribute to David Coffey, General Secretary to the Baptist Union of Great Britain, my friend and superior. He has been consistently supportive and helpful with this task, as with my regular duties as a General Superintendent. I am grateful to the Baptist Union for allowing me a sabbatical in 1994 to get the work started, and some extra study weeks to get it finished. Two of my colleagues, David Harper and Peter Tongeman, graciously undertook extra duties to cover these periods. The Metropolitan Area Pastoral Committee and the chairman, John Newby, were particularly supportive and I am grateful to them. The London Baptist Association was also immensely helpful, as ever so ably led by the secretary, my friend and colleague Peter Wortley. When energy flagged, many London ministers showed the kind of interest in my theme that persuaded me to get down to it again. I pay tribute to them and to my team of regional ministers who serve them and me with such dedication. None of this would have been possible without the support of Ian Randall, my supervisor, Tutor in Church History at Spurgeon's College. He is a fount of knowlege of the period about which I write. He is, moreover, an enthusiast for research, and I am deeply in his debt for his perceptive advice and counsel, and for his great gift of encouragement.

I express my gratitude to Christine, my wife, who is unfailing in her loyalty, support, and love, and whom, together with the family that continues to grow with the addition of beautiful granddaughters, wonderful grandsons and most recently a charming new daughter-in-law as the wife to Graham, I hold as the most precious part of my life next to the Saviour.

I dedicate this work to the memory of another truly remarkable woman of God, E. Lois Chapple, who died in 1989 in her ninety-second year. Lois was baptised in 1907 in Bessels Green, at the age of 10. In 1923 she went to China as a missionary with the Baptist Missionary Society, working in rural areas and teaching in a girls school. On her return home in 1940 she served the Baptist Union as the secretary for the Women's Department of those days with the Baptist Women's League. It was in 1968 that the Holy Spirit visited her in a renewing way. In all her subsequent years her humble, truthful, astute yet commonsense witness, as a member and deacon of an inner-suburban Baptist church in Lewin Road, Streatham, revealed what it means to be really renewed, fully charismatic and truly Christian. May we emulate Lois in our day with the balance of all these characteristics and with many spiritual gifts too. If this offering helps to that end, I shall be well satisfied.

Douglas McBain
Advent, 1996

Early Stirring

1

Roots by the Stream

(Jeremiah 17:8)

It is now a well-documented fact of British Church history that in the late 1950s and early 1960s a fresh movement began to make its presence felt throughout the United Kingdom, to become known as the charismatic movement. It arrived here as a migrant from California on the western coast of the USA, a part of the world renowned for the many extravagant forms of fundamentalist evangelical faith which flourish there. Few would have predicted the widespread effects of its arrival in Britain or even its survival in a religious climate so different from that of its home. Yet what began in Britain as a minority interest for a few, within a decade had become a matter of serious enquiry for many, before becoming the major characteristic for a large section of the evangelical and the wider Christian world.

As in California so also in the UK, this movement made its first appeal to members of several well-established historic denominations, mainly though never exclusively among conservative evangelicals. Soon another range of Churches from non-Pentecostal denominations was affected, and by 1967 it had broken out from Protestantism and was evidently to be seen as an active force among Roman Catholics too.[1]

Nor has the movement peaked and moved into inevitable decline. According to authoritative world Christian statisticians, it is expected that by the start of the third millennium it will have grown from its position in 1990 of holding the allegiance of 25 per cent of the world Christian population to a new all-time high of 30 per cent. Far from slackening off, the indications are that the rate of growth is still increasing, making it potentially an even stronger force everywhere in the world in the twenty-first century.[2]

It is not my intention to attempt to cover the whole of this remarkable story as it has unfolded so far. Rather, I am concentrating on what has happened among British Baptists, with whom it has been my privilege to serve for the whole of my ministry. I do so for more than personal reasons, which may be briefly summarised at this point. First, Baptists are more comprehensively evangelical in their theology today than most of the other denominations. To trace the story of renewal among them is to see the story through the experience of the evangelicals, commonly regarded as the most growing section of the whole Church. Second, they also have a restorationist history. The rise of the new Church streams is an important development in renewal. The Baptists provide a point of contact for other Churches, bewildered by a development for which Baptists have an instinctive sympathy and a wide experience. Incidentally, this explains why they have been vulnerable to more departures into restorationism than others. It is also the case that they have often provided a safe re-entry point for those wounded by the extremist tendencies of a few modern restorationists. Further, they have a long tradition for ecumenical involvement. From Thomas Helwys in 1612, through to William Carey, John Howard Shakespeare, Ernest Payne and David Russell, they have provided statesmen robustly committed to the awareness of the incompleteness of any Church which lacks meaningful fellowship with others. The story of renewal among Baptists is interwoven with the tensions of ecumenical debate. So what happened among them casts significant light on the struggle in which we are all involved in our common pilgrimage. For all their foibles I hope that this story can be seen as a case history for other Churches too. As we shall see, whatever our Church allegiance, the effects are likely to be with us all for a long time ahead.

Anglicans lead

It is generally true that most fresh initiatives in Britain come from the national Churches, not from the other denominations. Perhaps they doubt the worth of their numerically stronger colleagues, from a sense of inverted spiritual snobbery. Maybe they lack a sense of security about their own value. For whatever reason, it is to be observed that the renewal movement made its impact elsewhere first among the Anglicans. News of this was brought to the attention of the wider Church through the articles and testimonies to be found in the magazine *Trinity*. Its special interest was to report what was happening between American Episcopalians and members of other historic denominations, and to plead for the rightful place of the Spirit in the life of the Church.[3] This magazine soon found its way to Britain through a Methodist minister, Charles Clarke, and copies were avidly read from cover to cover. Then an English Anglican theologian, Philip Edgcumbe Hughes, who had gained the reputation of being a diehard Protestant, met the editor, Mrs Jean Stone, and through her encountered these developments in California for himself. His comments were published in the magazine *The Churchman*, where he first described them somewhat whimsically as 'a flirtation between Episcopalianism and the extravagancies of Pentecostalism under the hot Californian sun'. However, within weeks, he was prepared to make more serious observations:

> The serene joy, love and devotion which marked these gatherings made a profound impression on me. They adore their Lord and Saviour; they feed eagerly upon His Word; they seek in the power of the Holy Spirit to be his witnesses daily in their living, and they testify to the most remarkable answers to their prayers in the lives of others, in bodily healing and spiritual blessing. Dare we deny that this is a movement of God's Sovereign Spirit?

He concludes thus: 'The breath of the living God is stirring among the dry bones of the major respectable old-established denominations, and particularly within the Episcopalian Church.'[4] As we shall see, the first major home for this new movement was the well-known Anglican centre for evangelical ministry in London's West End, All Soul's, Langham Place. The rector was the Revd John Stott and it is the case that, although these developments were fostered by three of his staff, John Lefroy, Martin Peppiatt and Michael Harper, he never felt at ease with them.[5] The ministry of this church has always appealed to many who are not Anglicans, without this causing any sense of disloyalty to the Anglican evangelical tradition or any offensiveness to those who come from other traditions.

So from first beginnings, Baptist churches throughout the United Kingdom were among those that became involved, largely through their contacts with their friends who were evangelical Anglicans. In the course of the following three decades not only has the charismatic movement grown but, as I shall attempt to demonstrate, it has grown into a distinctive and influential element colouring a large section of the life of the Baptist denomination whether or not particular churches have been actively involved in it.

The statistics available from the church surveys in *Turning the Tide: An Assessment of Baptist Church Growth* by Paul Beasley-Murray and Alan Wilkinson, published earlier in 1981, then in *Christian England* by Peter Brierley on evidence collected in 1989 and published in 1991, support this judgment.[6] They also provide a clear reason, for it is the nature of Baptist churches to seek to grow by gaining more conversions. If they cannot attract and hold new members then inevitably, in time, their existence is in question. Both these reports show the strength of charismatic evangelicalism within the total denomination, and are supported by H. Leon McBeth in his magisterial survey of Baptist witness over four centuries in the United States, Britain, Western Europe and elsewhere, *The Baptist Heritage*. He comments:

> The extent of charismatic presence among English Baptists cannot be minimised. Few churches are unaffected: one association reported two-thirds of its churches caught up in the movement. Pastors and denominational leaders alike name this as one of the most serious issues facing English Baptists in the 1980s.[7]

The Churches have taken note of the findings of the reports, and the deductions which they have drawn have been that it is in their own interest to make sure that their Church is both evangelical and charismatic.

Lest this should be read as a plea for an unquestioning endorsement of all that has subsequently occurred under the renewal banner, we must enter some caveats at this point. As we shall go on to show, this is not to say that all the consequences of this renewal have been unmitigated blessings. The evidence that is available does not support such a conclusion. It is to propose that many aspects of the renewal have been of positive value, while some have been less helpful. A study such as this therefore calls for measured judgements in the light of all that we can discover of God's purpose for his Church. It is to be hoped that as we consider the issues, we shall think more carefully about church life in the future than we have in the past. To study renewal is an inspiring task, for there is much to spur us on. Yet it is my conviction that this ongoing story must be set into a wider background and to a broader agenda. For the sake of the Gospel which the whole Church must share and to which the whole Church is held accountable, the view that I shall advance is that the renewal we need is much bigger than the renewal we know so far.

What is this renewal?

Before we go any further, it will help us if we unpack the meaning of some of the terms used and the issues that are raised as a consequence. Though it is the impact of the charismatic movement that we are seeking to investigate, this is not as easy as it may seem. Among the first major denominations into the field seeking to understand renewal theologically was the Church of Scotland. They produced a report of the Panel on Doctrine in 1974[8] and in it declared that there is a legitimate place in the Church of Scotland for 'neo-Pentecostals', as charismatics were often described at this time. The report raised questions about a theology of subsequence in terms of a second blessing experience being necessary to empower the believer for service, as if the grace received at baptism or conversion was to be regarded as inadequate. They therefore raised questions on the use of the phrase 'baptism in the Spirit', though they did not question the legitimacy of the experience of those who testified to a renewal experience.[9] *Charismatic Renewal – a Baptist View* was published in 1980. This includes the report of a working party together with a commentary on it by Paul Fiddes. This shows the same attitude of respect for the testimony of those who had offered submissions and a similar unease over the terminology of baptism in the Spirit. At the same time, this working party discovered that there was no coherent interpre-

tation offered to the precise nature of the renewal encounter.
They had found the greatest help in this from the teaching of
T.A. Smail, the then director of the Fountain Trust, who
expressly rejected the Pentecostalist view of a necessary second
blessing. They expressed disappointment that there was no evidence for an enlivened approach to Church government
through the church meeting, but some signs of a fresh intolerance of the role of women in office in the Church.[10]

The next year the Church of England followed suit in identifying the difficulty of precise definitions in their report *The
Charismatic Movement in the Church of England*. However, few
would argue with its tentative suggestion that it is the overwhelming sense of the presence and power of a God not
previously known in such a combination of otherness and
immediacy that is the outstanding quality of renewal.[11] 'Fresh
encounter with God in our own experience' is the pithy
summary of one booklet on the subject by Bob Gordon. He
adds to that the dimensions of a fresh insight into the workings
of God's Spirit, a fresh understanding of the significance of
Jesus, and a fresh grasp of Christian hope.[12]

Perhaps the phrase that most aptly encapsulates the discovery
of the Spirit that renewal people are keen to share is in the
title of a mammoth compilation of no less than 104 official or
semi-official reports gathered by the Catholic theologian Kilian
McDonnell. It is *Presence, Power and Praise*.[13] In short, the
message of renewal by this brief definition is not to do with
tongues-speaking, second blessings, or demonstrations of
phenomena. Rather, it is to do with the recovery of both the
immanence of the Spirit of God with the people of God and
of his transcendence beyond them. It is about the application of
the vitality of the Spirit to every situation of need, by means
of God's gifts of grace. It is to do with the context of the
Spirit's activity in our worship which embraces the Father,
the Son and the Spirit in our corporate devotion, and our
willing service for him in the world he loves.

Spirit baptism

We should now reflect on the phrase which the renewal has
used for induction into the renewal experience. The term

which linked Charismatic Renewal with the historic Wesleyan Holiness movements of the eighteenth century and the Pentecostal movement is 'baptism in the Spirit'. It is a phrase capable of receiving numerous interpretations. In discussing the understanding of D. Martyn Lloyd Jones on this, Michael Eaton refers to no less than six.[14] For our purposes we may reduce that number to two. First, it has to be faced that, from the beginnings in the 1960s, the majority have accepted the Pentecostalist understanding that it is a further blessing for Christians to seek, to empower them for their service, and that it is often, if not always, accompanied by the evidence of the gift of speaking in tongues. I find that a theological defence of this is difficult to sustain. It is not what I believe to be the case, but the renewal of the 1960s largely inherited this view from Pentecostalism without dispute.[15] Second, some teachers in renewal have consistently rejected the notion of the theology of subsequence that suggests that this is a necessary second blessing for Christians who are otherwise incomplete without it. For them this term is understood experientially and aptly describes what the induction into the renewal seemed to be like – an encounter that felt like a baptism or soaking into the Spirit.[16] Instead of seeing this as a higher form of baptism, this is to be understood as a part of the constellation of blessings, including conversion and Christian baptism, that together mark our Christian beginnings. Seen in this light, Spirit baptism can be seen as the experiential confirmation of all that is sacramentally expressed in Christian baptism. It is not necessarily subsequent to either conversion or baptism, but is part of both. The natural place for this aspect of encounter with the Spirit would therefore be at their Christian baptism as a believer in Christ.[17] But it has to be admitted that the phrase in question has had a vexed history and that this has been a cause of much debate. Taking account of that, it is best understood to mean a definite act of receiving God's given Spirit, which is a part of the totality of Christian initiation. In that sense a less pejorative phrase like 'receiving the Spirit' would serve just as well.

Beyond the issue of what terms to use to describe initiation into the renewal experience, the first focal point for earnest enquiry became the gift of tongues.[18] If it was not this gift that was received, then the claim to a renewing experience was usually characterised by a new experience of other spiritual gifts that are listed in 1 Corinthians 12 such as prophecy or healing.

Such unexpected developments as these raise many questions for us today, and it is our intention to attempt to unravel some of the answers to them as they apply to Baptists and other evangelicals. Before we do that, there is still another basic question to be faced. How was it that a movement that so clearly linked with Pentecostalism both in its practice and also in its theology could take root and flourish in the way that it has among Baptists? To understand the background to these developments in earlier Pentecostalism, and then in the modern Pentecostal movement, only serves to make the answers more tantalising.

Earlier Pentecostalism

We need to recall that twentieth-century Pentecostalism itself was anticipated by a movement of the Spirit in the 1820s, associated with Edward Irving, that led to the formation of the Catholic Apostolic Church. There are no direct links between his work and Pentecostalism or charismatic renewal. Yet the theological links are profound and need to be repeated for that reason alone. His mortal remains lie in the crypt of Glasgow Cathedral yet it is apparent 'that he still refuses to lie down', and he has become posthumously recognised as the forerunner to the Pentecostal movements that have followed.[19] Irving arrived at his conclusions about the potential of the activity of the Holy Spirit not on the basis of the testimonies of others, but mainly through his own theological study of the nature of the humanity of Jesus. It was his view that Christ's real humanity was fallen humanity with the inherent tendency to sin within it, and that the innate tendency to sinfulness in him was only overcome in him by the presence and power of the Holy Spirit. Moreover, he perceived that not only was Christ sinless through the operation of the Holy Spirit in him, but he was also charismatically powerful and able to work many miracles. It was this discovery that led him to an openness to the baptism in the Spirit which he then proceeded to seek for himself, though without success. For if the Spirit could achieve such

wonders in the person of Jesus, may he not work in a similar
way with those who share the same fallen nature and receive
the same anointing? Not only was this to be attended by the
evidence of speaking in tongues, and gifts of prophecy and
healing, but it was also to be the cause for the setting up of a
new structure of Church leadership in which all the New
Testament orders of prophets, apostles and angels would have
their roles. The new Church with its fully restored orders of
ministry, including a fully functioning apostolate, would anticipate the imminent return of Christ, and it was prophesied that
this would occur within the lifetime of the Twelve whom they
had appointed.[20]

Irving had come to London from his native Scotland after
earlier ministry in the Church of Scotland as the assistant to
Thomas Chalmers of Edinburgh. He possessed great preaching
skills. Soon he was gathering the largest attendances in London
to listen to him at the Church of Scotland Caledonian Chapel
in Hatton Gardens. Fresh buildings at Regent Square had to
be constructed for the congregations. For a brief period he was
a London celebrity. Though he had a cast in one eye, so that
he was nicknamed Dr Squintum by one lampoonist, William
Hazlitt, Bentham, Coleridge, Canning, Lord Liverpool, Charles
Lamb, the young Macaulay and even the youthful Gladstone
paid visits to listen to him. Sadly, his fame was short-lived.
Charges of heresy were laid against him by the London Presby-
tery of the Church of Scotland, because of his views on the
peccability of Christ's humanity in which he was yet tri-
umphantly sinless. He was found guilty and was
excommunicated from the Church, and therefore turned to his
friends in the Albury group who met at Albury Park near
Guildford largely for the study of eschatology. Albury Park was
the home of a wealthy banker, Henry Drummond, and within
this circle he shared in the design for the structure for a new
Church order as we have already described it.[21]

The weaknesses of this development are obvious. By
believing too much in the inspiration of their own words, and
holding too lightly to the whole tenor of Scripture and the
experience of the Church, the Catholic apostolics marked out
a path that many charismatic groups have subsequently followed. The return did not accord with their timetable. They

have ceased to exist in this country and their influence has gone, though not before they had been responsible for the early nurture of at least one notable minister, Edwin Robertson, the minister of Heath Street Baptist Church, Hampstead. But their legacy to us is more than the gift of this prolific writer, preacher and pastor. It needed to jump several generations to get here, but theologians of the renewal now see their indebtedness to Irving not just because of his understanding of the human nature of Jesus, with its repercussions on our understanding of all the needs of our own, but also for his emphasis on the priority of doctrine over experience. It is striking to discover such powerful theological teaching from the ministry of Irving. Here is a fresh source of study for those who want to recover Irving's strengths without lapsing into the weaknesses by which alone his work has been too frequently remembered. Let him speak for himself on his understanding of the incarnation and the Trinity:

> My Christ is the Trinity manifested. . . . I have the Father manifest in everything which He doth: for He did not His own will, but the will of His Father. I have the Son manifested, in uniting His Divinity to a humanity prepared for Him by the Father. And in making the two contrary things to meet and kiss each other . . . I have the Holy Spirit manifested in subduing, restraining, conquering the evil propensities of the fallen manhood, and making it an apt organ for expressing the will of the Father.[22]

The modern Pentecostal movement

The Pentecostalism that emerged in 1900 began like the modern charismatic movement on the western side of the United States. In that year a group of students in a Bible college in Topeka, Kansas, laid hands on one another and prayed that the Holy Spirit might be given to them with the accompanying sign of speaking in tongues. Their leader was Charles Parham, a man from whom the emerging movement soon chose to distance itself. One of Parham's pupils was a black Baptist pastor, W.J. Seymour. He was invited to Los Angeles where he hired some old Methodist church buildings in Azusa Street for his revivalist meetings. In April 1906 remarkable times were known there. The meetings were accompanied by a wide variety of physical demonstrations to reveal a vivid awareness to the presence of God. Fallings, writhings, visions, shakings, tremblings, laughter and tears were all there. In addition, they had the great sign of the gift of tongues. What made it all the more remarkable was that black pastors were ministering to white pastors without any racial tension – in a day in which fixed racist attitudes would insist on their separateness and on white superiority, as the Anglican Alexander Boddy observed.[23] Boddy was the much-travelled vicar of All Saints, Monkwearmouth, Sunderland, and for his reports on his travels he was awarded membership of the Royal Geographic Society. He invited T.B. Barratt, the English-born pastor of the Methodist church in Oslo, to Monkwearmouth, because of his own investigations into the revival that was occurring in South Wales, knowing that Barratt had already been to Azusa Street and had become a strong advocate for its blessings. The plaque on the wall of the church hall commorates the results of Barratt's ministry:

September 1907
When the fire of the Lord fell
It burned up the debt

Pentecostalism, already stimulated by the Welsh revival of 1904 under the ministry of Evan Roberts, had truly arrived in the UK. Many believed that God had given them the blessed baptism in the Spirit with the confirming evidence of the gift of tongues, and soon began to share their testimony about this.

The power that fell at Pentecost
When in the upper room
Upon the watching waiting ones
The Holy Ghost had come.[24]

Higher life teaching in the Lakes

At the same time, a new movement had been gathering influence among evangelical Christians through the work of the Keswick Convention. The Keswick message was derived from the same American Holiness teachers who encouraged the notion of the second crisis experience of the Spirit subsequent to conversion which enabled believers to live a consistent

Christian life. For some Keswick teachers, this second blessing initiated a life of sinless perfection, but for most such a claim was repudiated. None the less, such discussions led on to a profound interest in the baptism in the Spirit. F.B. Meyer was a leading Baptist participant in the Keswick movement, and so was drawn to the teaching of a baptism in the Spirit which empowered for service but also sanctified from the power of inward sin. He was minister in Priory Street, York, from 1872 to 1874, and while he was there he met the evangelist D.L. Moody, then at the beginning of a two-year mission in Britain that was to lead to his lasting international fame. Moody included vivid testimony to the effects of a dramatic experience of baptism in the Spirit which deeply impressed Meyer. Later on, in 1887, he was preaching at Keswick yet again. He was tired, too exhausted to pray much, and so he left a prayer meeting in order to spend time on his own with God.

> I was too tired to agonise, so I left the prayer meeting and as I walked I said, My father, if there is one soul more than another within the circle of these hills that needs the gift of Pentecost it is I. I want the Holy Spirit but I do not know how to receive Him and I am too weary to think or feel or pray intensely. Then a voice said to me, 'As you took forgiveness from the hand of the dying Christ, take the Holy Spirit from the hand of the living Christ and reckon that the gift is thine. . . . According to thy faith be it unto thee.'

Meyer did as he was bidden and thereafter preached in the light of this experience.[25]

Meyer was a close friend and colleague of J.H. Shakespeare, the general secretary of the Baptist Union. They gave each other much mutual support. Though much of Meyer's ministry took him off on world preaching tours, he none the less maintained a close link with the Baptist Union. He devoted considerable effort on behalf of the Union in supporting Shakespeare's Sustentation Fund appeal for £250,000 and became the chief spokesman for it. He was the initiator of the Ministers' Prayer Union, which he established in 1897. In this all ministers were, and are, encouraged to remember their fellow ministers each Sunday morning and to pray for the further enduement of the Holy Spirit upon them. In 1902, while in Estonia, he witnessed the gift of tongues in operation in Baptist churches and he promised himself the opportunity to study the Scriptures more on this subject. In many ways Meyer can be regarded as one of the best of loyal and gifted Baptist ministers who none the less exercised much of his ministry among evangelical organisations and only from time to time within the life of the denomination. He did not have any great interest in the matter of spiritual gifts, yet his interest in entering into the life of the Spirit by a definite faith encounter with Christ certainly slanted his ministry towards an expectation for fresh actions by the Holy Spirit in the life of the believer. A hunger for such encounters takes us close to the heart of all that renewal has subsequently attempted to say. As to whether he would have rejoiced in the charismatic renewal we cannot say. There are fewer uncertainties about the views of his fellow Baptists who also shared in the ministry at Keswick but who were uncompromisingly opposed to Pentecostalism. W. Graham Scroggie was Baptist minister in Sunderland while Alexander Boddy was fulfilling his Pentecostally inspired ministry among the Anglicans across the River Wear in Monkwearmouth.

> I could fill pages with reports from the authorised literature of the movement which would only serve to perpetuate the dishonour to which I have referred. . . . But there are not a few authenticated instances of the up-breaking of home, of lunacy, of immorality, not to speak of fanatical displays of impropriety in public. . . . Surely no work which is genuinely Divine could permit, far less be productive of such things.[26]

It is not for us judge the respective qualities of goodness and godliness of such men as Meyer or Scroggie. Among the tantalising qualities of this movement of renewal, one of the greatest which has been there from the beginning is the vehemence with which the equally godly can adopt strongly opposing views on what is happening. Having surveyed these early scenes by the side of a river, we can move on to consider the development of the first fruits.

2

Roots Below – Fruits Above

(2 Kings 19:30)

To follow our theme, we now need to leapfrog over the years of the two world wars and move on to the post-war British evangelical world of the 1950s. This had been dynamically transformed by the effects of the ministry of the American evangelist Dr Billy Graham. His Greater London Crusade of 1954 had lasted for twelve weeks and had thrust him into national and international prominence. With 12 000 people making their way to a dismal barn of an auditorium in the Harringay Arena every night, and with a grand total of 1 300 000 hearing his message there, Billy Graham's ministry was front-page news. When relay services and other meetings were taken into account the attendance topped over two million. It seemed like a mighty religious revival. The crowds on the buses and the tube trains going to and coming from the arena were so filled with confidence that they came and went singing: 'This is my story, this is my song, praising my Saviour all the day long.' And London had never seen anything like it before. This crusade concluded with special meetings at the White City and then in Wembley Stadium. No less than 185 000 were there, and Archbishop Geoffrey Fisher pronounced the blessing at the conclusion as thousands made their way over the Wembley turf to register their decision for Christ. After taking account of the opposition with which the crusade was greeted by the press and also parliament, and the coolness of the Church too, it was a triumph of hope over scepticism. The imagination of the English-speaking world had been captivated by the youthful American preacher. He returned in 1955, and again in 1966–7, with significant effectiveness but never with as much power as in 1954.[1] Although there has been much debate about the long-term effectiveness of his ministry, there is no doubt about his success in getting a hearing for the Gospel in an age of growing religious indifference. Billy Graham was preparing the Evangelical Church for the culture in which the hope of revival would flourish.

Capital ministries

In the post-war era, the domestic side of the evangelical world was dominated by two more major ministries, both located in London and both renowned for their expository preaching and their vibrant spiritual life. John Stott was rector of All Souls, Langham Place, and D. Martyn Lloyd Jones was minister at Westminster Chapel. While other central London churches were beginning to feel the chill of departing congregations, both were capable through their effective preaching of filling their large church buildings to capacity. In the 1950s the two had frequently worked together in the university missions run under the auspices of the Inter-Varsity Fellowship.[2]

In spite of the beneficial effects of the Billy Graham missions, the statistics continued to show the fact that, with few exceptions, church attendances were shrinking on all sides.[3] The two men held each other's ministries in high regard, even though they did not necessarily see eye to eye on every point of doctrine. This was partly due, no doubt, to the differences in their backgrounds. Lloyd Jones came from a Welsh Presbyterian home and had trained initially as a physician. He was outstandingly able, and was soon appointed as assistant to Sir Thomas Horder at St Bartholomew's Hospital. From him he learned a clinical diagnostic ability, the principles of which he retained in his subsequent preaching ministry. In every sermon his aim was so to build logically from first principles so that the argument would move to only one inevitable conclusion. His understanding of the preaching ministry was that it was the greatest single need in the present-day Church.[4] Moreover, Lloyd Jones was an enthusiastic devotee of the Puritan era. He believed that evangelical Christianity was seriously jeopardised by an appeal to the emotions. He was not prepared to identify with the message about the life of Christian victory over sin that was given by the Keswick Convention. Even more controversially, he would not go along with the evangelism of Billy Graham, which he thought was man-centred rather than God-centred.

The younger man, Stott, preserved a much more open-minded approach to these issues and many others. He shared a medical background in that his father had been a physician to the royal household. Educated at Rugby and Cambridge University, Adrian Hastings describes him as the 'quintessence of Evangelical upper-class establishmentarianism'.[5] Unlike Lloyd Jones, he supported the Keswick movement. He gave the Bible readings at the Convention in 1966. He never wavered in his support for Billy Graham and was instrumental in introducing the evangelist to the queen and to the royal household. He remained open to the insights of Christians from other traditions, and was prepared to enter into debate with them. In any case, he was committed to the broadening influences inevitable with the Church–State relationship of Anglicanism. Another of his major goals was to strengthen the commitment of evangelical Anglicans to the Church of England and thus increase its evangelical ministry throughout the land.

While both preachers were committed conservative evangelicals, it was Dr Lloyd Jones who developed a fervent longing for revival. He was looking for a spiritual awakening in which the total religious and moral life of the land would be transformed by a life-changing awareness of the claims of Christ and our necessary response of faith and repentance to him. He believed that this could only be achieved by a sovereign move of the Holy Spirit, not by our prayers, our preaching or our achievements, although this theme became increasingly evident through his preaching in this period.[6] He was affected even more by the significance of the centenary of the last great revival which had occurred in 1859 and which was known as the Evangelical Revival. J. Edwin Orr was a noted historian of that revival, and promoted speculation of the possibilities of a similar movement at this time.[7]

In 1960, Stott was interested in the possibility of this but was less committed to the probability of such a development. He had given himself and his staff the task of joining together in the study of the doctrine of the person and work of the Holy Spirit. He had listened to accounts of revivals in East

Africa, and in 1948 on the Isle of Lewis in the Outer Hebrides. It was for this reason that Stott was prepared to listen to the first news of the Californian experiences, relayed through the testimony of an Anglican evangelical with whom he been in touch, with a view to the possibility of forming a body later to be known as the Evangelical Fellowship in the Anglican Communion. His name was Frank Maguire.[8]

Maguire was an Irish-American, and was rector of the Church of the Holy Spirit, Monterey Park, California. It was there that Dennis Bennett was baptised in the Holy Spirit. Largely through his story in the book *Nine O'Clock in the Morning*, Bennett went on to become a leading figure in the early days of renewal, though Maguire soon faded from prominence.

Although Stott shortly distanced himself from the emphasis that was now beginning to make its impact chiefly through the work of Michael Harper, who was still on his staff, it was the fact that so much of the focus for this was in no less a centre than All Souls, Langham Place, that the wider evangelical world sat up and took notice of all that was beginning to occur in Bible studies, prayer meetings and unofficial gatherings of one kind or another.[9]

It was a similar story regarding the influence of the ministry of Dr Lloyd Jones in Westminster. From 1955 to 1958 he was engaged in a detailed exposition of the Epistle to the Ephesians on Sunday mornings. In the course of these studies he dealt comprehensively with the theme of baptism in the Spirit, and concluded that this was a special blessing not known by all believers and distinctively different from conversion experience. As already indicated, when Lloyd Jones dealt with a subject, he treated it exhaustively. This led him to his emphasis on the great need of the Church for a sovereign move of the Spirit in revival. In addition to his Sunday preaching from the early 1950s onwards, he had also held a regular meeting for ministers of all denominations but of committed evangelical convictions, known as the Westminster Fellowship. It was into this arena that he introduced without comment the enthusiastic testimony of Dennis Bennett and the reports of the otherwise sober P.E. Hughes on the phenomena associated with the Californian experience.[10]

This raised the whole issue of charismatic experience for evangelical debate. When Michael Harper entered into baptism in the Spirit in September 1962 he wasted no time in sharing the news with the doctor, who also invited David Watson of Cambridge and John Collins, then rector of St Mark's, Gillingham, to meet with them both. Having heard their testimony, Lloyd Jones supported the view that they had indeed been baptised in the Spirit and encouraged them to go on in the new spiritual vitality all had found, though warning them strenuously against any theory of sinless perfectionism.[11]

Since he was based in London, Harper then joined the Westminster Fellowship, remaining in membership until this group splintered over issues relating to ecumenical matters in 1965. Among those who gathered in this fellowship were many well-known and influential Baptist ministers, mainly from the London area. Geoffrey King, Theo Bamber, Angus McMillan, W.G. Channon and Arthur Thompson were all members of this fellowship, which was an opportunity for evangelical ministers of all persuasions to meet and to debate whatever were the major issues of the day. By this time Stott had rejected the notion of a subsequent work of the Spirit to regeneration in favour of the view that baptism in the Spirit is another term for the conversion experience and that, if one were converted, it followed that one was already baptised in the Spirit. In 1964 he delivered a series of addresses on this theme to the Islington Clerical Conference; and his talks were subsequently published, so that there was no doubt about his opinion.[12]

The alternative view was being advanced by Lloyd Jones, which was enough to give it an imprimatur of theological respectability in the evangelical world as a whole. The flames of interest in renewal had thus been lit for Baptists as well as for others. Among the Baptists of the Westminster Fellowship were three ministers all of whom were to enter into the baptism in the Spirit: Harold Owen of Carey, Reading; Henry Tyler of Buckhurst Hill; and David Pawson of Gold Hill, Chalfont St Peter. They were also members of the Baptist Revival Fellowship, where much further debate was about to take place.[13]

Denominational concerns

In the 1960s the attention of the Baptist Union was firmly
fixed on much more mundane matters than stories of foreign
revivals or modern renewals, a programme that had been agreed
on in the council in November 1956. It was to mark the Terjubilee of the Union in 1963 by four years of campaigning
leading up to that date. In 1959–60 the theme was to be the
Church Alive to the Gospel; in 1960–1, the Church Alive to
Christian Education and Training; in 1961–2, the Church Alive
to the Neighbourhood, Nation and World; and in 1962–3, the
Church Alive to our Heritage and Opportunity. It was the aim
of the terjubilee to raise the sum of £300 000 which was to
be applied in four equal sums to the Loan Fund, ministerial
training, the Home Work Fund and specific objects relating to
the terjubilee.[14] Though the financial target was missed by some
£20 000, none the less the campaign as a whole was well
received and adjudged to be a sign of real progress. It clearly
marked out the intentions of the general secretary, Ernest Payne,
who saw it as an opportunity to challenge the whole denomination to be true to its calling to mission at home and abroad.
The denominational pulse had been quickened by the jubilee
and also by the Denominational Conference attended by 271
people in 1961, as a part of the total celebration. In the statement agreed by the conference, the accent was put on the need
for local churches to realise the need for interdependence as
the supplement to our independence. There was no suggestion
that the Union should become a connexional body determining
the policy of each of its member churches, but the importance
of the life of associations was stressed. When Ernest Payne
presented his annual report to the assembly of 1964 he
responded to some critics of the process with what Dr Morris
West describes as an impassioned speech:

> Would to God we had set the heather alight as did Whitefield and
> Wesley in the eighteenth century, but it seems that the leaves
> and the twigs are not yet dry enough for the fire from heaven to
> descend. . . . What certainly has happened is that there are few
> churches that have not been challenged by that uncomfortable
> word evangelism . . . all our churches have been called to a spiritual
> check-up. All over the country there are those who have been

challenged, encouraged and helped to be more venturesome in their witness. All this has been worth doing.[15]

Unexpected signs

At this time the Baptist Union had also commissioned a new hymn book, a new history, written by Dr Payne, and a new minister's service book entitled *Orders and Prayers for Christian Worship*.[16] This was written and collated by Ernest Payne and Stephen Winward, then minister in Highams Park, Walthamstow. Winward had already become widely known because he combined in himself and his pastoral ministry scholarship, evangelical zeal, a deep devotional life and considerable preaching and pastoral skills. Stephen Winward was the best kind of evangelical minister. He made it his practice to take a real interest in the work of his younger colleagues at the outset of their ministries. Those of us who had the benefit of knowing him appreciated his wisdom and his fatherly care. His sanctity was of a rare quality. He was best known through the books and manuals he co-authored with his friend Godfrey Robinson, in which they gave basic teaching on the early steps of Christian discipleship. One of Winward's main aims was to enable non-liturgical Churches to achieve a better balance between Word and Sacrament, and freedom and order in the normal diet of Sunday worship. In the introduction to *Orders and Prayers* the authors declare emphatically: 'It is a departure from apostolic worship to celebrate the Lord's Supper infrequently or to regard it as a brief appendage following another complete service. Christian worship is essentially Eucharistic.'[17]

Winward expanded this theme into an influential book in which he developed his own evangelical yet High Church views on ministry.[18] In the brief essay that he contributed to *Orders and Prayers*, he went on to make observations about another aspect of our current patterns of worship he thought needed attention, although possibly not in the way in which it received it in due course:

It would be seriously defective to describe Christian worship as having its dual origin in the synagogue and the Upper Room if we were to leave out of account the person and work of the Holy

Spirit. Full Christian worship is not only scriptural and sacramental; it is also pentecostal. The Calvary–Easter event from which we derive our Eucharistic worship was followed by the Day of Pentecost, the outpouring of the Holy Spirit upon the Church. The Holy Spirit endows believers with manifold 'gifts' some of which enable them to participate in the worship of the assembly. In the earliest description of Christian worship (1 Corinth. 14), we see a congregation under the inspiration of the Holy Spirit free to contribute and participate actively in the common worship. This element of congregational participation needs to be restored today which, apart from the singing of the hymns, is often the monopoly of the minister.[19]

As to the extent that either of the authors was aware of the prophetic significance of these words in the light of all that was to transpire in the decade of the 1960s through charismatic renewal, it is impossible to say. However, Ernest Payne was well aware of the new interest that was being shown in ecumenical circles concerning Pentecostalism, and it may be that this influenced him in writing thus.

Ernest Payne was held in immense respect in much wider circles than the Baptist Union, of which he was general secretary from 1951 to 1967. He served for 21 years on the Central Committee of the World Council of Churches, 14 of those years as the vice-chairman and 7 as a member of the praesidium. He was certainly aware of the views expressed by Bishop Lesslie Newbigin in his Kerr Lectures on the nature of the Church delivered at Glasgow University in 1954 and subsequently printed under the title *The Household of God*. In these lectures Newbigin urged that the Protestant Church should take into account not only its own emphasis on the central question, 'What think ye of Christ?', and the Catholic emphasis on the question, 'What think ye of the Church?', to find the appropriate place for the Pentecostal emphasis framed in the words, 'Did ye receive the Holy Spirit when you believed?' He foresaw that there is indeed a third major stream in world Christianity which needed to be included in the total understanding of the Church.[20]

The same point was substantially reiterated in 1955 and again in 1958 by Henry Pitt Van Dusen, president emeritus of the

Union Theological Seminary in New York, who declared Pentecostalism to be the third force in Christendom.[21]

The warmth of Payne's interest in Pentecostalism was also demonstrated by the respect he showed to the Scandinavian Nils Bloech-Hoell, whose book on Pentecostalism was favourably reviewed by him in the *Baptist Times*.[22] When as acute an observer as Paul Rowntree Clifford drew attention to Pentecostalism as a challenge of the first importance to any Christian thinking about renewal, it became evident that an increasing number of substantial theologians and leaders, including Newbigin and Payne, agreed with it too.[23]

At one level, therefore, it is likely that those who guided the official life of the Baptist Union in the early 1960s were more aware of what was emerging in our midst at this time than most others. Yet the Baptist leaders shared the same weaknesses that are common to all Church leaders removed from the normal demands of parish and congregation through being caught up with the running of ecclesiastical systems. Hence it is also probable that they never foresaw the impact with which the new charismatic movement was to make within the denominations in the near future.

Fundamentalists

Unlike the Churches which operate through a centralised executive, Baptist life has never been tidily contained by the activities of the Union, its council, assembly or office bearers. This is inevitably so with a body which prizes the independence of the local over the control of the connexional. It bears a marked similarity to the freedom with which the Anglican Church works within its own parish boundaries. It is always the case for both Anglicans and Baptists that it is in the local church that the real action always takes place first, and it is often the cause of mutual suspicion between local churches and all denominational offices. If in turn those called to serve the churches through denominational staff appointments choose to describe themselves and their work using the military metaphor of 'headquarters staff', or the executive language of business management, these tensions are only increased, and more culturally sensitive terms are needed.

While Pentecostalism was making its mark in the ecumenical world scene in the ways already indicated, many Baptists who prized their evangelicalism highly and who regarded denominational life with more than reasonable suspicion were members of an organisation known as the Baptist Revival Fellowship. This group emerged in 1938 out of an informal meeting of London Baptist ministers who were burdened by the low level of spiritual life in their churches. As they prayed and studied the Scriptures together they saw the need for personal renewal, and for revival in the Church. From 1954 onwards the BRF held an annual conference, mainly but not exclusively for ministers. They published quarterly bulletins, arranged district fellowship groups and sponsored special rallies from time to time in London and the provinces. Although their common concern was that of revival in the churches, it is plain that they gave focus to the sense of concern and unease within the denomination with what they perceived to be the growth of theological liberalism and the consequent lack of evangelical concern within the councils of the leadership of the Union. Hence much time was spent in discussing tactics for dealing with the Union, and giving expression to the viewpoint of those who, while in it, scarcely saw themselves as being of it in the way in which they conducted their ministry. Lacking self-confidence in their ability to change things in the Union, and fearing the strength of the influence of theological liberalism, they saw little hope of the Union changing in the future. As far as they were concerned, they were firmly wedded to a conservative evangelicalism which gave no quarter to other views and took no prisoners in its theological battles. They did not flinch from expressing the most critical views of their own denomination, as a pamphlet entitled *Liberty in the Lord* made clear.[24]

It is not the case that all members of the BRF shared the same views on the state of the Union. This is clear from the fact that Dr George Beasley-Murray was a speaker at their conference in 1960 and chose to speak on the subject of baptism. The Baptist debate on baptism was beginning at this point as between those who saw the rite in only symbolic terms, representing the entrance into new life for the Christian, and those like Beasley-Murray who interpreted it sacramentally as 'The Word of God in Action'.[25]

It speaks well of the influence of a minority in the leadership of the BRF that it was possible for George Beasley-Murray to deliver such a paper at their conference. Events were to prove, however, that the greater proportion of the BRF took a much more critical stance than leaders such as George Beasley-Murray, Stanley Voke and Geoffrey King, who had no intention of abandoning the denomination. For the most part, however, the leadership of the Union saw no reason for doubting that the BRF represented the extremist evangelical wing of the denomination. In this they were simultaneously both right and wrong. The BRF was the gathering for a grouping of those evangelicals who shared a longing for revival, and were concerned with their own agenda of protest concerning the Baptist Union. The source for this agenda was to be found in the discussions of the Westminster Fellowship under the chairmanship of Dr Lloyd Jones. He was becoming increasingly concerned about what he saw as the threat of the ecumenical movement. But the main body of the Union has been shown to hold more firmly to a much clearer conservative evangelicalism than its leaders thought likely in the early 1960s.

A popular tale

While the ecumenical world was becoming increasingly aware of Pentecostalism, many evangelicals were becoming increasingly tense over ecumenism. This was becoming a major theme in the Westminster Fellowship and the reason for its disruption. Members who could not in conscience sign a statement to the effect that they intended to resign their membership of their denomination when that body had committed itself to a scheme for ecumenical unity had to leave the Fellowship. Those who were confident that they would do so come the day were able to stay. A good number of those who stayed in the Fellowship decided that the time had now come to sever their denominational links. This affected a number of Anglican ministers who resigned their Orders and also some newly charismatical Baptists like Henry Tyler and Harold Owen who finally resigned from the Baptist Union over later controversy.[26]

At this point two small books were published. The first was by the Anglican bishop of Woolwich entitled '*Honest to God*'.[27] It was his attempt to popularise the theology of Paul Tillich and Rudolph Bultmann in expressing the nature of God in acceptable modern language, no more as Heavenly Father but now as the ground of our being, whose son is now the window into ultimate reality rather than the crucified and risen saviour of the world. Its publication at this point only served to underline the fears that many conservative evangelicals were expressing. The second book could scarcely have been more different, and yet in the end was just as significant. It was about the ministry of an American Pentecostalist pastor named David Wilkerson, and the book *The Cross and the Switchblade*. From his own experience of working with those addicted to heroin and other hard drugs, Wilkerson claimed that through faith in Christ, and the power of the Spirit, not only was it possible for addicts to be cured of their addiction, but Christian Churches could successfully evangelise a generation that was otherwise totally bereft of hope and life. *The Cross and the Switchblade* sold like the proverbial hot cakes, and the story circled round the globe, partly through the good offices of the *Reader's Digest* magazine that carried a section of it in its editions.[28]

All evangelical Christians heard of this tale, Baptists among them. Certainly this was the case concerning the Baptists in central Scotland. Together with their Presbyterian neighbours in the Church of Scotland, with Methodists, and Pentecostals as well, a small group of young ministers came together in Motherwell and Wishaw to study and pray together about the life of the Spirit. Some of them had entered into a new form of experience about which they were somewhat embarrassed, marked by their possession of the gift of tongues.

By 1963, renewal had survived the antenatal pressures of pregnancy and was born. As to whether there would be a healthy infancy was not yet clear. But for those who were involved from the beginning, the kindergarten for charismatic experience was to be the local church.

Growing Years

3

Like a Tree planted by the Streams

(Psalms 1:3)

We have seen that there are numerous sources from which the charismatic movement drew in its first beginnings. In the period now under review, 1964–71, the most influential force for the renewal was the Fountain Trust which was conceived and born within the spiritual family of All Souls, Langham Place. The date for the birth was 29 September 1964 and the place, the flat occupied by Michael Harper as a curate at All Souls at 76a Cavendish Street.[1]

Michael Harper was appointed the full-time general secretary. The absence of an alternative equally strong Baptist Church in central London offering high-quality expository ministry with a clear evangelistic purpose simply meant that what happened in the All Souls environment had a much wider effect on Baptists than would otherwise have been likely. This was especially the case when it appeared that a fascinating new movement was beginning to emerge under the nose of the well-known rector who plainly did not altogether approve of it. We thus need to record the steps leading to the inauguration of this new body, the ethos of which was in evangelical Anglicanism.

As we do so it is helpful to indicate how this period demonstrates four recurrent themes which are interwoven with the fabric of early charismatic renewal. First, it is plain that the renewal initiative was taken by Anglicans, not Baptists, to whom it came by a process of gentle osmosis from the Anglicans. Second, there were few headline-catching Baptist ministers involved at the start other than J.D. Pawson, whose early ministry was with the Methodists, not the Baptists. Third,

the movement nevertheless grew at grass roots level, where
there were many ill-defined signs of hope for spiritual revival.
Fourth, the leadership of the Baptist denomination was apparently indifferent to what was happening in their midst. They
had their reasons for great caution in that many of the renewed
were committed to an agenda of protest, not because of the
issues raised by their enlivening renewal experience but because
of the legacy of deeply held suspicions with the agreed policy of
the Baptist Union over ecumenism.

How, therefore, did the renewal launched in Anglicanism
produce such marked changes among Baptists?

Michael Harper and the Fountain Trust

To put this event into context we need to draw upon the
experience of Michael Harper and others in the preceding 18
months, back to 1962. In September of that year Harper was
due to speak at a Christian house party in Farnham and his
chosen subject was the prayers of Paul in the letter to the
Ephesians. Up to this point his testimony was similar to that of
a great number of other evangelical Anglican clergymen. He
had been converted while a student at Cambridge University,
and his ministry reflected the normal interests and persuasions
of young evangelical Anglican ministers at this time in his
earnest desire to live the life of a Christian and to win the lost
for Christ. As he prepared his talks on this occasion, however,
he became totally absorbed by the significance of Paul's prayers
for revelation and empowerment. Indeed, the train journey to
Farnham from Waterloo, through the south-western suburbs
and the Surrey countryside, became a time of spiritual quick-
ening as he reflected further on the Bible passages on which
he was going to speak. God's power was coming upon him in
a special way. All this was confirmed by his experience at the
conference. It was transforming for those who were listening
to his words, as it was for the speaker. Now he knew the
presence of God with him as never before. However he was to
describe this experience, he knew God had met with him and
blessed him very deeply, though at this stage without the
outward manifestation which was to become the hallmark of
this movement, the gift of tongues.[2]

In the background for Michael Harper there were three Anglican laymen, all of whom had been baptised in the Spirit and all of whom had also received the gift of tongues.[3] They were Eric Houfe, an architect whose practice was housed not far from All Souls, Bill Grant, and a retired missionary to India, George Ingram. George Ingram and his wife May were great prayer warriors much involved in prayer for revival in general around the world, and also for their own Church in particular. They had agreed to pray for the clergy at All Souls and that the principal target for their intercessions should be Curate Michael. When he returned from the Farnham experience he described to the church fellowship what had happened to him, and to them the change was obvious. As they understood it, Harper had been baptised in the Spirit. Through Houfe, Harper received a copy of the magazine that was just beginning to be produced by the American Episcopalians, called *Trinity*. This magazine enjoyed only a short life, from 1961 to 1965. It was well presented and sold at an exorbitant price for those days, 10s. 6d. per copy. Yet though only a few copies of each edition were sold in the UK, the influence of the magazine was very significant. The editor was Mrs Jean Stone, the wife of an executive with the Lockheed Air Corporation, Don Stone. It was in *Trinity* that Harper read the story of Dennis Bennett and what had happened to him in Van Nuys. But the one thing that he found hard to take in the stories printed in the magazine was the seemingly inevitable way in which these American Episcopalians received the gift of tongues along with their refreshing baptism in the Spirit.[4] It was at this point that Frank Maguire came into Harper's story, in May 1963. It was Maguire who helped Michael Harper to understand his own experience in the context of full initiation into Christ rather than as a second blessing Pentecostal experience. He cautioned Harper on the sort of speakers to invite and, without perceiving the extent to which the renewal in Britain would draw upon the teaching and testimony of North Americans in due course, counselled him not to welcome all travelling American charismatics uncritically.

The first visitor he commended was Larry Christenson, pastor of the Trinity Lutheran Church in San Pedro, California. Since Christenson was passing through London later in the summer, Harper arranged for him to speak at some meetings for ministers and leaders, in which not only did he speak about the movement as one among the historic Churches, but he also laid stress on it being one in which the Spirit was calling Christians to repentance for their own sins and those of the whole Church. During this time, Christenson gave Harper personal advice about the gift of tongues which was to become very helpful to Harper in his own pilgrimage. 'Do you speak in tongues yet?' asked Christenson. 'No – but I want to,' was Harper's candid reply. 'Have you tried to?' asked Christenson. 'You see, when we speak in tongues, we do the speaking, while the Holy Spirit provides the language.' That advice unlocked the puzzle of tongues for Harper who, during the night after this conversation, found that the gift was his. 'From now onwards surprises followed thick and fast,' was Harper's testimony.[5]

Thereafter, Michael Harper had the opportunity to spend some time away in the country reading and writing. One of the articles he wrote for the *Church of England Newspaper* soon became the first of many booklets for which he was responsible. It was on the gift of prophecy and was simply entitled *Prophecy – A Gift for the Body of Christ*.[6]

He also arranged a meeting for another extraordinary visitor from across the Atlantic in the person of David du Plessis, a South African Pentecostal then resident in the USA. The story he had to tell was truly remarkable, and went back to his years as the youthful general secretary of a lively young Pentecostal denomination in South Africa, the Apostolic Faith Mission. One morning in 1936 his office routine was disturbed by the sudden and unannounced arrival of Smith Wigglesworth, a Pentecostal evangelist from Bradford, who has been recognised as one of the giants of the early Pentecostal movement. He was conducting missions in the locality but he also specialised in delivering personal directive prophecies to individuals without forewarning, apology or aftercare for the shock element which his words would convey. So it was for du Plessis as Wigglesworth burst into his presence:

> There is a revival coming that at present the world knows nothing about. It will come through the churches. It will come in a fresh way. . . . It will eclipse anything that has been known in history.

Empty buildings, empty cathedrals, will be packed again with worshippers. . . . The Lord intends to use you for this revival. For you have been in Jerusalem for long enough. The Lord will send you to the uttermost parts of the earth.[7]

So du Plessis became involved in the renewal from an early stage, not only as an experienced Pentecostal, but more so as a warm-hearted advocate for the development of genuine ecumenical relationships, even though such an attitude was almost entirely foreign to his own denomination. His influence on the renewal was crucial in its early years. He was dubbed 'Mr Pentecost', and Harper introduced him to the emerging British scene. Several people were prayed for at a meeting held in the Londoner Hotel in October 1963. It was the strength of his ecumenical commitment and his growing influence on Harper and the Fountain Trust that caused Dr Lloyd Jones to rapidly reassess the future worth of the renewal. He now began to perceive new and dangerous ecumenical agendas within it through what he regarded as a deliberate attempt by du Plessis to downgrade doctrine in favour of induced experience.[8]

By February 1964, Harper had organised his very first charismatic conference. It was to be held at an Anglican retreat house and conference centre in Stoke Poges, for those who had already experienced some new life in the Spirit. The speaker was to be Arthur Wallis, whose ministry at a later stage was to become significantly divisive for charismatics. However, at the last minute he was unable to come because of illness, so his place was taken by a soft-spoken Scot from the Christian Brethren who soon impressed Harper by the worth of his devotional preaching. His name was Campbell McAlpine, and the consequence to his ministry was that many were baptised in the Spirit there. In June of the same year he organised a second Stoke Poges conference, this time for ministers or pastors either already into or at least sympathetic with this new movement. Three Baptists were among those who came, Frank Wilson then of Willesborough in Kent, W.J. James of Gresham Chapel, Brixton, and formerly a deacon at Westminster Chapel, and J.D. Pawson. David Pawson soon struck up a friendship with an independent Bible teacher also present named Harry Greenwood, whom he asked to pray for him. As a result of this

contact, Pawson invited Greenwood to Gold Hill Baptist
Church, and the work of renewal headed up through Harper's
experience and ministry began to influence many Baptist
churches, where the worth of David Pawson's ministry was
being increasingly recognised.[9]

The second Stoke Poges conference prepared the way for
Michael Harper to launch out into a new ministry through the
new Fountain Trust. In July 1964 he left the staff of All Souls
and in September began his work for the new Trust. Already
his story was in the public domain. Harper's conviction concerning the relationship of this renewal to the existing Churches
was expressed in his newsletter.[10] 'We feel called to serve every
section of the Church without fear or favour. We are seeing
the Holy Spirit moving in unlikely places today, and we rejoice
in his power to bring men of different traditions together.' The
Fountain Trust saw that its purpose was that of a service agency,
and therefore it did not seek a membership of its own. Its aims,
which were to be printed in the *Renewal* magazine that appeared
later, were:

1. To encourage Christians of all Churches to receive the power
   of the Holy Spirit and to glorify Christ by manifesting in
   their lives the fruit and the gifts of the same Spirit so that
   they may enrich their worship, strengthen their witness and
   deepen their fellowship.
2. To encourage local churches to experience renewal in the
   Holy Spirit and to recover the full ministry of the Holy
   Spirit, including that of healing.
3. To encourage Christians to expect and pray for worldwide
   revival.[11]

Since it was born in the mecca of evangelical Anglicanism, was
led by a wise and cultivated pioneer in Michael Harper whose
evangelical credentials were impeccable, and its sympathies were
broadly ecumenical, it was certain to have a considerable impact
among Baptists as among others. This turned out to be the
case for the rest of the decade and beyond.

The Scottish scene

In the different ethos of Scotland, events taking place in a fashionable church in the west end of London were not of pressing significance. None the less, there were other means by which the news got around, in this case by print, the magazine *Trinity*. Brian Casebow was minister of the parish church of St Margaret, situated on a new housing scheme in Netherton, on the outskirts of Motherwell. On the night of Sunday, 27 May 1962, with the day's services over, Casebow retired to his study and, after reading a copy of *Trinity*, felt an impulse to fall on his knees before God and begin to pray. Never having heard tongues for himself he had no idea what it sounded like, yet he found himself praying using words that sounded Russian, and he found himself uttering them with great emotion. Though he spent wretched weeks doubting the reality of the experience, it was soon apparent that his life had changed and that he had received the baptism, and that this gift of tongues came with the experience.

As the Glasgow *Sunday Mail* and the Scottish *Daily Express* got hold of the story of what was happening in St Margaret's, the news was soon everywhere. 'A veil of secrecy was clamped down on a Scots church last night after a mysterious new form of worship bordering on the supernatural is being practised,' they claimed, to which they then added, 'but speaking in tongues has Church of Scotland officials baffled.'[12] Perhaps it can be simply affirmed that it is not unknown for Church officials to be baffled by events bordering on the supernatural!

The story of what was happening with the unlikely Casebow travelled far and wide throughout the district in central industrial Scotland. It was not long before he was holding special meetings for prayer and for healing, and creating a stir of interest among his ministerial colleagues including ministers of the local Lanarkshire Baptist Association fraternal to which he was invited to speak. He was soon requesting the use of local Baptist churches in order to baptise new converts by total immersion. To their chagrin, it was soon evident that he, a Presbyterian, was making and baptising considerably more converts than his more evangelistically minded Baptist neighbours. His nearest Baptist neighbour was the minister of the Motherwell church,

Douglas Ross. Ross was also editor of the monthly magazine for Scottish Baptists, and decided to ask his nearest neighbour, who happened to be me, to investigate and report on what was happening in the parish of St Margaret. This then involved attending meetings at St Margaret's, against my own better judgement, but with challenging personal consequences. Though not sought after because of its Pentecostal associations, I too received a vivid renewing experience and the gift of tongues was a part of it.

Soon, a group of ministers gathered together to study the Scriptures, to pray and to listen to one another's story of what God was doing in our midst. They included Douglas Ross, Josiah Beecham, a Congregationalist, Gerald Ladlow, an Elim Pentecostalist, John Handley, Brian Casebow, and later Hugh Bain and Tom Smail of the Church of Scotland, Ken McDougall who was a Methodist but was later to transfer into Baptist ministry, and me. The ministers' group met together weekly and provided a safe haven for discussion, intercession, study of the Scriptures, and the first faltering attempts at mutual encouragement in the exercise of the gifts of tongues, interpretation, prophecy, and healing ministry. It is true to say that Motherwell became a focus for charismatic activity, and several American visitors came to Motherwell in the course of their visits to the United Kingdom. John Handley, Church of Scotland minister at Clason Memorial Church, made his buildings available for their meetings. The first to travel north was the editor of *Trinity* magazine, Mrs Stone, on Monday, 27 April 1964. Her meetings created a local sensation.[13] John Handley recorded the effect in his parish magazine:

> Nothing could have been more unconducive to emotional stimulus than the form of this evening meeting; nothing more matter of fact than the voice of Jean Stone as she spoke of the mighty acts of God in His Church today; and yet when the meeting ended and only those deeply interested and desirous of prayer were invited to remain, scarcely any left the building. For not a few this Monday 27 April will go down as a day of new beginnings in the life of the Spirit.[14]

Rapid spread

While there was considerable movement in central Scotland at this time, developments elsewhere were slow but there was nevertheless news of further interest being shown. *Crusade* magazine had already carried an article by Gilbert Kirby on the phenomenal spread of the Pentecostal Churches as long ago as September 1962.[15] In January 1964 they published another article by an Elim minister on the staff of the Evangelical Alliance, J. Hywel Davies, entitled 'The New Pentecostalism'. It was introduced in the following way:

> 'Outburst of tongues' was how *Christianity Today*, the respected American theological journal, headlined the subject. 'Baptism in the Spirit' announces the *Church of England Newspaper*. 'Tongues in a Church of England Parish' is the *English Churchman*'s headline. A 'form of worship bordering on the supernatural' was the unintentionally funny phrase chosen by the Scottish *Sunday Mail*.

The article concluded: 'News of what was taking place in America found its way across the Atlantic, and the same pattern seems to be presenting itself in Britain.'[16]

In the same month the Islington Clerical Conference gathered in the Assembly Hall of Church House, Westminster, under the theme: 'The Holy Spirit in the Life of the Church.' It was here that John Stott delivered his paper on the 'Baptism and Fullness of the Holy Spirit' which was soon to be published as a booklet with that title, and in which he distanced himself from the teaching of Michael Harper, still on his staff at that time, and indeed from other members of the All Souls' ministry team.[17]

Not to be outdone, the *Baptist Times* published an article by Godfrey Robinson, minister at Main Road, Romford, on the subject of 'The Power of the Spirit'. It was totally uncontroversial, however, and without any reference to the issues that were gripping the minds of a large section of the readership. 'How do we receive God's Spirit?' asks Robinson. 'We begin by trusting in Christ, by committing our lives to Him.' Quoting approvingly from William Barclay he goes on: 'The only way to receive the Spirit is silently and prayerfully to wait upon the Spirit.'[18] Later in the same year the editor decided to report further on this theme by drawing attention to the words of

Archbishop Coggan preaching at the annual Lee Abbey service at St Paul's Cathedral with this appeal, 'Don't neglect the Pentecostals.' Reminding his hearers that four out of every five non-Catholics in South America are Pentecostals, he affirmed that they cannot be dismissed as a sect: 'To pass by on the other side and neglect what is one of the most extraordinary features of religious life in the twentieth century is to show a lack of responsibility, or our unreadiness to face the evidence.'[19]

This was soon reinforced by news of the one Pentecostalist organisation that made a great impact as charismatic renewal was beginning. This was the Full Gospel Business Men's Fellowship International, and they too came from the USA. In 1965 they decided that the Lord had told them to descend in great numbers on London for a great conference that was to lead on to outstanding spiritual revival. To this end they charted planes, booked hotels and arranged meetings in London, concluding with a rally at the Royal Albert Hall. There was no doubt about their zeal, and since they were mainly affluent businessmen there was little shortage of funds for their efforts. If, in fact, it was soon clear that there had been no revival (at least in the way that Britons would use the term), there were a number of Baptist ministers who were impressed and who consequently gave their support to the emerging movement. They included the late Tom Rogers, who went on to have significant ministry as the secretary for evangelism for the Baptist Union, Edmund Heddle, Frank Payne of Henley, and Gordon Thomas, then minister at Thornhill, Southampton, but later to become pastor/secretary for the Berkshire Association. This meeting was duly reported in the *Baptist Times*.[20]

The journal waited until 1971 before it risked a major article positively commending renewal. However, when the BMS held their annual New Year Prayer Service on 1 January 1965 at Bloomsbury, the preacher was J.D. Pawson. He had no hesitation in saying that baptism in the Spirit was the secret of the success of the early Church, as it would be ours too.[21]

Baptist Revival Fellowship concerns

The natural focus for issues to do with spiritual renewal was in the Baptist Revival Fellowship, and from 1964 to 1966 this was the main subject for their annual conference. In November 1964 the BRF held their annual conference and the speaker was to be Leith Samuel from Southampton. He was ill, however, and at the last minute his place was taken by J.D. Pawson, who spoke on the theme of the Holy Spirit. Harold Owen had heard Pawson give the same address on a previous occasion and Pawson, being aware of this, apologised in advance that some would have heard his material before. As far as Owen was concerned there was no need for an apology. There was a significant difference this time in the speaker if not in his text. So he enquired afterwards whether in fact Pawson had now received the baptism in the Spirit. Pawson confirmed this to Owen and at this point Owen retired to his room, affirming that he would not reappear until God had met with him and blessed him too. God soon responded to Owen's hunger, and when his close friend Henry Tyler also testified to having received the baptism at this time, it was evident that charismatic activity was going to become the focus for considerable fresh interest among the members of the BRF. Richard Kayes of Everton, Michael Pusey of Farnborough, and Barney Coombes of East Acton were also involved in this move.[22] In 1965 they gathered again at The Hayes, Swanwick, for the largest gathering so far to consider the subject of the Person and the Work of the Holy Spirit. Three speakers took part: Geoffrey King, Dr J.I. Packer and Arthur Wallis.[23]

Then again in 1966 David Pawson was invited to return when, together with Stanley Voke and Glyn Morris, he was to speak on the Doctrine and Life of the Church. But if these were the themes for their public sessions, there was another agenda running that affected the relationships of the BRF with the main life of the Baptist Union. It was all to do with the issue of ecumenical relationships, and the discussions these precipitated were to come to a major crisis in 1971. Since many of the combatants were known to be charismatic, it was no surprise that the leadership of the Baptist Union assumed that when they were representing their anti-ecumenical views, they were identical to their charismatic convictions too. Inasmuch as the Fountain Trust was helping to formulate a charismatic approach to current Church issues, plainly this was not the case.

Within the Fountain Trust the ecumenical tide was flowing in.[24]

The unity issue

The Baptist Union had been in membership with both the British Council of Churches and the World Council of Churches since their beginnings in 1944 and 1948 respectively.[25] In 1964 the BCC held a conference at Nottingham on Faith and Order in which it was proposed that churches in England should covenant together for unity by 1980, in order to be 'One Church renewed for mission'. The Baptist Union as a constituent member was bound to respond to the proposal and did so by the appointment of an Advisory Committee for Church Relations through the Baptist Union Council. This committee was charged by the council to produce a comprehensive statement to help clarify and shape Baptist opinion and policy regarding both the changing patterns of Church relations in the UK and the more general question of Christian unity. They were to take account of the forbidding list of differences within the denomination over these issues. Eventually the strong committee that had been assembled produced a formidable report for the council entitled *Baptists and Unity*, which was received and adopted by council in March 1967. It was also to be sent to all the Churches and associations in membership with the Union for their study, as well as to the BCC, WCC, and other national and international Baptist bodies. The committee was to consider the results that came to them with a view to a further report to the council not later than November 1968.[26]

Since these issues were under permanent discussion from 1964 onwards, and they were ones in which it was known that at the grass roots the Churches were greatly split over them, it is understandable that the Baptist Union gave to them the lion's share of their interest. In the event, *Baptists and Unity* was a well-argued document but its recommendations were ecumenically cautious. There were no suggestions of the sell-out of evangelical truth that some were fearing. The writers found that while in their view we could not afford to remain out of the ecumenical process that was being envisaged, yet at the same time there was no way that the Baptist Union could encourage its member churches to seek to join the covenant. It encouraged discussion and debate but not commitment. It encouraged co-operation, especially in the designation of 'areas of ecumenical experiment', but it declared unequivocally that 'it would be a mistake for the Baptist Union to press for the idea of organic union by 1980, lest it endanger denominational unity, and thereby seriously weaken the witness Baptists have to make'.[27]

In the background, as far as Baptists were concerned, other voices were making a strong contribution to the debate, particularly among conservative evangelicals attracted to Martyn Lloyd Jones because of his theologically reformed views. He saw the ecumenical issue as a major threat to the effectiveness of an evangelical witness. He was deeply concerned, since his perception was that the World Council of Churches was the body that was going to produce a single world Church for which evangelicals would be hopelessly unprepared and from which they would either be ejected because of their Gospel convictions, or they would be unable to stay for fear of Gospel compromise. As we have already noted, he was greatly alarmed at the influence of David du Plessis. As far as England was concerned, he was convinced that the plan was for a single comprehensive Church in this country that would obviously include a basically unreformed Roman Catholic Church which might conceivably present some cosmetic changes to conceal the inward reality of what it remained. The forum for decision on these issues for Lloyd Jones was initially his own church meeting. The members of Westminster Chapel had no hesitation in endorsing the views taken by their minister, and the Westminster Chapel left the Congregational Federation and opted for its own independence. In addition, however, this subject had remained on the agenda of the Westminster Fellowship, which had grown in both size and significance. There the discussion raged to and fro, over many meetings over several years. By 1965, Dr Lloyd Jones had had enough of discussion and his patience was exhausted. He had become convinced that there could be no future for the meeting since it was split between those who accepted his ecumenical prognosis, and those who took a less stringent line both on the ecumenical movement and on the participation in it of their denomination. In 1966 the meeting was therefore brought to a close.[28]

To gain a measure of the strength of conviction with which this debate was conducted, we must take note of what happened at this time in the wider conservative evangelical constituency beyond the denomination. In the same year, 1966, the Evangelical Alliance held a National Assembly of Evangelicals at Westminster Central Hall. The subject again was Christian unity, and the assembly was preceded by the publication of a 12-page report in which they declared their findings: 'There is no widespread demand at this present time for the setting up of a united evangelical Church on denominational lines. . . . This does not mean that there could not be an effective fellowship or federation of evangelical churches at both the local and the national level.'[29]

The chairmen of the committee making this finding known were the Baptists Godfrey Robinson and John Caiger. In spite of this, Lloyd Jones was the invited preacher at the main rally although it was known that his views were different from these findings. The chairman was John Stott. Lloyd Jones's address raised the temperature of evangelical discussions on ecumenical levels in an extraordinary way, leading to a public confrontation between the speaker and the chairman and the polarising of views in the evangelical world over ecumenical issues in an unheard of way.[30] It is the repercussions of this debate that ran on throughout the evangelical world for a considerable period, and it can still be seen that many evangelicals have remained unable to revisit the arguments and resolve the problems raised. We shall come to this matter again later.

At the heart of the Lloyd Jones address lay his convictions that the ecumenical movement would inevitably lead to a situation in which all the Protestant denominations would ultimately become nothing more than an evangelical segment of a Church dominated by Rome. The reason was that ecumenical people would appeal to the primacy of fellowship over doctrine, whereas the evangelical priority is first doctrinal agreement out of which true fellowship would arise. Hence in 1966, with the public fracas between its two leading exponents, evangelical unity was shattered. As far as the Evangelical Alliance was concerned it was left to Morgan Derham, the newly appointed general secretary of the Alliance and a Baptist minister, to pick up the pieces and to begin to patiently put together the broken parts. In 1967 a new Westminster Ministers' Fellowship began for those conservative evangelicals who were grieved by what they saw as compromise on these issues, yet who treasured the goal of true evangelical unity. In order to join, ministers were required to sign a form indicating the fact that, if necessary and if possible, they would be willing to leave their denominations as and when the new super Church arrived. Since Lloyd Jones's influence profoundly affected many Baptist ministers, it is not surprising that the Baptist Union Report for the year made reference to these decisions.

> Some associated with the Evangelical Alliance and Martyn Lloyd Jones's Westminster Fellowship favour withdrawal from our Union. . . . The Baptist Union Council appeals to ministers to think hard and long with a maximum of fair and full consultation with other Baptists before any action is taken.[31]

Since many charismatic Baptists had a close affinity to Lloyd Jones because of his greater sympathy for the notion of baptism in the Spirit over the views of Stott, who interpreted this in terms of conversion initiation into the life of the Spirit, the heated debate between them over ecumenism inevitably had its effect on the development of charismatic renewal at a time when the Fountain Trust was promoting much warmer ecumenical sympathies. Because of the evidence of further division, the Union decided as a consequence to set up an appropriate committee in 1967 to examine the causes of dissension in their midst.[32] Up to this point, their leaders had never seriously taken account of the growing strength of conservative evangelicalism. They were meticulously careful in their handling of the ecumenical issues causing tension but, since they had not familiarised themselves with the ministry of Lloyd Jones or Stott, they were in no position to give wise counsel to those whose world was falling apart through the division both leaders represented.

4

A Day of Good News?

(2 Kings 7:9)

Lest we should imagine that this strong, theologically polarising debate among evangelicals was robbing the renewal of its first fervour, we need to retrace our steps to 1965 and the significant visit of the American Pentecostal businessmen in the Full Gospel Business Men's Fellowship International, founded in 1952 by a Texan millionaire, Demos Shakarian. On the wider scene their coming was significant for a further reason. The infant Fountain Trust had decided to take the considerable risk of launching a bi-monthly magazine entitled *Renewal*, which has continued in circulation without interruption ever since. The first edition was in January 1966, and the main news item it carried was that of the impact of the visit of the Full Gospel team to London.[1] The work of the Fountain Trust continued to thrive as the magazine gradually built up its circulation. By 1967 Michael Harper was able to express the most confident predictions in its pages:

> The overwhelming evidence of the last few years points to the fact that the day of world revival has dawned. In spite of the persistent opposition of some, and the excesses of others, there are ample grounds for much rejoicing. God is pouring out His Spirit on the worldwide Church on a scale hitherto unknown. Careful though we must be concerning the dangers of the counterfeit, and sensitive to the guidance of the Spirit, we would be grieving God if we suggested that what is happening is anything less than the firstfruits of world revival.[2]

Regular conferences were now being held such as the one for ministers and Christian workers at High Leigh, Hoddesdon, 12–15 June 1967. The subject was the Holy Spirit and the

Church, and the speakers were J.D. Pawson, John Collins of St Mark's, Gillingham, and Pastor Arnold Bittlinger of the Lutheran Church, who was to go on to help found an ecumenical charismatic centre in Schloss Craheim, and later to serve on the staff of the World Council of Churches. Among the participants were Jim Baker from North Hanwell, David Betts from Slough, Roger Gandy from Chiswick, Johnny Johnson of Woodstock Road, Oxford, D.S. Lock from Brockley, C.N. Mobbs from Bristol Baptist College, Ron Park from Muswell Hill, Michael Pusey from Farnborough, Walter Wands from Glasgow and myself from Wishaw. In fact, it was through Michael Harper's generosity that four of us from Scotland travelled together for this occasion. Tom Smail, then Presbyterian, and Ken McDougall, at that time Methodist, completed the Scottish quartet who took advantage of the kind offer.[3]

While J.D. Pawson's expositions from Romans 9–11 were memorable, Arnold Bittlinger's treatment of the Gifts of the Spirit from 1 Corinthians 12 was unique in that he combined spiritual perceptiveness and critical scholarship. This was no traditional evangelical conference, nor was it in any way a typical Pentecostal gathering. For all the informality of the occasion and the warmth of the fellowship, it felt like the beginning stages of a movement of massive significance especially since the greater proportion of those attending were in their early years of ministry.[4]

Another participant at the High Leigh conference was Morgan Derham, who was seeking to recover a mediating position in interdenominational evangelicalism after the showdown at Westminster Central Hall in 1966. The Evangelical Alliance could not have been led by a more diplomatic general secretary for the critical needs they faced. While not identifying himself with the renewal, he was prepared to give support for the reason for its growth, in what he described as 'the spiritual barrenness, formality and dullness of much that passed for "sound" Christianity'. He went on to state, 'The kind of Spirit-controlled, joy-saturated, dynamic Christian living described [in the New Testament] was not very often experienced among us.'[5]

All of this indicates that charismatic growth was largely at the grass roots level of local church life. As led by the Fountain

Trust, it was also positive in its approach to ecumenical issues. When Douglas Ross of Motherwell visited the Fountain Trust conference in June 1968 he commented:

> There were Baptists there – one from Scotland and quite a number from England. But there was a strong contingent of Anglo-Catholics and there were some members of the Brethren. The Church of Scotland was there, one or two Pentecostalists, the Dutch Reformed Church, the Salvation Army, an Irish Presbyterian, two members of the Anglican Community of the Resurrection – and one day there was even a Roman Catholic, a university chaplain.[6]

Coming to the boil

Nevertheless, the onward growth of the renewal among Baptists could not fail to be affected by the atmosphere of growing crisis that permeated the life of the denomination. The publication of *Baptists and Unity* led to two further booklets being circulated. The first was entitled *Baptists for Unity*,[7] which represented the convictions of the ecumenical enthusiasts who were almost to a man among the theological liberals. They advocated immediate negotiation for organic integration with other denominations. In the absence of these negotiations, they threatened unilateral local action by individual churches joining with other local denominations. The opposite view was espoused by David Kingdon, the youthful principal of the Irish Baptist College and a member of the BRF. His booklet, *Baptists at the Crossroads*, produced by the BRF, brought forth a stormy response.[8] For him there were three ways through the crisis: inaction; reformation, leading to the clear enunciation of our biblical understanding for fellowship; or secession. There was little doubt which of these he favoured. J.D. Pawson was asked to comment on this for *The Christian* newspaper, and characteristically proposed not three possible responses at the crossroads, but five. One, to stop where we were; two, to retrace our steps to the good old days; three, to turn left and go for absorption with a larger group though with appropriate safeguards for baptism; four, to turn right and go for a closer set of links with others generally regarded as outside the normal ecumenical field; five, to move forward into a Baptist Union whose extreme wings had left for other pastures, seeking both reformation according to the Word of God and revival by the Spirit of God for the future.[9]

The Assembly of the Baptist Union in 1969 decided the matter of our continued involvement in the ecumenical bodies whose thinking was behind the covenanting proposals. It must have been a considerable relief to the leadership that in fact the Assembly agreed with the recommendation of our continuance in both the BCC and the WCC by a vote of 1125 in favour and 356 against the proposition. This was in spite of much campaigning by the BRF to oppose membership of both bodies.[10] Hence the BRF set up their own subcommittee to explore the possibilities for those evangelical Baptists who could not work with a denomination which had a link with the WCC. This was with the deep regret of G.R. King but the reasoning behind it was expressed in a letter from the BRF chairman Theo Bamber that appeared in the *Baptist Times* on 15 January 1970: 'For my part, I am reluctant to leave the Baptist Union. It is a lifelong association but what is one to do? If one thinks it is going to rain, must one be condemned for buying an umbrella?'[11]

The storm breaks

Events in the Union underlined the sense of gathering gloom. Dr Ernest Payne's service as general secretary came to an end in July 1967. He was widely acknowledged as an immensely able administrator and greatly respected for the integrity of his service to the work not only of the Baptist Union but also of the ecumenical movement, serving as chairman on a number of significant committees, and also as one of the British presidents of the World Council of Churches. This major commitment was not universally popular, for obvious reasons. It is a fair estimate to say that Dr Payne's service was better appreciated by the wider Church and the overseas Church than by the denomination from which he came.[12]

He was replaced by Dr David Russell. Almost as soon as he was appointed, the committee set up in 1967 to examine the causes of dissension reported back that there were three. They were uncertainty about the ecumenical commitment of the

Union, unhappiness with the Declaration of Principle, and fear of centralising tendencies militating against the independence of the local church.[13] To these causes the Baptist Union soon added a fourth cause for profound dismay. It took the form of a report from a specially convened commission on the subject of the realistic possibilities for full-time pastoral ministry in Baptist churches. It was entitled *The Ministry Tomorrow* and was completed and released in 1969. As a report it had several positive suggestions to offer on a range of ministerial issues, but particularly concerning the training and deployment of a new category of supplementary ministers. They were those called to a secular occupation but able to give part of their time to ministerial service. They would be fully trained and accredited. Yet the report could not have been less helpful in terms of its overall message to the denomination, with its morale rattled by all the other factors that were around at this time. As Dr George Beasley-Murray, then principal at Spurgeon's College, commented, it advocated a policy of general retrenchment which could not be justified in the light of the Great Commission. It lacked any sense of a strategy for mission. In short, together with the devastating graph it produced indicating the virtual extinction of the Baptists by about the year 2000, it promoted little more than the idea of a seemly denominational funeral.[14] What had happened to the bright dawn of the first Denominational Conference of 1961 marking the terjubilee celebrations? At that time it was thought that the advance of the Baptists was such that they would never look back, yet the report predicted that within 10 years no more than about 400 full-time ministers would be required to serve the churches.[15] With this prediction it seemed as if hope for the future was being effectively extinguished. The general superintendent of the metropolitan area at the time was Geoffrey Haden. The forebodings that *The Ministry Tomorrow* produced were well illustrated by his comments addressed to ministers on this matter in his annual report in the London Baptist Association directory for 1970:

> It has been assumed wrongly . . . that there might be some plan to reduce the number of full-time ministers to 400. Let them be reassured that if they have been called and are now ministers of

churches, that the denomination will continue to support them as long as they are able to exercise an effective ministry.[16]

It must be open to question as to whether these comments were as soothing as they were doubtless intended to be. But then it is the lot of those who serve as Baptist general superintendents on occasions to be shown to be far more provocative than they had believed they could be even when they tried!

In 1970 another denominational conference was held at Swanwick. Many papers were produced for it over a full range of subjects, and the conference was adjudged a success. The overall impact of the renewal within the ranks of the Baptist establishment was adversely affected by one detail at this time. J.D. Pawson had been invited to take part by leading the conference in a Bible study. This he did with an address from the Book of Joel on the need for the restoring of the wasted years consumed by the locusts. However it was intended, to those present it appeared to be a severe and untimely attack not only upon them, but also upon their predecessors over many years. The one high-profile Baptist in renewal was Pawson because of his notable ministry at Gold Hill, Chalfont St Peter. Many other charismatics had never shown any great interest in gaining the approval of the Union leadership. Several were moving ever nearer the point of severing their Baptist links altogether. Pawson hoped that the Baptist Union would be both reformed according to Scripture and revived by the power of the Spirit. To cautious but responsible leaders words such as his at this time gave ample confirmation of the wisdom of their indifference to his other well-known interests. Pawson's standing among denominational leaders was thus severely damaged at this point.[17]

To compound matters even more, in 1971 an address was given at the National Assembly of the Baptist Union on the subject of the Humanity of Jesus that could not have been designed more expertly if the purpose was to divide and destroy the common witness of Baptists. The speaker was Michael Taylor, the principal of the Northern Baptist College. His title was 'The Incarnate Presence – How much of a man was Jesus Christ?' His argument was clear and his conclusions precise. As Taylor understood Jesus, there was no difference in kind between Christ's humanity and our own, nor in the way in which God was in Christ and in ourselves. It appeared that however much Taylor went on to affirm his acceptance of traditional Christology, in fact he thought its formulations to be irrelevant and did not believe a word of them. As an attempt to restructure those formulations, Taylor's work in a theological lecture hall where he was open to question and debate would have served well. On the platform of the Baptist Union Annual Assembly, and from the pulpit of Westminster Chapel of all places, it sounded as if he was endorsing a view of the Person of Christ that was heresy.[18]

Even though the congregation rose to a man to cheer the address, many were deeply distressed by it. Dr David Russell sensed the mood of the denomination accurately: 'I must confess that as I listened to him, I sank lower and lower in my chair. I knew for a certainty that following the Assembly, the storm would break! And it did!'[19]

As to the repercussions of the Taylor affair, we must wait at this point. Suffice it to say that when the popular minister of the Park Road Church, Bromley, Godfrey Robinson, newly appointed as vice-president of the Baptist Union, collapsed and died in his sleep in June 1971, hopes for the Baptist Union emerging from these troubles unscathed reached their nadir.[20]

Guildford, 1971

While these critical issues were being debated by the Baptists, the work of charismatic renewal continued unabated as far the Fountain Trust was concerned. By now Michael Harper had gained considerable experience and expertise in handling the demands of an itinerant ministry, and the time seemed ripe for him to stage a major international conference. This took place at Surrey University, Guildford, from 12 to 17 July 1971 and was described by James Dunn as the Coming of Age of the Renewal. Harper cited four reasons for this: first, it was international in its appeal and overseas delegates as well as overseas speakers participated; second, it was ecumenical, including over 40 Lutherans and 30 Roman Catholics; third, it was unifying, and the intention was to bring together rather than polarise those who attended; last, it was also didactic, and highly qualified theologians were able to begin to grapple with the major issues of the doctrine of the Holy Spirit.[21]

Though the participation of Catholics was publicly criticised by some Pentecostal leaders, it was clear that this conference set a new high-water mark in the life of the renewal movement. David Pawson had moved from Gold Hill and was now minister of the Guildford Baptist Church and beginning his most productive period as an exceptionally gifted Bible teacher and preacher. He approached this conference with considerable misgivings because one of the speakers was a Methodist known to Pawson from his Methodist days, and also known as a liberal-evangelical, Leslie Davison. In the event, after the diplomatic Michael Harper had managed to allay his fears, Pawson enthusiastically supported it.

This was not the case, however, for Harold Owen, now of Woking. His judgement mirrored the tensions among the Baptists to which we have already referred and which have remained a part of the backcloth for the whole renewal drama, coming to a head when restorationism became a major and separate sub-plot as the movement advanced. Owen did not feel he could give it much support because of the presence of a Roman Catholic speaker in Kevin Ranaghan.[22]

The versatile team of speakers also included Robert Frost, Rodman Williams and Ralph Wilkerson, all from the USA. David Watson and Arthur Wallis from England were part of it. 'Mr Pentecost', David du Plessis, was also there. While only a few Baptist ministers booked in, many others attended, including R.E. Maycocks and Alan Braybrooks.[23]

Nevertheless, the ongoing impact on Baptist churches was to be shown to be great. At first the leadership of the Union did not realise that a new movement was taking place before their eyes. It was not the property of the evangelical fundamentalists, though it was passionately evangelical. It was not owned by the conservative evangelicals. If anything they felt somewhat upstaged as a diminishing number continued to react, because of the evidence of the more liberated spirituality among the renewed. It succeeded in promoting good ecumenical relationships, but it was not tied in to the ambiguities of the ecumenical movement. Many leaders of the mainline Pentecostal denominations were deeply suspicious, and very few renewal leaders had any desire to be closely identified with their views anyway. The trouble for the Union was that, while an increasing number of ministers and members were enthusiastically counting themselves in, their denominational leaders had not even been looking in the right direction. Guildford began to change all that, as the carefully modulated comments on the conference in the minute book of the influential Advisory Committee on Church Relations stated: 'It was clear that blanket condemnation is no longer possible of the charismatic movement. It would be important for us to consider how best to keep in contact with those participating in the movement.'[24]

However, in keeping with the best traditions of ecclesiastical committees of all descriptions, they began the process by the application of a more easily controlled process, namely the drawing up of an appropriate book list for further study.

Crisis and Hope

5

Contending for the Faith

(Jude 3)

The decade of the 1970s were years of mixed and contrasting
fortunes for the Church in Britain. For Baptists, in particular,
they began with a period of theological strife that could have
been terminal for the national Union. They concluded with a
report written by the general secretary of the Baptist Union,
Dr David Russell, entitled *Signs of Hope*.[1] For the charismatic
renewal as represented by the Fountain Trust, the developments
were diametrically opposed. The decade began with the affir-
mation that followed their first highly successful international
conference at Guildford in 1971 that they were a movement
that had come of age.[2] They concluded with the announcement that, as from 1 January 1981, the Fountain Trust would
cease its operations.[3] Such a reversal of the respective fortunes
of a historic denominational body battered by controversy, and
a new and respected charismatic trust that was a stabilising
factor among the renewed and a trusted representative of their
views by the wider Church, was the last thing expected at the
start of the decade.

As we shall see, the closure of the Fountain Trust did not
signify the end of the renewal movement. In terms of our
theme the closure, and the erosion of the influence of the Trust
that lay behind it, was significant in both positive and negative
ways. It aided the development of a new ethos in which charismatic Baptists could be themselves without the inhibitions of
being a minority grouping under Anglican patronage. Towards
the end of the decade we have the emergence of Mainstream
which provided that setting within a broader alliance that was
itself a substantial contribution to healthy renewal for a period.
At the same time the removal of a body with a strong bias

towards the Established Church meant the ending of some of the checks implicit in all experiences of *de facto* ecumenism. Thus some Baptists began to look towards the emerging restorationists, who were convinced that the days of all forms of denominationalism other than their own were over. Since strong restorationists believed that all true Christians with a vital experience of the Spirit would inevitably gravitate to their new Churches, Baptists who followed this teaching could only do so by somewhat detaching themselves from their proper roots.[4] It is one of the ironies of Protestant Church history that new Church groupings, which so often begin with a strong desire to repudiate the exclusive ties that they perceive as the supreme weakness of those from whom they separate, almost invariably go on to promote even greater degrees of exclusiveness for themselves.

In following these developments, further major points about the renewal so far masked by the excitement of its beginnings become clearer. Plainly, they indicate one of its continuing characteristics in the relatively short life of many of its apparently stable centralities. More significantly, they clarify the point that in and of itself charismatic renewal is a corrective for the whole body of Christ rather than a fresh revelation about its essential nature. As a corrective, renewal assumes but does not express the wholeness of the Gospel which brings the Church into being, which defines the nature of the Church, and which is the mandate of its ministry. Renewal underlines the importance of aspects of the Gospel the Church has long neglected in the need for vital and continuous encounters with the living Spirit of God. To put it another way, renewal as a corrective acts like an immunising agent for the health of the body. It deters what Archbishop Michael Ramsey described as 'the mistake of ecclesiasticism'.[5] It protects from the condition of spiritual dryness. But taken exclusively by itself, the renewal virus breeds other diseases it was designed to combat because it lacks the compensating factors that come from the rest of the body. Hence in this period we deal with both the glory and the shame of the renewal, strong as the servant of the Church yet weak once it becomes the master. Its message has the capacity to initiate fresh discoveries of the grace of God but it lacks the ability to mature the characters of the renewed. It is these contrasting effects that we must now examine, beginning with the fraught condition of the Baptist Union in 1971.

Another downgrade

As we have seen, the upset caused by the address given by Michael Taylor on 20 May 1971 at the Annual Assembly was due to many other factors besides the theological convictions he expressed then. As we have already suggested with the benefit of hindsight, had the address been given in a lecture room and subjected to the normal questions it raised, there would not have been the controversy that it stirred. Whether or not that is the case, far-reaching debate was inevitable.

In evidence of this, the minutes of the council of the Baptist Union for the period make it clear that it occupied major time in the life of the council throughout the subsequent period from 1971 to 1972. It was the subject of further Assembly action in 1972. The repercussions continued in the life of the churches of the Union throughout 1972, 1973 and even after that.[6]

At the heart of the debate was the theology of the address to which we have already referred. The subject was 'The Incarnate Presence: How much of a man was Jesus Christ?' In the course of his carefully scripted argument, Taylor said:

God indwells Jesus in the same way as he indwells his greatest saints and all of us. God is in Christ as God is in all men. Jesus is not of a different kind of stuff or substance. But Jesus is unique because God did something quite unique in Jesus. That uniqueness is not in the presence – 'God was in Christ'. It is in the activity 'reconciling the world to himself'. God is always active in the world, and his actions are never out of character, but he does different things at different times and what he did in Jesus is unique. He had never done it before and he has not done it again: he showed with unrivalled clarity that he loves the world, is involved in its struggles, is suffering to death for its salvation. He acted in a decisive way for the reconciliation of man to himself and for the healing of the whole of creation. He raised the Nazarene to life, the firstfruits of the harvest of the dead. Of no other can it be said that God did in him what God did in Jesus.[7]

Taylor made it clear that he had no great enthusiasm for

making the kind of argument that he offered as a confession of faith, since to him there was a far more significant way of expressing the significance of Jesus 'by starting at the other end'.

What is the significance of Jesus for us in here? How does Jesus illuminate this situation? What is the God who is active in Jesus doing now, and how do we co-operate with him? Where in this concrete set of circumstances can we celebrate and say 'Yes' and where must we say 'No' and how are we called to respond?

In the light of the furore all this unleashed it was amazing that Taylor had been given the brief of speaking on such a theme at such a time. At the end of the Assembly there is always a brief meeting of the council to transact small items of business like the co-options of a certain number of candidates to serve on the council alongside those appointed by ballot. This meeting duly took place on 28 April 1971. After the necessary business had been done, Stanley Voke raised the question of the theology of the address and urged the council to repudiate the views that had been expressed in it, and reaffirm its acceptance of the doctrinal clauses of the Declaration of Principle. Discussion on the issue was short-circuited, however, when Dr Payne moved the adjournment of the council on the grounds that Taylor was not there to defend his viewpoint. This duly happened, and it was agreed that any repercussions to the address would be handled at the discretion of the general secretary.[9] During May and June letters began to arrive on the general secretary's desk. The Superintendents' Board became increasingly uneasy and asked for copies of the address to be made available to them. The superintendents were correct in their understanding of a groundswell of unease that was building up.

By October 1971 a small group of young London ministers had arranged another meeting to attempt a statement of Christology which was clear, unashamedly evangelical and orthodox in its doctrinal content. They invited their best-known colleague to make it and he agreed to do so. This was J.D. Pawson. His subject was 'How much of a God is Jesus?' The address was given to a packed Bloomsbury Chapel on 2 October 1971 and was fully reported in the *Baptist Times*. For his efforts, some supporters of the controversial views expressed by Taylor now attacked Pawson, charging him with Docetism, Apollinarianism and Arianism among various other heresies.[10] Others expressed the wish that now that both wings of the denomination had vented their views, it was time to call a halt, but this was not to be. Having failed to make any public statement in April, the General Purposes Committee of the Baptist Union agreed to prepare a statement which was delivered to the council in their November meeting. It was a comprehensive summary acknowledging the extent of the distress that was being felt as a result of the address and now the debate. It affirmed the need for theological reflection, and supported the integrity of Michael Taylor. It reaffirmed the doctrinal clauses in the Declaration of Principle.

At the council the debate moved forward to a major confrontation in the Union by two steps that were taken. First, in order to free himself from the responsibilities and limitations of being chairman of the council, George Beasley-Murray resigned from that position. He was convinced that this issue was of such enormous significance that he needed to marshal all his theological skills to help the denomination repudiate heresy. To this end he wrote a paper entitled *The Christological Controversy in the Baptist Union*, and sent it to all accredited Baptist ministers.[11]

Second, the council agreed the text of the recommendation from their committee with minor amendments but added an addendum to it that was seriously damaging in its consequences in the wider constituency. At its heart were these words:

Not only is it [the denomination] characterised by evangelical and missionary zeal; it possesses a treasured heritage of liberty of opinion and utterance and since the seventeenth century has shared in the struggle for religious toleration and the freeing of men's minds and consciences from intellectual and civil fetters. Accordingly the Union has always contained within its fellowship those of different theological opinions and emphases, believing that its claim for toleration involves tolerance and mutual respect within its own ranks.[12]

When this addition was released to the churches, the storm cones in the denomination were in full view. A number of ministers forthwith resigned from the lists of accredited ministers. The BRF at their annual conference in Swanwick declared, 'We cannot in conscience remain associated with the life of a Union which has decided to tolerate the denial of the deity of our Lord Jesus Christ. How we translate this conviction into action will be a matter of individual judgement.'[13] By January 1972, the council realised belatedly that not only was there enormous unease throughout the whole family but that the former president of the Union Sir Cyril Black and George Beasley-Murray were determined to act on this. In March the council agreed to a motion expressing regret at the confusion caused by the addendum. But on 26 April 1972, a year less a day from the utterance that caused the trouble, by a massive majority of 1800 to 46 with 72 abstentions the Assembly affirmed the Black resolution. This declared

> that the Declaration of Principle represents the basic requirement for fellowship in the Baptist denomination and that we attach high importance to the loyal and wholehearted acceptance of it. In particular, we assert the unacceptableness of any interpretation of the person and work of Jesus Christ Our Lord which would obscure or deny the fundamental tenet of the Christian faith that Jesus Christ is Lord and Saviour, truly God and truly man.[14]

So the issue was resolved. As Dr Russell said at the conclusion of a debate that was the centre-piece of the Assembly, 'May we all leave older and wiser.' In total, it eventually transpired that the 38 churches that removed themselves from fellowship in the Baptist Union were soon joined by eight more. It was a grievous wound to the life of the Union, and the division in the body had gone deep. David Russell confessed that he was not convinced that this was the best outcome, and E.A. Payne was reported by *The Times* religious affairs correspondent Clifford Longley as believing that the denomination had taken 'a lurch to the right'.[15] With these words he demonstrated that although he was still undoubtedly the outstanding Baptist leader of these days, he was out of touch with the grass roots convictions of those whom he represented. David Russell now had the unenviable job of seeking to bind up the wounds by finding, then applying, the healing balm of a new common vision for the future of the Union.

Renewal advances

The striking success of the Guildford conference in 1971 continued to make its impact on the Baptists throughout late 1971 and 1972. One of the major factors in this change of mind concerning the renewal was the emergence of Roman Catholic Charismatic Renewal, which had already surfaced at Guildford through the presence of Kevin Ranaghan on the speaking team. By far the most significant development to begin to emerge followed this up and was of major ecumenical significance. It was in the form of the interest and later commitment of one of the senior Roman Catholic cardinals, the primate of Belgium, Cardinal Suenens. It was not long before his commitment to renewal led him to publicly testify to the blessing of the baptism in the Spirit, to commend the practice of speaking in tongues, and to urge his Church and all Churches to embrace the renewal as a genuine movement of the Holy Spirit.[16] Hence Suenens became a major spokesman for the renewal movement, and it is true to say that his participation raised the awareness of the wider Church, including Baptists, to renewal issues.

Created cardinal in 1962 by Pope John XXIII, Suenens was heavily involved in the arrangements and the business of the second Vatican council in 1962 for whom he was one of the four moderators. He was widely regarded as the leader of the reforming group of the council. Clearly, with his involvement, it was no longer a case of dealing with a few Pentecostal extremists. Suenens was a friend of Pope Paul VI, and a close collaborator and joint author with Archbishop Michael Ramsey. He certainly could not be ignored. Suenens had chosen the phrase, 'In the Holy Spirit' when he became a bishop. His charismatic pilgrimage commenced while on a lecture tour in the USA. There he encountered some charismatic nuns in Philadelphia who told him of the wonderful changes the Spirit had been achieving in their lives. Soon he was able to speak of his own response to baptism in the Spirit, which he interpreted as a release of the Spirit already received at baptism, confirmation, and Eucharist. He described tongues speaking as a way of God showing us that the Spirit of God is with us to help us to pray in depth, and as another of his 'surprises'.[17]

Essentially, Suenens saw the renewal supplying the spiritual dynamic for the institutional changes that Vatican II had set in train. He perceived that it would be an enormous boost to the quest for Christian unity, of which he was a strong and passionate advocate. As a senior member of the Roman hierarchy there is no doubt that he saw the future of a united and dramatically reformed Church within the see of Rome. He did not appear as a speaker on the platform of the Fountain Trust until the international conference at Westminster in August 1977, where to great applause Tom Smail introduced him with the words, 'Bienvenue, M. le Cardinale'. Nevertheless, his influence throughout the movement had grown before then through the meetings of the Catholic renewal agencies and the European charismatic leaders' conference. He formed a strong friendship with Tom Smail, and he and his theologian Paul Lebeau much admired Smail's robust summaries of Protestant and Reformed theology.

In the summer of 1976, the meeting for European charismatic leaders convened at Mechelen and the theme was *koinonia* – fellowship. Theological papers were given, and there was serious discussion on the theme proposed by David Pawson on the place of the Virgin Mary in our salvation. Although no agreement was reached, some positive propositions were arrived at. The cardinal presided over a Eucharist, held in the chapel at Mechelen in which Cardinal Mercier is buried, the initiator of the first Anglican–Roman Catholic conversations which had taken place some 50 years previously. So, throughout the years from 1971 to 1977, the Roman Church was usually represented at major conferences organised by the Fountain Trust.[18] The support of the cardinal was crucial. Nor was he disposed to be exclusively concerned with Roman Catholic Charismatic Renewal. For instance, he was happy to come as the special guest to a dinner arranged by the Baptist philanthropist and former president of the Baptist Union, Sir Cyril Black. He seemed to be quite as much at home among evangelicals as he was in his own Church.

To return to 1973, this was the year for the next international Conference following the successful meeting in Surrey in 1971. Nottingham was the venue, and the theme was 'Gathered for Power'. This was also the title of the book written by Graham Pulkingham to describe the remarkable transformation that had taken place in the Church of the Redeemer Episcopal Church in Houston, Texas, during his ministry there, and he was a main speaker at Nottingham. Michael Harper managed to complete his own book on the same ministry before the conference, entitling it *A New Way of Living*.[19] Essentially, Pulkingham was claiming that renewal leads on to a form of community sharing that enables the Church to break through the barriers of personal isolation in society and family, especially as this is experienced by the lonely single or those with special problem conditions through medical or psychological causes. He advocated a new adventure in extended family homes in which the members of the new family contributed all their possessions and their earnings by agreement. Each household was to be led by strong, dependable and resourceful men, who together formed a corporate church eldership. They expected total loyalty from their new family and total compliance from their spouse and nuclear family. He believed that new charismatic communities dominated by 'intense love, indomitable faith, and a spirit of praise' would make a dramatic impact on the secular western world of the 1970s. The result would be in significant evangelistic advance.[20] Harper used the words of Eliza Doolittle, the heroine of *Pygmalion*, to make the point:

> We are sick of sermons, books, discussions, theologies, Bible lectures. We are not interested in hymns, anthems and choruses. Don't spout poetry at us. Show us. Give us a demonstration. We want to see action. Words are not enough. Your words make us sick and we won't listen to you any more.[21]

Harper had been so hugely affected by his own experience of the new lifestyle of the Houston church that there is little doubt that Nottingham was designed at least in part as a launch pad for Pulkingham and the highly talented musical group he had brought with him, known as The Fisherfolk. Within a year Pulkingham had moved to England to set up his own ministry community. They were placed under the guidance of the bishop of Coventry, Cuthbert Bardsley, and became known as The Community of Celebration. Another of Pulkingham's admirers was Dr George McLeod, then head of the Iona Community. He was also a speaker determined to share his own insights on the needs of the hour. For him, spiritual renewal was crucial

but not in itself complete. He looked for a political expression
of the love of Christ in a willingness to serve the whole community for Christ's sake.

> What does it mean to be in Christ, not just in personal regeneration
> but in political obligation? To love God might be called the vertical
> of the cross but to love our neighbour is the horizontal. . . . I pray
> God that Nottingham will nail us to the cross, that buried with
> Christ we may rise with Christ to full stature.[22]

He contributed in this way at the conference, but also gave
his backing to the work that Pulkingham had set his hand to.
Bishop Bill Burnett of Grahamstown, who was to go on
to become the last white South African archbishop of Cape
Town, was also a speaker. David Pawson redeemed a promise
made to Michael Harper in 1971 by speaking on the Freedom
of the Spirit, from the letter to the Galatians.[23]
With such a galaxy of speakers, and a full attendance, the
Nottingham conference was considered another notable success
for the Fountain Trust. Among those who attended was
Emmanuel Sullivan, an American Franciscan who had already
written sympathetically on the potential for the renewal to
renew the Churches in a survey prepared for the British Council
of Churches.[24] He wrote in glowing terms of his experience at
Nottingham:

> There was nothing narrow about the spirit of Nottingham. There
> was no Orthodox presence and a limited Roman Catholic one.
> Yet the spiritual witness of both these historic Churches was
> appreciated. There was ecumenical witness throughout the confer-
> ence but proselytism never raised its ugly head. . . . It has been said
> that at Guildford the charismatic renewal movement came of age.
> At Nottingham it was evident that the movement was becoming
> mature.[25]

In the matter of finance, however, the Nottingham conference did not pay its way, but there was more to it than this.
The central issue advocated at Nottingham was that of extended
family living. It was expected to be a major breakthrough for
the renewal. Certainly attempts were made to take it up and
community living was promoted with great zeal. The following
year the same emphasis was brought from California in a visit
by Ken Pagaard, pastor of First Baptist Church, Chula Vista,

near San Diego, linked with the American Baptist Convention. His church was replicating the Houston experience in a different setting close to the border with Mexico, in southern California, and from a Baptist base. In his ministry in England he made contact with a number of Baptist churches and ministers and encouraged their experimentations with forms of extended family living.[26]

Soon this development produced more threatening results which presaged the decline of the Fountain Trust. The immediate consequence was a crop of damaged families, broken marriages, severed relationships, and troubled people. Apart from the highly organised exception of the Jesus Family Bugbrooke, extended family living soon lost its attractiveness and support and the interests of the renewal moved on to different territory. We shall return to the story of the Bugbrooke Community later, but note at this point that it was for a variety of reasons that they were never accepted within the mainstream of the renewal, just as they were also to be out of fellowship with the Evangelical Alliance and the Baptist Union.

The main problem in extended family living ultimately arose over the issue of the marriage covenant between the two persons of the husband and the wife, and the teachings of Scripture on the nature of the marriage bond. At Nottingham, Pulkingham had arrived in Britain with an extraordinary reinterpretation of the teaching of the Scriptures on this basic issue, which encouraged such a strengthening of the commitment of the married to the extended family in the Church of which they were members that inevitably there was a lowering of their commitment to their spouse and their nuclear family. Ultimately, it took Tom Smail to expose the theological issues of Pulkingham's ministry with a robust restatement of the uniqueness of the covenant of Christian marriage.[27] In the course of our own travels, my wife and I visited the Chula Vista Church in 1976 and found that, while the teaching there had not been as extreme as in the case of Pulkingham's ministry, the church itself and the homes which we visited were quite unhappy conglomerate gatherings, not happy extended families.

At this point some of the inherent weaknesses began to emerge as far as renewal as a whole was concerned. For one thing, the Pulkingham episode exposed the way in which the

British expression of renewal has consistently depended upon the insights of North American teachers who either claim or are soon invested with the status of the all-wise guru. Their North American achievements are impressive when compared with those of our own less successful preachers who are attempting a very different task set amid the challenges of the very different Western European spiritual atmosphere now overwhelmingly secularised. Renewal seldom takes due account of those differences, and does itself few favours by these unwise promotions and comparisons.

More than this, it demonstrated one of the least attractive characteristics of the renewal, which is to adopt a fresh enthusiasm for a brief period. For a while it is conceived and promoted as being in itself the total answer to the needs of the Church, the one missing piece in the jigsaw of the purposes of God which, once it is found and put in place, will secure the ever elusive revival about which the renewal constantly affirms its faith. When the one theme does not deliver what is expected of it, the tendency has been to drop it without further ado in pursuit of its successor. But the truth is that these enthusiasms pursue each other with restless haste across the stage of the consciousness of renewal, each one consuming its predecessor with cannibalistic ferocity. No one biblical truth can deliver all that its discoverers promise, and the great revival remains but a distant mirage.

The lesson that Nottingham was underlining was a familiar one for us all, but it was not yet learned by the charismatic movement. It is that ill-considered, theologically insecure insights offering the promise of long-term blessings through short-term schemes are doomed to disappoint. Pulkingham has had many counterparts, all of whom have ultimately become a danger to the survival and growth of the renewal which first gave them prominence. We should never refuse to listen to the teaching of those who come from other lands. Many of our most reliable and helpful visitors come to us from North America and commend their ministry by the modesty with which they give it. But beware the words of the guru. Like each of us, they all have feet of clay. We know that the power of the Gospel is made known in the self-offering love of Christ upon the cross. The triumphs of the early church rejoicing in the glorious presence of the Spirit in their midst were won at the cost of much sacrifice and heroic confessions of personal weakness and inadequacy. If the renewal attempts to draw us away from our crucial centre in Christ's Calvary or in our own reflection of that experience, it is false teaching indeed. So supporters of charismatic renewal must never forget the lesson that in the life of the Spirit there are never any short cuts to success.

Teaching and Integrity

(Titus 2:7)

Tom Smail had joined the staff of the Fountain Trust from the post of minister at Whiteabbey Presbyterian Church, Belfast, in September 1972. He was one of the group of Scottish ministers in central Scotland who had entered into renewal in the 1960s, and for him the ministry of Dennis Bennett had been crucial. He is a Scot, born and bred. It was in Scotland that he had received most of his education. He had graduated in arts at Glasgow University with first-class honours before going on to New College, Edinburgh, for his BD, which he gained with a distinction in systematic theology. He had also studied for a further year in Basel under Karl Barth, and so was well qualified to take part in the theological debate raised by the renewal. In this, Smail has remained a unique figure in the renewal scene in Britain, though latterly a larger number of trained theologians have begun to emerge.[1]

With Smail's appointment as director of the trust, there were necessary adjustments to be made to the role of Michael Harper. While he remained the editor of *Renewal* and the chairman of the executive, room had to be made available for Smail to exercise his ministry, which was of a different calibre to Harper's. By temperament and gifting Harper is supremely a pioneer. He enjoys planning ahead, he is not disturbed by risk-taking adventures and his instincts are always entrepreneurial. Although these characteristics are usually associated with the flamboyance of the extrovert, with Harper they are much more carefully displayed. He is nothing if he is not a discreet and charming middle-class Englishman. He had started the work of the trust more or less single handedly and without any financial security for the difficult early days. By contrast, Smail is naturally a more cautious man not given to dangerous escapades. He is the theologian who weighs the implications of his own ministry and that of other teachers. He is also a gifted preacher capable of giving vivid inspiration to his listeners, often with the use of sharp phrases and memorable humour. His concern has never been for the more bizarre aspects of renewal that shock people by their novelty, but for the unitive factors that renew the Church by drawing us back to the basis for the Church's whole existence in Christ.[2]

One of the consequences of the advent of Smail into senior renewal leadership was that the restless rush of the enthusiasms we have already noted was somewhat curbed. For Smail these were unnecessary activities that were doomed to disappoint those who accepted their prescriptions, and that led inevitably to their greater immaturity. It has to be admitted that, for all the fact that the Fountain Trust was by far the most responsible body in the renewal scene at the time, the trust had promoted an interest in a vast range of additional possibilities for the amusement of the renewed. They included the pursuit of unusual healing techniques like the healing of the memory, the understanding of Frank Lake with his emphasis on clinical theology and the notion of the significance of reliving the birth trauma, the possibilities that behind most of our personal problems or the difficulties of Church life lay demonic influences, witchcraft or ley lines. We were encouraged to consider the ministry of exorcism, or the value of continuously praising God under all circumstances, or the special significance of using the gift of tongues for considerable periods of prayer, or communitarian living. Many visiting preachers from South America as well as North America encouraged ideas of authoritarian leadership. Others accounted for the superiority of their ministerial results on the basis of their greater faith and stressed the legitimacy of asking for and receiving 'anything you ask' from God, be it the healing of the sick, the raising of the dead, or receiving lots of money for our particular ministry.

This is to name only some of the passing interests of charismatic believers up to this point. Smail soon scrutinised the value of these different phases and wisely concluded that at best they were of only marginal significance. Most of them were promoted by those whose personal lifestyle was opulent, and there seemed to be a direct connection between the rhetorical skills of the promoter and the level of their expectancies for financial rewards. Only a few of these emphases were taken up immediately by British preachers, perhaps for reasons to do with the limited cash flow in the churches in the United Kingdom, but later on some of the restoration churches were drawn towards these themes at least for a period. Smail saw that, at worst, some of this teaching was potentially destructive: for example, the view that Christians have such power in prayer that they can receive all the healing they need, providing they ask for it with the proper formulae and with sufficient faith, is no help to the chronically or terminally sick sufferer for whom God's answer to their prayer has not been as they had hoped. It is clear that healing is not always appropriate or within his purposes. Smail knew of pastoral instances where this was the case. He did not hesitate to expose the folly in such teaching nor the tendencies to extremism that it represented, even when to do so exposed him to many suspicious comments from those who were most in need of his help.[3]

He also commenced the publication of *Theological Renewal*, claiming that unless the renewal found an adequate theological framework, its influence was bound to be limited.[4] He was responsible for moving the emphasis away from spectacular ministry to teaching. Fountain Trust night schools were inaugurated in 1975.[5] Together with new study sections in *Renewal* magazine, which also started in 1975, and the weighty editorial commentary in *Theological Renewal*, they became the characteristics of the leadership he was to go on to give.

Had it not been for Harper the pioneer, it is probable that the charismatic movement would never have taken hold in the mainline Churches in the way that it did. But the pioneer had to give way to the theologian. Hence in June 1975 it was announced that Michael Harper would be relinquishing his position as director of the Fountain Trust that September, his place being taken by Smail. He saw that his mission was to relate the renewal to the wider Trinitarian faith of the Church and to its essential mission. He interpreted his own experience of renewal and that of the movement as a whole by considering its teaching through the prism of his own classical reformed theology.

The restriction of the pursuit of novelty inevitably led to other developments for the Fountain Trust. At the tenth anniversary of the trust in October 1974, Harper had been quick to identify triumphalism as a recurrent failure, leading to arrogance and injudicious statements, and confessed: 'We have on occasions lacked the boldness of love and substituted an arrogant conceit.'[6] But by August 1976 Smail was confessing: 'The surface sparkle has rather faded from the charismatic renewal. . . . Not all the healings have taken place, not all the prophecies have been fulfilled, and amidst the blessings we have discovered what problems to ourselves and others we still are.'[7]

To summarise the later history of the trust, the following factors combined to make the closure in 1980 inevitable. First, there was the loss of a hunger for novelty in renewal. This led to a diminishing of the excitement level at the meetings of the trust, and hence support for them died down. They became much tamer and more respectable affairs, not dissimilar from other large gatherings to be found in most Christian circles from time to time.

Second, there was a growing financial problem with the loss of novelty appeal. The money required to mount the major conferences and alternatives was beginning to become available elsewhere, especially through the house church movement, as restoration was originally called. Their meetings were strong at the very points where the trust had now little desire to be strong, so the work of the trust became less significant.

Third, the meetings became less eventful as obvious demonstrations of the presence of the Spirit, particularly with the public exercise of the gift of tongues, with interpretation, and the phenomenon of singing in the Spirit, became fewer. Added to this was the fact that, since by now many churches had embraced the new worship style of renewal which allowed space for the exercise of spiritual gifts, they scarcely needed more meetings to model this for them.

Fourth, during this period some Anglicans who were not from the majority background of conservative evangelicalism became increasingly convinced of the need for a renewal approach that was more geared to their own spirituality. Denominational renewal therefore grew chiefly among them at the same time as the restoration movement became attractive to many non-Anglicans.

Fifth, we need to consider the impact of the fresh confidence among non-charismatic evangelicals through the emerging teaching on church growth. It appeared to offer many of the benefits associated with renewal with far fewer of the painful losses that renewal brought, through challenging the sufficiency of a non-charismatic evangelical experience.

Finally, the consequence to the theological discussions with a group of evangelical Anglicans led by John Stott was the issuing of a joint statement with them and Harper and Smail and others entitled *Gospel and Spirit*.[8] In the end this indicated that, differences of terminology apart, they were a group of thinkers among whom there were few differences of theological substance.

Bringing all these factors together at the end of the 1970s, the closure of the trust was inevitable.

Smail left the service of the Fountain Trust in September 1979 to take up an appointment as vice-principal of St John's College, Nottingham, and Michael Barling was appointed in his place. As Smail left, with typical honesty and without denying his indebtedness, he spelt out his own sense of personal frustration and disappointment with the renewal in a way that was bound to produce shock waves for those still uncritically committed:

> One of my convictions at the moment is that the charismatic movement, as a thing in itself, is just about over. The approach that was so fruitful in the mid-sixties has almost exhausted its usefulness by the late seventies. It is a movement that, for all its stated desire to do so, has not shown that it has, within itself, the resources to deal with its exclusiveness and immaturity. . . . I believe that the charismatic phase that is nearly over needs to give way to a deeper and wider renewal in the Church. . . . I feel in my bones that the Spirit is saying to us that your renewal, so far, has been too small and is calling us to a humble repentance from that smallness to something immeasurably larger which will add still more new dimensions to the basic conviction that Jesus is Lord.[9]

The restoration challenge

Although the house church movement only began to surface in the early 1970s, its origins go back considerably further. According to Andrew Walker they are drawn from the twin roots of the Irvingite movement of the Catholic Apostolics, and Brethrenism. It was in 1951 that Arthur Wallis emerged from his background with the Open Brethren through an early experience of baptism in the Spirit. In 1956 he published his work on revival entitled *In the Day of thy Power*, in which he expressed his great desire for a latter-day Pentecost, preceding the return of Christ. Wallis was joined by David Lillie, who was also from a Brethren background. Together they organised a conference in 1958 at Mamhead Park near Exeter on the theme of 'The Church of Jesus Christ – Its Purity, Power, Pattern and Programme in the Context of Today'. It was attended by future leaders of the restoration movement such as Bryn Jones and Graham Perrins, and also by Campbell McAlpine and Dennis Clark whose subsequent links were more in the renewal setting than that of the restoration movement.[10]

During the 1960s the charismatic renewal overshadowed much development among the restorationists. According to Walker, the rise of the renewal was so phenomenal that this was inevitable. Wallis and McAlpine commended themselves to a wide variety of charismatics because of their gracious manners and their scriptural ministries, so they had no difficulty in ministering alongside other leaders from the historic Churches. Moreover, the fact that Michael Harper, Tom Smail, Peter Hocken, Colin Urquhart, David Pawson and a host of others had no desire to leave their Churches, since they were confident that God could renew the existing structures, militated against the notion that to be faithful to the will of God, new non-denominational structures were a vital ingredient.[11]

As the pace of the renewal activities diminished, however, the convictions of Wallis became more urgent, as he plainly indicated in 1974:

Jesus Christ is not coming back for Anglicans and Methodists, Baptists and Brethren, Presbyterians and Pentecostals, he is coming back for His Bride without spot [the mark of adolescent immaturity] or wrinkle [the mark of old age]. I see no future for denominations, but a glorious future for the body of Christ.[12]

By 1980 he was sure that not only had the renewal peaked and moved into decline but that there was one reason over and above all the others we have already registered. It was 'the absence of biblical radicalism' among charismatic leaders, their compromise over the most basic issues of their spiritual loyalty to Christ.[13] His charge at this time in part reflected a similar challenge from Lloyd Jones to evangelicals in 1966 to be willing to abandon their denominations because of their ecumenical involvement. So Wallis now affirmed that the radical nature of the Church of Christ was not being tackled by charismatics, who were compromised by their loyalties to the denominations to which their churches belong, for which he saw no future.

To Wallis there was soon added a considerable number of future leaders of restorationism. John Noble emerged in 1967, having been a friend of Michael Harper in his days at All Souls. Gerald Coates emerged in the late 1960s. Barney Coombs was a part of the new movement, and Terry Virgo, Roger Forster, Peter Lyne and Harry Greenwood were soon with them, together with Maurice Smith, George Tarleton, David Mansell and Wally North. While they were sympathetic with the work of renewal, they were not at home in the meetings led by the Fountain Trust nor in the style of their conferences. At a Fountain Trust conference, the highlight was usually a dramatic and colourful Eucharist, celebrated according to a form of the Series 3 rite in the Alternative Service Book. The more outrageously flamboyant the vestments on these occasions for Anglicans, the more most of the crowds loved the event. Not only was this difficult for the minority of less liturgically minded Baptists, it made little sense at all to former members of the Brethren and independent evangelical Churches to whom the appeal of the new, pure Church was far more relevant.

Bible weeks became the platform for propagating the new message, beginning with the Capel Bible Week in 1973. This led on to the Lakes Bible Week which soon became Dales Bible Week in 1976. The Downs Week followed, led by Terry Virgo, and it was evident that here was a powerful new force, somewhat charismatic and certainly sectarian, which had a great appeal to the minds and hearts of charismatic Nonconformists.[14]

It is a matter of some significance to note that probably the strongest of the networks of churches that have now emerged is New Frontiers led by Terry Virgo. He grew up in the Baptist Church at Holland Road, Hove, and was trained for ministry at the London Bible College. Like a large number of his associates there is a strong commitment to the reformed teaching of Lloyd Jones and a love of good Bible teaching. This underlines the point that the call from Arthur Wallis to charismatics to have done with their compromising associations was an extension of the Lloyd Jones view to which we have already drawn attention. At a personal level there was never any animosity from Arthur Wallis towards those who disagreed with his analysis. In a very real sense it can be claimed that British restorationism of the 1970s was the reinvention in the twentieth century of the Baptist wheel of the seventeenth century.[15] Baptists should therefore be the last ones to respond in a hostile way to the restoration development of which he was a senior statesman.

In the light of these similarities we notice that, like our Baptist forefathers, they have a hearty dislike for all forms of establishment religion and a strong commitment to Biblical authority. They are warmly evangelical in their general outlook and hold to the necessity of demonstrating their enthusiasm in their worship. Unlike our forefathers, they model their worship not so much on the passages in the New Testament that usually apply but on their own understanding of Davidic worship in the Old Testament.[16]

Moreover, they see themselves as a Church for the end times. According to Pawson they are 'the post-millennial imperialists' of the day because they believe that the world and its society will be ruled by Christians prior to the Return.[17] At the heart of their distinctiveness, however, is their conviction that not only do we need a restoration in our worship but also in our ideas of church government and order, for which they believe there is a single authoritative blueprint in the New Testament. On this basis they have decided that 'democracy' (*sic*) in church government is out, and leadership by teams of elders who act with authority is in. The notion of the church members meeting together to find the mind of Christ on important governmental issues ceases. On their reading of the New Testament there is little place for congregational meetings making major decisions. They may meet for a family night to be informed about the decisions that need to be taken, and their views may be listened to by those who carry this responsibility. But they are to be ruled paternalistically by the appointed leaders within the church who will in turn submit to apostolic leaders from outside the church who will give oversight to the leaders and the whole fellowship. This pattern accords with their understanding of a crucial passage on church order in Ephesians 4:11–12: 'The ascended Christ gave some to be apostles, some to be prophets, some to be evangelists, and some to be pastors and teachers, to prepare God's people for works of service so that the body of Christ may be built up.' As Hebrews 13:17 expresses it, believers are to 'Obey your leaders and submit to their authority.'

So herein are the patterns for the restoration of primitive New Testament order for which the quest is on. To be a renewed and restored believer in the fullest sense, it is essential that we submit to the authority of these passages and apply these principles to our church practices. In these new patterns, even though they reveal much misunderstanding of basic Baptist principles about the need for the whole body of Christ to seek his mind for corporate decisions, there are obvious attractions for Baptists in renewal. Harold Owen was one of the first Baptists to be involved in the renewal scene in the 1960s, but withdrew from the Baptist Union as a result of the Taylor controversy we have already described. He was also a strong supporter of the reformed theological emphasis of Lloyd Jones. He was dismayed by the presence of Leslie Davison on the teaching team at Guildford in 1971.[18] Hence it was not surprising that, as a consequence, he soon found himself linked up loosely with the restoration networks, before a more formal link with Terry Virgo.

Others were in a similar position to him. Lloyd Jones had appealed for the gathering together of all evangelicals because of the threats of ecumenism. His evangelical federation would not have been hidebound over secondary doctrinal matters, but clear on the primary issues of the faith, and above all on the authority of Scripture. However, he scarcely had time to get his ideas adequately advanced: he had left all that too late to implement them. Now there were others who were adamant that new structures were needed, not just on the ground of doctrinal purity, but also for the sake of the experiential life of the fellowship, true to the Word and alive in the Spirit. The challenge of restorationism has remained a far stronger threat to the vitality of the Baptist Union than the message of the renewal ever was.

Moreover, the appeal of the restorationists has been on the ground of their great success. In this connection a glance at any of their publications is enough to show that they have a level of promotional expertise from which many other Church bodies can learn. There is often a vivid contrast in self-perception between the Baptist Union and the restorationists. Self-flagellation is usually the order of the day for the former, who are more than willing to describe their weaknesses, failures and fears. Not so the restorationists, if anything leaning towards over-optimism in the statements they make about themselves and their vital statistics.[19] Whereas the appeal of the Union has too often been on the grounds of the innate loyalty of its member churches, restorationists have appreciated the reality that, in a day of rapid change, support can only be gained by the strength of the vision that is communicated and the boldness of the scheme to which it points. For all their mistakes, restorationists have much to teach us, and we have much to learn from them.

The fact of the matter is that many normal, healthy, ambitious Baptist ministers without strong ties with the Baptist Union realise that very little commitment is required of them to stay within the ranks of its accredited ministers by the Baptist Union. In the light of this they have been quite prepared to accept at least for a period the claims of restorationism uncritically, while remaining only in a technical sense within the fellowship of the Union.[20] This is a reality to which the Baptist Union, with greater inner cohesiveness and sense of mission, must give attention.

Union recovery

After all the troubles through which the Baptist Union had passed at the beginning of this period, the main task for David Russell was that of supplying a new unifying lead to the whole family. He began that task in 1974 by a series of articles in the *Baptist Times* on the theme of the Wholeness of the Gospel. These were taken up with enthusiasm by the council and became a useful campaigning slogan for the Union in 1975. The Mission Department wrote mission kits for the churches on the general theme of the whole Gospel for the whole man for the whole world. They included material on the theme of the Vision of God, the Church, the interpretation of Scripture, and the World.[21]

These healthy developments were soon overtaken by even more promising possibilities. The Baptist Union was involved in the work of the Churches Unity Commission which led to proposals being sent to the Churches entitled 'Visible Unity: The Ten Propositions' in 1976. By 1977, however, the council agreed that it was impossible to present any unqualified recommendation to accept the Ten Propositions, though it urged the continuation of discussion about them. At the same time, it was apparent that there was widespread support in the wider Church for just the sort of evangelistic emphases that David Russell had been advocating with his theme of the Wholeness of the Gospel. Hence the Church of England Evangelical Council, the Billy Graham Association, the Evangelical Alliance, and the British Council of Churches embarked on a course leading to what became known as the Nationwide Initiative in Evangelism. The chief initiator of this was the archbishop of Canterbury, Dr Donald Coggan, and David Russell gave it his full support. David Pawson was also among its first initiators.[22]

Sad to relate, though much good work was done by this body its only immediate fruit was a conference on the task of evangelism in 1980, and the fears of the Baptist Council about it were confirmed, that all the effort would 'evaporate into the air as so many conferences on evangelism have done'. In the end, the NIE was well described as 'an unwanted child'.[23] At least, as far as the Baptists were concerned, it made its appeal at the point where Baptists are always at their strongest, in an emphasis on mission.

As the decade advanced so too did the interests of the Baptist Union and its leadership in the renewal. This was plainly seen in the pages of the *Baptist Times*. In November 1971 they published an article on the renewal which was seriously positive. It was written by Alan Braybrooks and was entitled 'Tongues . . . prophecy . . . charismatic movement is growing'.[24] In 1972 the editorial for Whitsun on 18 May was entitled 'The neglected Spirit' and commented favourably on the Pentecostalist emphasis on receiving the Spirit as an essential part of the total Christian experience and doctrine. Then, in November 1972, the paper ran a series of four articles on the same subject, with contributions from W.T.H. Richards of Slough Gospel Tabernacle, a traditional Pentecostal, W.J. Hollenweger, professor of missions at Birmingham University and author of *The Pentecostals*, myself, then minister at Lewin Road, Streatham, and James Dunn, lecturer at Nottingham and author of *Baptism in the Spirit* and *Jesus and the Spirit*.[25]

Clifford Longley wrote in *The Times* in March 1973: 'The Pentecostal movement seems to be growing like wildfire in the inflammable tinder of a generation seeking a meaning to life and not finding it in organised religion of the traditional kind.'[26]

Many denominations were stirred to set up commissions of enquiry about the renewal,[27] and this was one of the factors which prompted David Russell to set up an enquiry into the charismatic movement through a working group responsible to the Mission Department; this began its work in 1975. A further series of articles was written for the *Baptist Times* in 1975 on the theme of baptism in the Spirit, and again this stirred considerable interest.[28]

Thus, by the summer of 1975, the report of the Fountain Trust conference at Westminster entitled 'Glory in the Church' was very warm. Plainly the Baptists were beginning to appreciate the positive values that renewal was offering, especially as they were interpreted by Tom Smail. In 1978 the working group reported back positively, concluding that the denomination's churches have a great deal to learn about fellowship from those involved in renewal. They noted the dangers of authoritarianism that were creeping in, and the intolerance towards the ministry of women, that was to become almost a hallmark of orthodoxy for the majority of restorationists. Renewal was given a guarded endorsement and the report eventually appeared with a suitable theological commentary on it by Paul Fiddes.[29] At the same time Dr David Russell gave an even more guarded endorsement as a result of his participation in a conference organised by the British Council of Churches and the Fountain Trust.[30] In the light of these positive signs, it must be open to doubt as to whether any further stimulus was needed to encourage the development of healthy life within the body of the Union. However that question is answered, the Union soon faced another challenge in an unexpected way at the Annual Assembly in Nottingham in 1977.

Mainstream is born

The annual report of the Baptist Union is both a summary of the life of the Union in the previous year and an attempt by the general secretary to relate those activities to the prevailing situation in the wider community. The report for the year that was presented to the Assembly in 1977 was no different from any other in this respect. In it he commented on the continuing statistical decline that has been the unhappy history of all the mainline denominations and of the Baptists since 1906. His explanation of this was unfortunate – 'due to the fall in the birth rate and the prevailing social conditions'.[31] For two of the delegates this was not an adequate statement, not merely in the understanding that it expressed but also in the apparent complacency with which this condition was being faced. When the report was presented and received by the Assembly, the first delegate took the opportunity of drawing the Assembly's attention to the paragraph. He had never before met the other delegate, who soon became his colleague in the discussions that followed. The chairman was the newly elected president, the retired general secretary, Dr E.A. Payne. He wished to close the discussion as soon as he could and proceed with the rest of the business in an orderly manner. Dr Paul Beasley-Murray, the second delegate, was not going to allow the matter once raised to be thus disposed of, nor would David Russell agree. As a result of much public debate of the sort that National

Assemblies seldom enjoy, it was agreed that the council be requested to set up an interdepartmental commission to examine the causes of numerical and spiritual decline in the denomination, and this motion was overwhelmingly agreed by the Assembly.[32]

After the Assembly, the General Purposes Committee of the council appointed the appropriate body to begin work on this task both by analysis of the causes of the numerical decline and also with proposals for future action that might stimulate growth both numerically and spiritually. But this was not all. Within a week of returning home Paul Beasley-Murray phoned his new colleague to propose further action. His colleague was myself. There were numerous other phone calls and letters of support for the action taken, including contact from other ministers who now serve the Baptist Union in senior positions of responsibility.[33] So Paul Beasley-Murray and I met together on the morning of the 8 February 1978 at the home of the principal of Spurgeon's College, Dr Ray Brown, and the idea of the formation of a group of activists and thinkers, loyal to the Baptist Union but wholly committed to its reformation and renewal, was born.

Much work had to be done in order to achieve these ends. At the Assembly in 1978 to be held at Westminster Chapel it was agreed that the group would meet on the Wednesday evening after the missionary service. While they had no great secrets to hide, they also thought it wise to exercise great discretion about the gathering. Hence they met in the lounge of the vicarage of St Michael's, Chester Square, kindly made available by Teddy Saunders, then the vicar.[34] They arranged another meeting in September in Gorsley, near Ross-on-Wye, to formulate action plans for publications, for meetings and for raising the profile within the Union of any and all factors that would lead to a positive evangelical impact.

While in Gorsley the title Mainstream was chosen, and it was agreed that the explanatory phrase for it would be 'Baptists for Life and Growth'. The aim was for a group to span the divide between charismatic and non-charismatic evangelicals by allowing space for both viewpoints within the life of Mainstream, and for a common witness to the denomination on the basis of our commitment to the support of whatever contributed to life and growth within the denomination, along with wholehearted consent to the Declaration of Principle on which the Union is based. In the first executive Dr Ray Brown was president; Peter Grange, treasurer; Clifford Roseweir, secretary; Patrick Goodland, chairman; Dr Paul Beasley-Murray and me. Later on, when Dr Barrie White, principal at Regents Park, joined the executive, the basis for Mainstream was considerably strengthened. Jack Ramsbottom, David Warner and David Coffey were also involved in the early executive.

It was agreed that Mainstream would go public with a fringe meeting at the 1979 Assembly, and a Swanwick conference at the end of January 1980. Through the kindness of Sir Cyril Black it was possible for the necessary legal formalities to be arranged. The first newsletter was prepared in time for the 1979 Assembly with a leaflet summarising the aims of Mainstream.[35] It was with much trepidation that the executive came to the fringe meeting on 24 April 1979. They need not have been over-concerned. Though 500 was the highest number expected, in fact, over 700 came at the end of a busy day and an excellent Assembly evening. The *Baptist Times* commented: 'This stream brought strength, warmth and joy' and noted how the aim of Mainstream was to be an antidote to the curse of evangelicalism: fragmentation.[36]

John Capon, then editor of the evangelical magazine *Crusade*, went further. Under the title 'Charismatic cease-fire' he commented:

> I was glad to be at the inaugural meeting of the new Baptist 'ginger' group Mainstream in London in April, not only because of its unashamedly non-sectarian evangelical stance and the unexpectedly large response it attracted but, also, because it seemed to symbolise a long overdue cessation of hostilities between those who for want of a better label are called charismatics, and the rest of us.[37]

Dr Morris West, president of Bristol College and the incoming president of the Baptist Union for 1980, and widely regarded as a pillar to the Baptist establishment, wrote supportively too:

> So far as I read the purposes of the movement I have great sympathy with them and I thought I would take the opportunity of writing to share this reaction with you. I hope that the presidential address

this year, together with Donald English's address on the Tuesday evening, will pick up the emphases which Mainstream seeks to bring before the denomination.[38]

So Mainstream began and, as the conference that followed in January attracted another full house in Swanwick, it was plain that the new alliance was beginning to make its presence felt.[39]

The scene was thus set for the development of the contradictory trends we noted at the beginning of the chapter. The Baptist Union enquiry into the state of the denomination produced a positive report on the state of the churches entitled *Signs of Hope* and then followed it with a sixfold Call to Commitment, written by David Russell.[40] With the closure of the Fountain Trust, the field was open to the restoration movement to make significant advance. Had it done so among Baptists, it is likely that the genius of the renewal would have been lost to the Union and that renewal would have been just one more cause for the factionalism the *Baptist Times* report had rightly commented on as a curse in evangelicalism. To prevent this, a broader-based renewal emphasis needed to return to the charismatic foreground with a distinctively different message and agenda to that of the Fountain Trust which had acted as a renewal pioneer.

Non-charismatic renewal

As we approach the end of the decade, we note the point that there were other possible emphases beginning to emerge to challenge the exclusiveness of the charismatic approach to renewal. Chief among them was the church growth movement that was pioneered by Fuller Theological Seminary, where the Church Growth School was led by Donald McGavran.[41] In Britain Tom Houston saw the significance of this teaching and managed to persuade the Bible Society to extend their concern for promotion of the Scriptures to the promotion of this teaching.[42]

It might have been thought that these developments would lead to the eclipse of the charismatic movement by newer and less controversial emphases among evangelicals. However, this was not to be the case. We should not be surprised to discover that the new wave of charismatic life that was going to arise at this time would take account of the teachings of McGavran but supplement them with even stronger charismatic themes than had occurred up to this point. The expert who led this new wave soon used the term 'Third Wave' for this new move. His name was John Wimber.

Mixed Blessings

Christ's Power in Weakness

(2 Corinthians 12:9)

'Revival is just around the corner. The tide has turned for the first time in seventy years. All the signs of revival are here,' declared David Pawson in the early 1980s. The signs to which he was referring included the 100,000 house groups that he estimated were taking place each week, attended by one million people. To this he added a warning: 'But if Christians are not ready, the miracle will not happen.'[1]

Such confident predictions as this were being made frequently at this time, notwithstanding the closure of the Fountain Trust. The qualification about the need to be ready was usually included as an exhortation to more prayer. Furthermore, this was to become the decade of John Wimber, perhaps the best-known charismatic teacher up to the present time on the world evangelical stage. His influence has been at its strongest among Anglicans, with whom he has enjoyed very close relationships. It is also evident among Baptist charismatics and many of the new Church streams and, coupled with the growth in popularity and influence of the Spring Harvest Conference weeks, has been of the utmost significance in bringing charismatic renewal into a position of dominance in the evangelical world in general and among Baptists in particular. As we shall see, there is a paradox in all this, for it has been from this position of strength that the renewal has also provided ample evidence of its accompanying fragility. The setting for Wimber's ministry has always been the atmosphere of positive expectations of an imminent outbreak of significant revival.[2]

Wimber's expectations became very specific by the end of the decade, but he was not alone in declaring that the long-awaited revival was about to happen. Such words were also being uttered by many others, including John Noble and Colin Urquhart.[3] Yet, sad to say, the expectations of the end of the decade were no more fulfilled than those at its beginning. Revival did not happen in any way in which those who have anticipated it had expected. The decade of the 1980s thus concluded disappointingly, and the statistics continued to reveal the evidence of a major crisis of confidence and hope for the Churches in Britain.[4] There were the signs of growth among Baptist churches which were conservative in their theology and charismatic in their worship style and experience. Throughout the decade a number of such churches grew while many other mainline churches whose worship and churchmanship was more traditional shrank. Thus there was a proportionate increase in the growth of evangelical and charismatic influence. Yet these changes remain small when compared with the overall national picture, which remained one of continuing numerical shrinkage both in the attendance figures of those in regular Sunday worship, and also of those in committed membership of their local church. The goal of a widespread spiritual awakening has so far eluded the grasp of all evangelicals, including the charismatics. We therefore need to see how the renewal moved into such a strong position of power, yet at the same time give some explanation for the limitations of that success.

The importance of facing these issues is further emphasised when we take into account the fact that it was during the 1980s that the Church as a whole was persuaded to take charismatic renewal seriously and, as a movement, it grew greatly in its overall influence. The ambiguous consequences that have resulted inevitably raise the most relevant questions for us all. Why, then, the marked failure as well as the successes? Are there lessons to be learned from the 1980s that should be considered by us all now that we are well on into the next, the Decade of Evangelism, and poised on the edge of a fresh millennium? Is it all down to insufficient repentance, or the absence of strong prayer and the other spiritual disciplines for Christian living? Have we missed the significance of one or other of the different emphases in renewal teaching, perhaps to do with the powers of occultism and evil? Have we stumbled somewhere on the renewal pathway that leads on to the great revival, by becoming too cautious, too critical, or even too cynical about some it its trends? This last question reveals the assumption of some present-day charismatic leaders regarding those whom a few may count as their lapsed predecessors. That possibility may have more than a grain of truth within it. Yet in addition to these relevant dangers we should add the further possibility that what we have been pursuing is a somewhat illusory goal. The course of the progress of the renewal has always been uneven and spasmodic.

To begin to address these questions we need to recall the significant developments in the 1980s, especially as they impinged on the life of British Baptist churches. As we have already indicated, undoubtedly the most important factor was the emergence of John Wimber.

The Wimber story

John Wimber arrived late on the American Church scene. Converted in 1963 at the age of 29, his Christian roots were first in an Evangelical Quaker church in Yorba Linda, California. Some details from his personal life are relevant for our study. Wimber was the only child of a couple from the Midwest. When his father left home, his mother moved to California and remarried. His first love was music and from teenage years he was involved in the rock and roll scene, eventually forming a group named The Righteous Brothers, which topped the charts for a period. All this provided Wimber with an affluent lifestyle. In 1955 he married Carol, a non-practising Roman Catholic. It was shortly after the breakdown and then the recovery of their marriage that his conversion took place, and he and Carol soon gave themselves to the work of personal evangelism.[5]

In 1970, at the age of 36, Wimber entered the Azusa Pacific Bible College, named in commemoration of the Azusa Street revival in the early years of the century associated with the birth of Pentecostalism. During the three-year course, he co-pastored the Yorba Linda Friends Church. Soon he gained a reputation as a catalyst for growth in this church, and enrolled in the Doctor of Ministry course at Fuller Theological Seminary. Here he made the acquaintance of Dr Peter Wagner, the Donald McGavran Professor of Church Growth, in the School of World Mission. Wagner was so impressed with the potential of his student that he invited Wimber to head up the work of the Department of Church Growth. This led the way for Wimber to move into an extensive travelling ministry which gave him a comprehensive knowledge of the reality behind the outward appearance of success in much of the church life in North America. At the same time, in the School of World Mission, he was constantly encountering those who had first-hand experience of the enormous growth in the Evangelical Churches of the Third and Fourth Worlds, characterised as they were by their vitality, integrity, and above all by their Pentecostal spirituality.

From Wimber's spoken and written ministry, it is evident that he relies heavily on the spiritual perceptions of his wife. At this point, Carol was moved by a vivid dream not only to stop attacking those who claimed to have received the gift of tongues for themselves but also to begin to speak in tongues herself. Moreover, she inducted Wimber into the environment of a healing ministry, albeit unconsciously as far as he was concerned. This came about during a brief stay in a cabin in the mountains in January 1977. Carol Wimber was suffering from a painful bout of rheumatism in the shoulder. During the night while John slept, she placed his hand on her shoulder and prayed for healing. She felt a surge of heat through the shoulder and the pain left her immediately.[6] This personal incident carries the message of Carol's significant conviction about her husband, to which we shall return. Here is a person so imbued with the healing energy of God that, even when he is unconscious in his sleep, the power flows from him. Then she persuaded John to go to a prayer meeting in their home which she organised but which he always tried to avoid and rarely attended.

Despite his reservations about some of the outward manifestations, like the raising of hands in the singing of a moving song that would nevertheless soon be considered most restrained, Wimber was impressed by both the freedom and joy of the participants. When the prayer group, which had rapidly expanded, was then asked to leave the main church, they did so, but invited John Wimber to become their pastor. Soon healings, miracles and many other manifestations of the Spirit began to occur, all of which made hand-raising now seem tame. The Wimbers became familiar with scenes of holy confusion, as if their service had become a spiritual battlefield with bodies everywhere. Tongues, trembling, falling, weeping, wailing, and violent convulsions like electric shocks, became commonplace.

Initially Wimber himself was not happy about these developments. They were introduced to his church one Sunday through the testimony of a young man who had begun to attend, Lonnie Frisbee. After much reading, reflecting, praying and searching on Wimber's part, early one morning the phone rang with a call from a friend in Denver. That phone call settled the issue for Wimber. 'I'm sorry to call you early but I have something really strange to tell you. I don't know what it means, but God wants me to say, 'It's me, John.'[7] This was enough to persuade Wimber to involve himself in the ministry for which he has subsequently became world famous. The pervasive influence of a new expression of charismatic renewal which was to flourish throughout the English-speaking world and, particularly, in the United Kingdom had been released

The initial link between Wimber's Californian ministry and the British evangelical churches was made through the ministry of the late David Watson. He was a regular visitor to Fuller, and in 1981 he accepted the invitation to visit the Vineyard and be introduced to Wimber. There were about 3000 at the Vineyard service. Watson was deeply impressed by the gentle, low-key ease in which the service was conducted together, and he appreciated the heartfelt but intimate praise. Above all, it was 'the signs and wonders' element that struck him. There were many stories of significant healings, which had begun to flow after a halting start. Watson encouraged Wimber to come with a team to England.[8]

Late in 1981 Roy Pointer, who was working for the Bible Society, contacted the newly formed Manna Ministries Trust of which I was director, with the suggestion that Wimber be invited to visit a number of Baptist churches and others, and an itinerary was arranged including visits to the north-west of England, central England, Surrey and South London. He had a team of about 30 young Californians with him and he was accompanied by Lonnie Frisbee, whose testimony had so impacted on Wimber's own ministry. Indeed, Frisbee played a

key role in Wimber's ministry at this period. The pattern was
to conclude the meeting with an opportunity for prayer ministry which Wimber called 'Clinic', in which the presence and
reality of the Spirit was sought through the ministry of Frisbee.
This practice soon became the Wimber hallmark. It began in
his church and was taken into the School of World Mission of
Fuller Theological Seminary, at which he was invited to teach
a course that soon became the most popular course in the
seminary. Wimber then continued with it as he embarked on
a series of overseas teaching missions. It became normal for
Wimber, or one of his close associates, to preside on these
occasions while teams of his younger supporters engaged in the
ministry to individuals.

Martyn Percy, a severe critic of Wimber's fundamentalist
presuppositions, reaches the conclusion that it is in a 'combination of charism, charm and a dependable ability to
demonstrate signs and wonders wherever he goes' which has
ensured that Wimber's international ministry has been so prolonged.[9] Yet initially, Wimber's laid-back presentation gave little
cause for an expectation for the scenes that have become well
known.

An affable teacher, a gentle style of worship and an absence
of the 'hype' element which often accompanies the ministry of
Californian preachers visiting the UK, all helped to create the
element of surprise in the sudden demonstrations that then
followed. Nigel Wright, senior pastor at Altrincham Baptist
Church, describes his own experience in 1982 in a way that
typifies this:

> After listening to John for an evening and a morning, stumbling
> through a worthy but boring exposition in lecture form of what
> he called 'power evangelism', . . . I was wondering whether I had
> made the wrong decision [to invite him to come] . . . but then it
> happened. After lunch John cut short his lecture, proclaiming that
> it was time to have some fun. He brought along his personal fun-
> maker in the guise of an ageing hippy called Lonnie Frisbee. Lonnie
> encouraged us to sing 'Majesty' twice and, after praying simply,
> invited the Holy Spirit to come. What then happened is exceed-
> ingly difficult to describe. Within seconds, the inside of our
> attractive Edwardian Baptist chapel was transformed into something
> resembling a battlefield. Holy carnage reigned. Not that I saw

much of it because, by this time, I was flat on my back, shaking under the power of the Holy Spirit and calling on the name of the Lord as I had never done before. Half the church was doing something similar . . . this was no case of hyped-up hysteria. We were changed. We remained permanently different. The same scenes were evident in Streatham, Peterborough, Holy Trinity, Brompton, and St Andrew's, Chorleywood. We heard the same reports from Wimber's visit to St Michael Le Belfrey, York.[10]

Such was the success of the Wimber visit in 1982 that Manna Ministries Trust took the initiative in organising a major international conference to be held in Westminster in 1984. It was here that many evangelical churches began to take notice of this new ministry, and the international advance was well launched from which Wimber has never looked back.[11] The title of this conference was 'Third Wave'. This phrase was originally the title of a book by the futurologist Alvin Toffler, in which he describes the dramatic changes that will happen to world conditions as a result of the accelerating speed of technological progress.[12] To Peter Wagner it seemed an appropriate term to use in describing the penetration of the supernatural dimension of the Holy Spirit into the life of evangelical churches which are neither Pentecostal in doctrine nor charismatic in experience.

According to Wagner, the First and Second Waves were represented by Pentecostalism in the 1900s and charismatic renewal in the 1960s. In this Third Wave, he foresaw the possibility of evangelical Christians participating in the dynamism associated with renewal without moving or even intending to move from their own denominational preference. This was to make for a much less threatening and confrontational approach, yet one that was simultaneously much more dramatic in its overall effects. Wagner linked Third Wave with the ministry of Wimber. Wimber was happy to become a warm advocate for this and soon assumed the role of its chief proponent. Such was Wimber's impact that he captured the interest and support of the overwhelming majority of charismatic churches.[13] Many more evangelicals soon became involved. As we shall see, there were also a few among them who would soon discover that Wimber's ministry raised many questions that it did not solve.[14] This was not immediately apparent, however, and the work of attempting to disentangle some complex charismatic knots was left on one side for a while. Nevertheless, questions would not go away, and it is therefore vital to summarise the teaching that Wimber gave that contains the blend of attractive yet also potentially alarming elements.

The Wimber teaching

John Wimber presented himself as a straightforward conservative evangelical Christian. The basis for this was his confidence in the authority of Scripture. Though some regard him as no more than a somewhat sophisticated fundamentalist, Wimber is keen to stand firmly within the evangelical tradition.[15] Wimber has consistently declared that the Scriptures are without error and are our guide in all areas of faith, morals and practice. Moreover, he believes that it is his call to expound more fully the purpose of Scripture in the development of our personal relationship with Jesus Christ, to enable us to place our faith in Scripture with greater confidence.[16] From this he deduces that the New Testament, and particularly the record it contains of the experience of Jesus, are to be normative for the Church of today.

This view of the significance of Jesus is seminal to Wimber's teaching, as Martyn Percy points out, quoting from Wimber's earliest writings, *Signs, Wonders and Church Growth*:

> Jesus came not only to bring the Kingdom of God, to save and to heal people, but also to impart to others this healing ministry that they might share in bringing people under the Rule of God. We as the Church, were commissioned by Jesus almost 2,000 years ago to announce the good news to all creation through the healing 'signs' that would accompany and authenticate the message wherever it was preached . . . the transference of Jesus' healing ministry to others . . . and the powerful exercise of it today is of the utmost importance if we hope to see the Kingdom of God reach the ends of the earth.[17]

This then led him to his primary analysis of the true state of western evangelicalism. He judged that many evangelicals have lost the significance of the Gospel record of the ministry of Jesus, particularly that to do with his miracles, because of the pervasive influence of the rationalism springing out of the age of the Enlightenment. This was the period in the eighteenth century and after which marked a growing optimism about the power of human reason. For many it meant that the need for divine revelation was reduced, indeed, the effects of human sinfulness were regarded as diminishing in the light of the inevitable progress of mankind. Karl Barth characterised it as: 'A system founded upon the presumption of faith in the omnipotence of human ability.'[18] According to Wimber, the effect in the twentieth century was that intellectual doubts were honoured and a scepticism which opposed the miraculous in real-life situations was accepted even among evangelicals. Hence he thought that many evangelical believers were predisposed against the possibility of signs and wonders and needed a 'paradigm shift' in order to recognise their relevance.[19]

It is at this point that we can see the significance of a second basic element in his teaching in his expectations of growth which emerged from his own discoveries in the area of church growth. The statistics available from the research work of David Barrett and others show that not only have the Pentecostals maintained astonishingly high levels of numerical growth in the developing world, but that in North America, the UK and in the English-speaking world, it is the charismatics who have been showing signs of numerical growth. Often, as in the UK, this has happened against all the other denominational statistical trends. Many churches in the United Kingdom are in serious numerical decline. Charismatic evangelical churches of all denominations not only show signs of growth but also a capacity to attract and hold a younger age group, so that the future is more hopeful than in those churches where it is the senior generations that dominate. This applies most obviously in the new Churches. The same statistical analyses show that Pentecostal and charismatic growth is now being equalled by those evangelical churches which are increasingly involved in the Third Wave.[20] Wimber expects an increasing number of orthodox evangelicals to open up to Third Wave ministry and Third Wave church life. The evidence is that, through Wimber's teaching, evangelical Christianity has been and is still being reshaped by this message. The suggestion of one leading Ang-

lican on the extent of his impact on Anglicanism may be applied
with equal force to other denominations too: 'Wimber has had
a greater impact than any one since John Wesley'.[21]

A further important strand in Wimber's thinking contributes
positively to the process. It is in his theological contention that
the purpose of the ministry of Jesus is in his inauguration
of the Kingdom of God which is always perceived in terms of
its opposition to the rule of Satan.[22] He owes this insight to
the work of the renowned conservative scholar G.E. Ladd.[23]
From this starting-point Wimber perceives that the signs and
wonders, the miracles, the healings, the exorcisms of the ministry of Jesus are all the evidence for the breaking into this
world of the Kingdom of God. Moreover, the coming of the
Kingdom always involves a spiritual struggle with the powers
of this world under the lordship of the devil. While the devil
has been decisively overcome through the victory of Christ at
Calvary, Wimber believes with Oscar Cullman that the Calvary
triumph is the D-Day of victory prior to the final celebration
which will take place at the end of the age.[24]

Hence, in the light of the facts that Scripture is normative
for the Church today and that the ministry of Jesus is to be
replicated by the Church today, the present tension for us is
that of living between the times after the inauguration of the
victory process, but before it is finalised in Christ's return and
ultimate triumph. This leads Wimber to the conclusion that
every stage in the interim period is marked by spiritual warfare.
The reality of this conflict means that the Church is to engage
in much prayer, many exorcisms, and possibly much suffering
due to the ebb and flow of the spiritual battle in which we are
often unconsciously involved. For instance, Wimber attributed
the death of David Watson prior to the Westminster conference
in 1984 to a satanic attack. 'The devil murdered David Watson,'
he declared, but went on to say, 'but we will make him pay!'[25]

It is in this context of a bitter spiritual battle taking place on
planet earth between believers and the powers of an unseen foe
that Wimber teaches the need for supernatural empowerment
through the Holy Spirit. This is not as a second blessing, nor
even as a completion of the initiation process begun for Christians at their conversion, or through their baptism. It is to
equip them as an anointing with power for ministry.[26] It is

undoubtedly the case that Wimber escapes the second-stage categories of Pentecostalism through this more dynamic understanding of the work of the Spirit. He writes:

> The concept of being baptised in the Spirit is a controversial doctrine. The term being found in Scripture, over the past 150 years Christians have understood its meaning in a variety of ways, almost always causing great misunderstanding and division among themselves. Satan has been particularly effective in stirring up controversy over the Holy Spirit.[27]

He goes on to offer his solution to the problems of terminology in suggesting that all Christians should submit our lives to the Spirit and ask him to actualise all that he has for us and to release the gifts.[28] As Wright makes clear, this view is much more attractive to other evangelicals than the more traditional two-stage induction teachings on this matter as proposed by Pentecostals and some charismatics.[29]

The rest of Wimber's teaching now follows. Spiritual gifts are part of the equipping process, but the overall effect is that individual believers begin to operate in the area of the supernatural. They begin to receive insights, suggestions about the real spiritual condition of those to whom they minister, and these are 'words of knowledge'. So armed, they move into ministries of healing. Their experience, and especially the experience of churches that commit themselves to these perceptions, is the experience of the miraculous in ever-increasing measure. As may be expected, Wimber has a considerable number of examples to quote in this regard. His teaching implies that church life should mirror that of his own Vineyard Christian Fellowship in Anaheim, California. About that he made an oft-quoted and extraordinary claim:

> Today we see hundreds of people healed every month. . . . Many more are healed as we pray for them in hospitals, on the streets, in homes. The blind see, the lame walk, the deaf hear. Cancer is disappearing. More importantly . . . the people are taking healing and other supernatural gifts on the streets.[30]

Taken together with the evidence he has accumulated for the relative inadequacy of what he describes as 'programme evangelism', by which he refers to presentation of the Gospel through preaching ministry alone, without an expectation for miracles and healings, Wimber pleaded for an openness to 'power evangelism'. He did so without dismissing the need for the declaration of all the central themes of the Gospel, even if they are substantially reoriented around his overall concept of power and the miraculous. As the leader of a large and growing Californian church with whom some 600 other congregations around the globe are now associated, he has gained a position of great authority. Having already demonstrated his view that signs and wonders lead to church growth through his own ministry, he has claimed that all this is to be seen writ large in the advance of the Church in the developing world, and witnessed to by Pentecostal and charismatic Christianity.

So, with his belief in the continuing ministry of power, the force of the Spirit, as in the time of Jesus, a desire for growth, a belief in the conflict with Satan as a context to the involvement of any believer in the ministry of power, Wimber came in his teaching to 'clinic'. He claimed that all this power would be demonstrated here and now in a conference or in a service in a local church which is committed to these understandings. Teams of workers then move among the congregation as the Spirit directs them or as he directs them. Those two factors are often perceived as one. Since his use of ordinary members rescues the ministry from all ideas of élitism, again, it has its own appeal. Ordinary believing people want to be used by God.

In UK terms, it is interesting to notice that the local churches which have entered this new phase not only include Anglican, Baptist and the new Churches but also British Catholics. Whereas the first part of his strategy was to serve and service other churches, particularly in the area of church growth based on the doctrine of signs and wonders, the second stage in his strategy now emerging focuses on planting churches in the United States and abroad. At this point, only about 20 churches have been planted in the UK but he entertains the vision of creating a vast extension of this in terms of 10 000 churches worldwide within his lifetime. There are an increasing number of Vineyard churches affiliated to John Wimber's international network. Ever since 1984 a good number of churches from different denominations continue to receive visits from Vineyard representatives.

By the late 1980s, Wimber's teaching about the place of the miraculous received a further impetus through his encounters with the ministry of a church in Kansas City known as the Kansas City Fellowship. Mike Bickle, the pastor, was presiding over a fellowship in which the ministry of prophetic revelations had come to the forefront. The most notable of their prophets was an older man, Paul Cain, who had much experience and an extraordinary testimony to which I have drawn attention in *Discerning the Spirits*, and about whom there is more to say later.[31] Although in fact the partnership between Wimber and Cain proved to be short-lived, from 1988 onwards Wimber's expectations were framed by the prophetic ministry of Paul Cain. He declared at a Vineyard conference in August 1989: 'And I believe that revival will probably find its starting-point here in October, when the Lord just starts to move throughout London and throughout England.'[32]

This provoked no small measure of discussion even among those who fervently believed in the absolute reliability of Cain's words. But in July 1990 he went further: 'I stand by every word I prophesied. . . . Thus saith the Lord, revival will be released in England in October 1990. . . . Tokens of revival will come in October 1990.'[33] Wimber expected the conference he was to hold in the Docklands Arena, London, to be the start of this revival. It was to begin in among the people there and then spill on to the streets, leading to a massive nationwide turning to God.[34] This revival, in turn, was expected to have a massive worldwide effect. In acknowledging that manifestly this did not happen, Wimber affirms that his mistake was in the matter of the timing of this, not in the promise itself.[35]

Thus, Wimber's teaching, from the beginning of the long period of his substantial influence to the present time, has been characterised throughout by his announcement of the near advent of a new move of God's Spirit in a great revival world-wide which will precede the ending of the age and the return of Christ to the world to crown the endeavours of a triumphant Church. It has to be acknowledged that Wimber has succeeded because of his presentational skills, his wisdom in avoiding restrictive Pentecostal categories and the power of his claims for expertise in the areas of church growth, healing ministries, prophetic ministries and revivalist hopes. A large number of modern evangelicals have been swift to buy up the package he offers. The Third Wave continues to roll and Fourth and Fifth Waves are now expected from Toronto or elsewhere in North America.

Weighing up Wimber

This is not the place for a detailed examination of Wimber's teaching – others have begun that process elsewhere.[36] Here we are concerned only with his impact on the development of renewal. There is no doubt about the size of this, as I have already indicated in *Discerning the Spirits*.[37] In some places it is not putting matters too strongly to say that many of his followers not only respect him, they also revere him. In spite of the difficulties he has faced and the frequent changes in his main team of supporting teachers, he has managed to maintain his own authority. It would be the height of folly to underestimate the significance of John Wimber.

Yet the history of the renewal in the decade of the 1980s shows us that underestimation was not the danger facing churches already committed to renewal and, if anything, it was the opposite danger that applied. For many, Wimber has taken the uncomfortable position of being the guru of the movement, for which reason it has to be said that the majority of the tendencies that have led to the failures of renewal to deliver its most self-confident predictions are largely due to him.

Firstly, it is necessary to take issue with Wimber's claim to enormously high levels of numerical success in his healing ministry. We have already referred to the best known of these claims, but allusions to miracles are littered throughout his writings and his addresses. It is fair to say that Wimber has on occasions admitted he is puzzled by the infrequency of healings. Yet the overall message is that not only is he very familiar with striking examples of surprising healings, but so can his hearers be also. He has come to give away what he knows, for he adds characteristically that he is only a fat man trying to get to heaven. It seems more likely that his ministry is no more and no less effective than the normal prayer ministries of Christian believers when it comes to facing the problems of known, diagnosed organic conditions.[38] Even when there are the remarkable recoveries that Wimber has described, the specific role that prayer for healing has played as against that of normal medical procedures remains properly ambiguous.

This does not present us with a problem. We understand that God often uses both the normal and the special in his healing love for us. But this is not what Wimber is offering. For him, immediate healings are to be such dynamic demonstrations of the Kingdom that the Church is to engage in a signs and wonders ministry forthwith in order to speed on the advance of the Kingdom. So the lack of clear evidence that this is happening is a significant flaw which he appears to be slow to acknowledge. This is the charge levelled against him by Philip Jensen of Sydney, Australia, in his account of a three-hour-long interview in the course of which Wimber evidently acknowledged a much lower and more credible level of healings, but then refused to amend his teaching to take account of this admission. Jensen thus regards him as a confused and confusing teacher.[39]

To add to this, in his attempts to produce convincing evidence for the miraculous today according to the pattern of the ministry of the Lord as described in the Gospels, Wimber has shown no sign of coming to terms with the significance of the sociological setting for the healing miracles of Jesus. As Nigel Wright observes:

> The sign value of the works of Jesus has more to do with whom he was healing, than with what he was healing them from. . . . The objects of Jesus's compassion were normally the rejected, the helpless, the despised and the excluded. . . . It is difficult to see how this element is maintained when healing is being practised upon already wealthy and privileged Westerners.[40]

Martyn Percy makes a similar point more sharply:

> Jesus seldom healed his friends. Nor did he locate his healing ministry in a community of faith, in order to build up his congregation; it was more usually offered to those people who were explicitly or implicitly excluded from such gatherings.[41]

When we review Wimber's encounters with the ministry of

prophecy and prophets, however, not only has he failed to show any particular expertise, there is evidence rather of an alarming level of naïvety. Wimber declares that this new excursion came about at a time of major spiritual crisis for himself and his Vineyard organisation:

> In 1987 I had to admit that the Vineyard church movement for which I have responsibility was in a desperate condition. We had become dull spiritually and several of our key leaders had fallen into sin – but I sensed these were only symptoms of a more serious condition.[42]

Into this backslidden organisation came the word of the Lord through a Paul Cain prophecy about an earthquake in the area, which occured, as Wimber chronicles the event, at 3.38 a.m. on 3 December in Pasadena under the Rose Bowl.[43] So Wimber was open to receiving the ministry of the extraordinary Paul Cain, whose personal life story makes the strangest reading.[44] Cain gathered the Kansas City team of men with prophetic ministries under the care of John Wimber, and this interest persisted for Wimber up to the Docklands London Prophecy for 1990 and beyond. In 1995, however, Wimber himself confessed to having had enough of it and has ordered 'time out' for them: 'By giving the prophets a Vineyard platform, he gave them a credibility which impeded people's discernment; in other words, people thought that because John Wimber let them speak, they must be right. . . . I mishandled that one and I had to go back and repent.'[45]

As with prophecy, so also with the issue of the phenomena that Wimber has popularised since the beginning of his worldwide ministry. To him they are frequent accompaniments to the action of the Holy Spirit, and are similar to the responses recorded in a variety of disconnected Scriptures to the power of the Holy Spirit, including shaking, trembling, falling over, apparent drunkenness, bodily writhing, laughter, sobbing and prolonged praise. Not content with such a list of physical possibilities Wimber goes on to list the less obvious phenomena betraying the action of the Spirit. He describes slight trembling, fluttering of the eyelids, deep breathing, perspiration and heaviness.[46]

Yet the fact is that all of these manifestations may be nothing more than the conditioned results of the heightened excitement in which Wimber's ministry is usually conducted. As to what they signify, that is far from clear. Percy refers to the views of Christopher French in suggesting that, in exciting religious meetings, the body releases endorphins which produce the religious feel-good factor, and so we feel changed.[47] Wright comments that they are at best the human response to the divine presence. It is far from clear that they constitute a sign and evidence of the singular presence of the Spirit. Maybe this is what Wimber now concludes, but it is certainly not what he has taught or promoted.[48]

Wimber's widespread influence appears now to have moved into decline after this long period to the fore. He has suffered a massive heart attack, cancer, and more recently a stroke which has left him wheelchair bound for a while. Even if he recovers his health and strength, it is doubtful if he can retain his status as an unrivalled charismatic teacher. There are, of course, others waiting in the wings to take his place. Toronto appears to have been the turning-point, and we comment on this later. The probability is that his would-be successors are characterised by much less credibility but more claims to their own powers, which would make Wimber the soul of modesty.

From this brief survey it can be seen that there are many aspects of his ministry that remain positively helpful for the Church today. Above all we note his capacity to stimulate a consciousness of the presence and power of the Spirit of God among those who have attended his meetings. Time and again the testimony of respected charismatics has been that they have been introduced to a numinous awareness of the sacred and divine presence. Wimber has made a vital contribution in stimulating the morale of many charismatic churches severely shaken by the surge of restorationism. Yet as we review the total contribution there remain serious doctrinal weaknesses in his teaching. Having opted for a reinterpretation of the Gospel in terms of the theme of power he inevitably misses its real heart, which is the biblical theme of the unconditional grace of God brought to us in the person of his Son. Not only does this fail to do full justice to the true nature of Jesus as Son of Man and Son of God, it misses the point about the nature of the Trinity as the community of the persons of the Godhead.

To this intricate and fascinating theme we must return later, but for Wimber it is as if the Father becomes the hierarchical head of heaven, the Son a passive instrument, and the Spirit an unstoppable, almost brutal force unleashed by human inductors on earth. This impression is what follows his practice of invoking the presence of the Spirit for the times of personal ministry at the end of a worship service and evidently judging the effectiveness of the result of the Spirit's presence in terms of the phenomena, and not the moral consequences of the changed lives of those who are involved.[49]

Inevitably these assumptions ignore the reality of the incarnation, the sufferings of atonement, and the cost of redemption to God. There is no grappling with the problems of theodicy. The gentle fruits of the transforming Spirit which speak of the conversion of Christian character are omitted. There are profound grounds for concluding that a large amount of the fruit of Wimber's ministry has been to promote the sensational over the spiritual. It is no surprise to discover that, in the period when his power as a teacher was at its zenith, the inner qualities of the fruit of the Spirit were seriously devalued. But there are no short cuts to success by this route.

As we shall see later, the Church of the 1990s is spiritually poorer through overdosing on the spectacular. If in fact we are to become more faithful instruments for the purposes of Christ for the new millennium then much more will be required of us than this.

In an earlier generation, the ministry of the Chinese Church leader Watchman Nee had a similar widespread influence around the world. Angus Kinnear comments thus on the long-term significance of a similar emphasis in his ministry on spectacular manifestations:

> Over a period of a year or two a wave of spiritual excitement and a fresh emphasis on spiritual experience swept through the [Chinese] assemblies . . . jumping, clapping, laughter, unknown tongues, and a flood of dramatic healings, some undoubtedly real, but not a few mistaken. . . . Some revival methods, Watchman held, worked like spiritual opium. . . . Three years later . . . we find on looking back over this period that the gain has been rather trivial, and the loss quite large.[50]

Smail's conclusion about these emphases which can produce much more of a love of power that, in fact, can negate the power of love needs much more reflective thought:

> My own experience of charismatic renewal strongly suggests that if some of its leaders were as concerned with being men of love as they are with being men of power, because they saw that the only power the Spirit has is the power of love, it would be a more wholesome thing than it has sometimes been.[51]

Fire, Water and Abundance

(Psalm 66:12)

The Wimber message of signs and wonders became the popular orthodoxy for charismatics throughout the decade of the 1980s, and also succeeded in making a significant impact on the evangelical world in general. Baptists were responding favourably to the contributions from Mainstream, successfully launched at the Assembly in 1979, but for which there had been various antecedents with a similar agenda. One of the foremost was composed of a group of evangelical ministers who gathered around David Pawson of Guildford and held a 'think tank' conference over two days at Millmead in 1976. This led on to a three-day conference at Pilgrim Hall, Uckfield, held in May 1977 under the title 'Let My People Grow'. The purpose was to consider contemporary worship and issues to do with church growth, the impact of extended family living in a local church, and ecumenism from a charismatic perspective. The accommodation was fully taken up for this event, which showed the potential for a group that was distressed by the apparent indifference of the council and the staff of the Union to issues affecting the ongoing life of their churches and also determined to reform the life of Baptists from inside the Union.

From its inception, this was the goal that Mainstream set itself. It too was a coalition of different interest groups sharing a common evangelical heritage and the desire for the same agenda of life and growth within the churches and structures of the Baptist Union. Initially there were three broad groupings in Mainstream corresponding to a degree to the varying interests of the three ministers who had come together to form the body. The majority belonged to the traditional evangelical section represented by Dr Raymond Brown, then principal of Spurgeon's College and appointed president of Mainstream. He was a trusted Baptist leader, a greatly loved preacher in the churches, a distinguished college principal and a respected scholar. A younger evangelical contingent, less traditionally minded, more open to the new teaching on church growth advanced by the Bible Society, management methodology, counselling ministries and the like were represented by Dr Paul Beasley-Murray, then minister at Altrincham. Paul was to succeed Raymond as the principal at Spurgeon's College in 1986. The third section was for those who were involved in charismatic renewal, and in Mainstream at this time I was its leading representative and was still in pastorate in Streatham. Later, a less well-defined section emerged whose interests combined the renewal with the radical agenda of the Anabaptists.

It was to everyone's advantage that this core group was soon joined by a wider representation in Pat Goodland who became chairman, as he had been of the Millmead think tank, Peter Grange as treasurer, David Warner advised on publications, and Jack Ramsbottom looked after arrangements for the conferences. David Coffey, then of Torquay, came in as secretary. Undoubtedly the most significant addition at this stage, indicating the potential breadth of Mainstream and showing that it was no mere extremist fringe, was the appointment of Dr Barrie White to the executive, which took place following his address at the first Mainstream conference in January 1980. This talk also became the first booklet to be produced by Mainstream, entitled *Opening our Doors to God*. It was offered as a contribution to the denomination at the time of the Call to Commitment, but constituted an appeal for a far deeper appreciation of the two movements of the Spirit that Barrie White identified in both liturgical and charismatic renewal. More than this, it was a heartwarming exposition of the centrality of the Lord's Supper in our worship as the Lord's invitation to his people to give him the priority space and place in our lives:

> Can you not hear him knocking at our doors, over our prayers, our private prayers, our covenanting together to hold each other up to pray? Can you not hear him summoning us to give ourselves to that worship which feeds the hunger of God's people for him,

not only a hunger for programmes, not a hunger for theology only (though I believe theology is vitally important), not a hunger for numbers, not a hunger for new church buildings, but a hunger for him.[1]

In September 1981 a further sign of this breadth was in a one-day conference held at Tyndale Church, Bristol, on the covenanting proposals which were then being discussed between the Churches of Christ, the Church of England, the Methodists, the Moravians and the United Reformed Church. There were two speakers, Dr Morris West and Roger Nunn, then minister at Manvers Street, Bath, and now field secretary for the south of England for Churches Together in England. Dr West was president of the Bristol College at that time. It was well attended, highly informative and was adjudged a worthwhile exercise.

In spite of the successful launch and this broad agenda, nevertheless there were tensions in the Mainstream executive. Not surprisingly the chief cause was over issues to do with the renewal, with which I was much involved. I am therefore writing rather more autobiographically at this point.

The Swanwick crisis, 1982

The issues were raised by Paul Beasley-Murray in an editorial in the *Mainstream Newsletter* in April 1981 headed 'Mainstream – The Fountain Trust in another guise?' Paul argued that one did not need to be a 'card-carrying charismatic' in order to be a member of Mainstream but that, since the number of hands raised in the air in the worship sessions was greater than had ever been seen in all the Baptist Assemblies put together, this suspicion about Mainstream being a front behind which the charismatics were planning a takeover was understandable. Going on to insist that charismatics are often seen as those outside Mainstream and as problem people in problem churches, he urged far more positive openness in our attitudes. 'Brothers and sisters, if we want life and growth, let's be open to the Spirit: his grace is kaleidoscopic.'[2]

In spite of this appeal, all this came to a head at the 1982 conference at Swanwick. The theme on that occasion was

'Commitment to Caring'. The speakers were to be Bernard Green, shortly leaving the pastorate at Horfield, Bristol, to become the new general secretary of the Baptist Union in succession to Dr David Russell, Michael Eastman of the Frontier Youth Trust and the Scripture Union, Norman Wade who gave the Bible readings and served as minister in Richmond, Liverpool, and Bill Hancock, the superintendent for the south-eastern area.

I was due to take the communion service at the end of a conference which had turned out to be a relatively sedate affair. In spite of the best efforts of the speakers there was not a hint of radicalism in the air and this caused unrest among the more charismatically committed delegates. This had already shown through by the second day. I was on the point of launching out from the safe haven of a suburban pastorate where we had seen substantial growth and charismatic renewal without strife. My new ministry was dedicated to advancing the work of evangelism and renewal and was overseen by an independent trust named Manna Ministries. Moreover, I was tired of tepidity in all its forms. For me this was a major unacknowledged reason for the decline in influence and subsequent closure of the Fountain Trust. With the benefit of hindsight I was also unduly suspicious of the motives of the Baptist Union leaders whose response to the denominational enquiry set up through my intervention at the 1977 Assembly had been the production of *Call to Commitment*.[3] To my mind it went nowhere near far enough, since it concentrated its appeal to greater responsiveness on churches and ministers, but showed little awareness of the need for changes within the structured life of the Union. I had already expressed my views in a Mainstream publication, in the same series as the booklet by Barrie White, entitled *No Gentle Breeze*. This had been submitted in draft form to the whole of the Mainstream executive and after suitable amendments duly published. My views were well known:

> Now it is vital that our council, its executive and its committees become more of a catalyst for change than a talkshop about history. . . . The fundamental question which we must face is as to whether it is possible for the present institution to move reformingly with sufficient speed and conviction to keep a hold upon the new life which is emerging, whilst not losing touch with the

continuum of our tradition. I am forced to one conclusion regarding the prospects for Baptist life in Britain. It is that whatever timetable for change God may have adopted for other Christians, His time for us is now. If we do not take it then we sign a death warrant for our institutions. It will be executed in the name of financial economics.[4]

Perhaps to the surprise of many I conducted the communion service in the ordered way I favoured then and for which I still retain a preference. There were led prayers, common prayers, and times of open prayer too. We shared a united confession and later the exchange of the Peace. The worship songs were strong and rhythmic and we began with the grand hymn, 'The God of Abraham praise'. It was my address that caused the rumpus that followed. In all conscience it was not carefully designed as the swingeing attack on the Union and its structures that some took it to be. To be frank, I had not gone to Swanwick with a prepared text because I wanted to see how the programme would work out before I drew matters to a conclusion at the end. But I did feel in my bones that Mainstream under the careful and guarded leadership of Ray Brown was likely to become just another evangelical grouping in the Baptist Union, adept at sidestepping the challenges to the institution that I was sure were there through the renewal, and that the institution desperately needed to respond to in a positive and affirmative way. My words were meant to be a call to be true to our deepest convictions about the need for obedience to the leading of the Spirit without compromise. It provoked a vigorous response to which the executive attended at its next meeting scheduled for Gorsley in March 1982.

A postbag had been gathered summarising the letters received. Some were delighted by my outspokenness, which they had found to be a breath of fresh air within a turgid gathering. Rather more wrote to me and to the executive with weighty criticism. Typical of the two sides are these comments:

> I came away from the conference with a real burden for Mainstream, especially for the executive. . . . As Doug McBain shared at the communion service about Caleb and co. I thought about the ensuing narrative with the whole generation lost in the desert and the people brought 40 years on to the same place—needing

leadership to take them on. It would be an awful thing for that to be true of us.

What concerned me was to see the overt impatience among the charismatic brethren with this liaison. When on the Tuesday evening, Douglas McBain reported on behalf of his discussion group a demand for a much closer definition of renewal (obviously in charismatic terms) and an impatience with those who use the trimmings of renewal (such as its music) without going all the way with its demands, I think I could see the writing on the wall. . . . My chief concern is the public pronouncements that Douglas in particular is making about the Baptist Union at this time. His language, not only at the council, but especially at the Wednesday morning communion service, seemed to me intemperate, unconstructive, and somewhat rabble rousing. I fail to see how the likes of Bernard Green, or Ron Cowley and others found it possible to enter into the spirit of celebration and communion when the sermon had been an attack on the Union as an institution.[5]

Ray Brown was more uneasy about the emerging situation than his fellow principal, Barrie White. Prior to our arrival in Gorsley he circulated an article that had appeared in the *Grassroots* magazine, written by Tom Smail, former director of Fountain Trust, then vice-principal of St John's College, Nottingham. It was entitled 'Contextualising Renewal – the Way Forward for Charismatics'. The following words encapsulated Smail's article and clearly expressed Ray's own hopes at the time for the coalition in Mainstream:

The Holy Spirit is not the Spirit of separation and segregation but the Spirit of fellowship, who relates us not merely to those who are saying the same things as us, but to the brothers and sisters in Christ who have different experiences, insights, preferences and needs from our own. He is the Spirit of truth who does not want us to cling for dear life to the parts of the truth that are congenial to us, and in which we have found blessing in the past, but rather wants us to see this in the context of the whole truth of the Gospel into which he wants to lead us. . . . I believe it was a right discernment that led the Fountain Trust to see that it had to die to let the work of the Spirit deepen and grow. I believe that the whole charismatic renewal has to do the same. . . . This renewal is not just Pentecostal but Trinitarian, it does not just happen in upper rooms but bursts out into action, to declare with the church and in the world, that in all corners and concerns of creation Jesus is Lord to the glory of God the Father.[6]

Discussion ranged freely around the letters, the article and a brief paper I had produced at the request of the Executive to express how I saw the relationship between my own future ministry and that of the Baptist area superintendency. In this paper I stated that I saw that where fellowship is open there are no necessary problems and good relationships are possible between both sets of individuals. I suggested that some kind of consultancy status could be conceived for the apostles. I acknowledged that where an apostolate became authoritarian, anti-denominational or sectarian, then that would be a cause of strife. I also stated that, when the denomination becomes rigid, suspicious, inflexible and inward or backward looking, danger would also be present and that both tendencies would require careful working out with patience and tolerance in terms of the wider vision of the work of God's Kingdom nationally.[7]

As it happened, reflection on this paper and the discussion on the conference were both inevitably inconclusive. It was left to Alastair Campbell, newly appointed to the executive and the editor of the *Newsletter*, to sum up the discussion in a way that aptly summarised the functions of such a group:

> If it is the job of a conference to provoke people then the 1982 conference must be judged a great success! Many people have written searching questions about the purpose and direction of Mainstream . . . the aim of which is to be a forum, workshop, and gadfly in the service of the living and growing of our churches in the Holy Spirit. It should be a forum where ideas can be freely aired, a workshop where experience can be shared, and a gadfly from time to time piercing the hide of our Baptist churches, producing the occasional bellow of rage perhaps, but also, who knows, a little forward movement.[8]

Although confidence had been damaged by the experience, Mainstream had survived its first internal crisis.

Manna Ministries

All these concerns and criticisms were quite enough to be going on with and they were deeply felt on all sides, though by none more than me in the vulnerable isolation of an untried new form of parachurch ministry. They were further compounded as the news had now broken concerning my work with Manna Ministries and specific links that were being forged between a small group of pastors meeting in the north-west of England that were soon replicated in the South-west, the Midlands, and throughout the London area. I had stated quite openly that the work of the Manna Ministries Trust was to build relationships between churches and ministers open to renewal both within and outside the denomination. I envisaged a great deal of travel at home and overseas, leadership training, church planting and writing too. John Wimber was due to arrive in June 1982 for a national tour which I arranged together with Roy Pointer of the Bible Society on 'Evangelism with Signs Following'. We booked Kinmel Hall, Abergele, for a first residential conference with Bob Gordon, Jim Graham and Michael Harper as the speakers. Because of the pressures and in spite of the great help of Jim Graham on that occasion this was not an experiment I was prepared to repeat.

The specific links forged between a small group of pastors in the North-west was significant. Nigel Wright, then at Ansdell, Lytham St Anne's, was their leader, together with Mike Wood from Rochdale, Mike Huck of Heywood, and Geoff King, then pastor at Hawkshead Hill in the Lake District. They had been exploring the notion of what they described as committed covenant relationships for their own ministries in order to exercise a ministry of encouragement and correction towards one another and be enriched by opening themselves to one another's lives and ministries. They had three other purposes for their relationships with each other. First, to explore the New Testament vision for the church as a radical and spiritually powerful community and to encourage one another in the fulfilment of that vision in their churches. Second, to reach out to other ministers to encourage them to share the vision. Last, to explore the meaning of the translocal ministries of

Ephesians 4:11 and to work towards their implementation in their own lives and that of their churches.[9]

These aims resonated powerfully for me when I first heard them being enunciated, and have continued to do so ever since. One of the worst characteristics of Baptist ministry for its full-time pastors has always been its inevitable insularity if, in fact, the minister is not entirely in harmony with the team of leaders with whom the local vision must be fulfilled. Strong, uncompetitive, supporting fellowship with one's ministerial peer group is still a necessity but also something of a rarity in our midst, and the resulting loneliness can often produce grievous consequences. If the life of our churches is to develop more healthily in the future than it has in the past it must be the united aim of churches, ministers and superintendents together to address this issue in a more creative way in the future.

In July 1981 a consultation on these matters had been held in Ansdell, Lytham St Anne's, where Nigel was the pastor, taking up also the theme of renewal in Baptist churches and in particular discussing the ways in which it might be possible for Jim Graham of Gold Hill, Chalfont St Peter, and myself to exercise our wider ministries of encouragement and guidance towards those who came. Over 50 ministers attended, and another 45 informed us that they had wished to do so and wanted to be kept informed of developments. News soon reached the ears of the Baptist superintendent for the north-western area, Trevor Hubbard. Seeing the implications of all this developing around the country and wasting no time, Trevor contacted Bernard Green who wrote immediately to Nigel suggesting a meeting with the four ministers concerned, Trevor and myself. This duly took place, after the Mainstream conference, on 4 February 1982 at the large community home Mike Huck was then running with his Heywood pastorate. No one would blame Bernard Green for the concerns he must have felt at this time, with the heavy responsibilities of office about to descend upon him. The last thing he wanted was another difficult splinter group to cause further pressure in the life of the Union which, by its low-key nature, is always somewhat prone to fragmentation. He could not have been encouraged by the response he heard from his younger colleagues to his

appeal for careful strategic reflection and no rocking of the
Baptist boat.

'No rocking the boat – I would like to put my boot through
the bottom of the damned thing,' expostulated one of the more
outspoken northern brothers. In spite of the humour with
which this outburst was received, the skilful argumentation
proposed by Nigel, and my own earnest attempts to recover
the position, great damage had been done by the undiplomatic
outburst. Accepting that it was intemperate, none the less it
revealed the extent to which Union life at that time was a cause
of deep frustration. Subsequently, I discovered that this reaction
was by no means confined to the evangelicals and charismatics.
Many others felt disenfranchised by the leadership of the
denomination. One of Bernard Green's less obvious achievements was the extent to which he recognised and addressed
this problem, for there were significant changes during his
period in office, but at this stage my part in these encounters
only served to raise questions over my place in Mainstream
leadership now I was with Manna Ministries. I was a travelling
preacher, apparently toying with strange ideas about a Baptist
apostolate and out of step with the very people who might
have held me in check. My exploration into the freedom of
charismatic ministry opened me to the charge of irresponsibility.
Perhaps I was a loose cannon capable of inflicting serious
damage on the Baptist Union. Where would this radical and
outspoken form of renewal end?

In the North-west the covenanted brothers were advancing
their vision and organised a week-long Bible school at
Heywood on the theme of 'The Believer's Church', attended
by an average of 150 each night. They printed a booklet with
the text of the various addresses from the week entitled *The
Believer's Church*.[10]

The Dales Bible Week was providing the base for what
appeared to be a major threat from restorationism. Large
numbers were attending. Alastair Campbell commented thus:

> People are thirsty, thirsty for God, for the Living God. Not only
> the unchurched or the unbelieving (though they are), but Christ-
> ians, Baptist even, a thirst for reality and all too often finding the
> official channels are broken cisterns full of words. . . . In front of

me as I write is the programme for this year's Baptist Union Assembly. It is all very worthy, necessary, even inevitable. Above all it is a true reflection of our Baptist life, busy, caring and sensible, but it lacks passion. It will draw the loyal and the satisfied and they will be puzzled and hurt that we who are thirsty are unenthusiastic, but it will not make any difference in the Kingdom of God. Tear Fund presented the needs of the thirsty to us this year in the slogan, 'We are not just scratching the surface' – our churches and Mainstream could well adopt the same motto.[11]

Thus he explained the attraction of the Dales Bible Week. Similarly, he understood the attraction of the covenant relationships about which Mike Beaumont wrote enthusiastically at the same time.

In the event, life moved on for us all without the spilling of much more denominational blood, though doubtless with the raising of many more fears about the possibilities of disaster ahead. For me there was a further series of consultations with cluster groups of pastors in different parts of the country, but into the picture came John Wimber and the ministry we have already described. Having participated in its launch and having pioneered Wimber's first major international conference in Third Wave 1984, I was soon bound to review my own response to his claims and arrive at the conclusions about them I have already outlined. Although I found it exceedingly painful I had to withdraw somewhat not only from his methodology, but also from the thinking that lay behind it of the inevitability of a massive revival for which his ministry was the vital antecedent.

It was not only the matter of my diverging views on Wimber. By November 1984 Nigel, well aware of the difficulties I had experienced with Third Wave, wrote to me to urge a restriction of my tendencies to multiply ministries. He wanted me to concentrate on a greater level of commitment to a smaller group of churches sharing the vision he had enunciated in July 1981. I was reluctant to attempt to draw together a wider peer group into a travelling team to give support to those sharing these covenanted relationships. In my opinion, the people whom Nigel and the brethren from the North-west wished to involve in this way were far too busy with their own ministries to want this further work. I knew them and had worked with them on a number of occasions.

There was also the necessary practical matter of how I was to be funded without a guaranteed stipend. Experience had already taught me that to finance my own ministry I had to work very hard and certainly could not rely on the limited support that came from those churches with whom I was in regular committed relationships, although several of them led by Ansdell were most generous and dependable in their support. In any case, by 1985, while I was pulling away from the new and vigorously growing Third Wave circuit that I was partly instrumental in creating, a greater part of my younger colleagues were still well and truly in it up to the hilt, and travelling many miles across the country and across the Atlantic for a further intake of the same diet. For me the emphasis moved to leadership training, night schools, church planting and evangelism in inner London, and writing about the need for the exercise of much more perceptive gifts of spiritual discernment.[12]

Over the next two years I organised a series of evangelistic campaigns under the name of Mustard Seed Missions that were taken up by inner London churches of all denominations from Black Pentecostal to Roman Catholic. They were staffed by about 300 volunteers who gave a week or two to the missions. To this day I still come across those who joined a team or churches that received them and found the time to be a blessing, with a considerable number of converts on occasions. Unfortunately for Manna Ministries, we had not worked out the practical implications of funding such a venture, and so the work had to stop after two years.

The advance of the Wimber factor

As we have seen, the emergence of John Wimber gave a strong counterbalance to the attractions of restorationism. The 1984 conference had been highly successful, and one of the chief reasons for that was through his chosen way of working. His meetings followed the same pattern throughout this period. Relaxing, worship with simple and often beautiful music, characterised by its stress on our warm and intimate relations with God, would lead into teaching and then into the clinic sessions, which usually concentrated on healing ministry to those present on the basis of the 'words of knowledge' offered

by the Wimber team. His audiences found the presentation
fascinating. Things happened. The prescribed channel through
whom the influence of the Spirit would flow was Wimber or
one of his close colleagues, so these meetings were always
eventful. A perusal through the *Mainstream Newsletters* of the
period makes the attraction clear. For many, Wimber's ministry
was a call to mission:

> It is not enough that we trust God for miracles of convenience.
> We have to trust Him enough to go out preaching the kingdom
> where Christ is not named, without the benefit of high-publicity
> evangelists. We have to dare more, not just daring to believe but
> daring to go out. Above all we have to care more.[13]

For all it was an unforgettable experience. Under the heading,
'Riding along the crest of the third wave?' the *Newsletter*
included this testimony:

> It's all very well but are these people actually being helped? Reassur-
> ance came in one ministry session when a fellow Baptist minister
> felt prompted to lay hands on the lady next to him. When he
> did she promptly collapsed in the Spirit to his amazement and
> consternation.[14]

These meetings stimulated an interest in prophecy. Alastair
Campbell commented:

> Too often prophecies are pretentious in their claims, vacuous in
> their contents or attention-seeking in their motivation. How can
> we encourage mature believers to be open to the very possibility
> that they can receive the promptings of God's Spirit to speak out
> in faith words that cause God's will to be seen and done on earth
> as in heaven?[15]

Another described the impact of Wimber thus:

> What knocked me out was the sheer immediacy of the presence
> of God. Would that we knew that each week in our church. It
> wasn't the music – it was not the natural charisma of a good
> communicator. Neither was it the sheer volume of people who
> filled the hall with the sound of His praises. No, it was just that
> the faith expressed among the Wimber team released the power of
> God among us. They believed that God was there and that he
> could demonstrate himself in his power and that is exactly what
> happened. I was blessed. John Wimber is worth listening to. . . .

Beyond all this there was the awareness that the keys of the Kingdom were unlocking the truth of God now. . . . It was like a spring of joy that just kept flowing. I understand what it meant to have a river of living water flowing out from my inner self. The joy knew no bounds. The fact that I shouted and laughed and jumped for joy astounded me as much as it surprised my wife and my friends. I knew that God had touched and blessed me.

There were those who would travel to America not once but several times to experience a bit more and to catch the excitement of the occasions:

I have seen jumping, shaking, swaying, vomiting, whooping, crying, falling down, laughter, tears. Is not this the shaking away of obstacles and resistances to God and His work in us and through us? In this process we become significantly whole. Let us simplify in order to intensify.[16]

These positive viewpoints have remained strongly within the Mainstream constituency since 1984. They have been further re-emphasised from time to time, most markedly with the emergence of the 'Word and Spirit' network in the 1990s associated particularly with Rob Warner. But the contribution of David Coffey in Mainstream provided a balancing factor. How his efforts and then the work of Derek Tidball helped to centralise the reforming energies of the renewed within the structures of the Union must now occupy us.

Back on course

The growth of the influence of Wimber's teaching has not dimmed the chief Mainstream characteristic, which has been to serve as a catalyst for life and growth within the main structures of the Baptist Union. After the lively consequences of 1982, the 1983 conference took the theme of 'Authority', and was led by the genial Lewis Misselbrook as chairman. This was far from being an occasion for the gathering of a group of Baptist anarchists, as some might have feared. Jamie Wallace described it thus:

As for Union-bashing radicals? Here were the Baptist Union president and general secretary, two heads of departments, with other church and mission house staff, four area superintendents and a college principal. Its radical address is, to misquote Monica Furlong, 'to the Union with love'. Last week I tried Mainstream in conference. And I don't propose to ditch it.[17]

In 1985 Paul Beasley-Murray addressed the annual conference on the priority of mission in our churches. He called for the adoption of church growth principles, a more radical approach to church planting, experimentation of cross-cultural mission, and the development of effective training courses. He suggested the need for much more short-term and long-term planning. Alan Pain of Sutton Coldfield once more rehearsed the Wimber teaching on evangelism with signs following, but it was the Methodist Donald English who raised the theological issues of what constituted the signs of the Gospel and what was the much more important substance that lay behind them.

In 1986 I was asked to speak on the theme, 'Where the Breeze blows now: the current state of Renewal'. I attempted to identify both the strengths and weaknesses of renewal teaching, summarising the former in terms of the deepening and releasing of new gifts, with fresh commitment to mission, a fresh quest of ecumenical harmony, and a prophetic vision for the growth of a Union committed to numerical and spiritual growth. I described the latter under the four heads of authoritarianism, exclusivism, illuminism, and what I described as charismatic Scargillism after the well-known extremist trade union official Arthur Scargill. By this I was referring to the tendency to raise expectations to such a point of unreality that many people were bound to be disappointed in the end. But fresh encounters with God should lead on to fresh adventure in mission. The fact that I was prepared to make such a statement no doubt contributed to a degree to some rehabilitation of confidence that the wider group of evangelical Baptists were ready to place in me. Without doubt it also led to a certain loss of confidence for those who were now as thoroughly convinced about the reliability of Wimber as I was unconvinced of this very factor. They were unhappy with my greater caution.

By 1986 the wisdom of a more guarded approach was justified in the election of David Coffey to the presidency of the Baptist Union. His presidential address was on the necessity of the Christian ministry of reconciliation which he fulfilled in his own church and in his wider ministry and expressed in his book *Build that Bridge*: 'Though we can never expect renewal without tears, we should strive for the reformation of congregational life without needless division and carnal schism.' Neither was he afraid to challenge either the more traditional: 'We need to be more open to God: re-examining our theology, reappraising our methods, and rediscovering the breadth of our ministry', or the charismatic because of

the apparent gap between the spirit of power on the platform and the spirit of truth in the classroom. The saccharine spirituality which always presents the Gospel in terms of need fulfilment. Have you grasped part of God's truth and in your enthusiasm mistaken the part for the whole?[18]

With Raymond Brown ending his principalship of Spurgeon's College partly because he found the renewal issues to be too difficult to accommodate, Paul Beasley-Murray was appointed as his successor. For David Bebbington this appointment was evidence of the way in which the Baptist denomination was accommodating itself to the new influences that renewal was creating.[19] Add to this the advancement of David Coffey and it was plain that the Baptist family was more than ready to endorse a renewal that avoided extremism.

By 1988 David Coffey was ready to accept the call of the Baptist Union to become the Secretary for Evangelism. With his appointment into the central life of the Baptist Union it was plain that Mainstream was enjoying significant recognition. The capacity for Mainstream to exercise influence on the making of such appointments and through them the shaping of the policies of the Union was increasingly clear, once more within a broad agenda for the life of the churches. In the previous year Derek Tidball was responsible for gathering the material for a weighty contribution from Mainstream writers to the debate on Baptist Identity, created by the lectures given by Brian Haymes on this subject and subsequently published by the Yorkshire Baptist Association.[20]

The Mainstream articles, while not expressing total agreement with these lectures, in some ways complemented them and even extended the argument, particularly over the issues of mission and association. Again it was evident that those who wrote them were keen to contribute positively to the shared life of the Baptists.[21] By 1989, therefore, it was time for Mainstream to pause to reflect about its future. The result was its intention to recruit new members from the ranks of younger leaders and to find a new agenda which would include the recovery of a distinctive Baptist identity, the advocacy of biblical reform in the local church and the Association, and the appointment of men and women to positions of denominational responsibility who were mission-minded and forward-thinking.[22]

In the same year the Baptist Union was due to hold a critical debate at its Assembly to be held in Leicester, concerning membership of the newly formed national ecumenical body. The former British Council of Churches was being replaced by a body that was less centrally and more locally structured, that was more mission-oriented than ecclesiastically involved with issues to do with major church mergers, yet without losing sight of the goal of a pilgrimage to unity.

The inclusion of the Roman Catholic Church in the new body, known as Churches Together in England, was a fresh development of great significance and with enormous disruptive potential for such a body as the Baptist Union. Having an awareness of the amount of stress such an issue had stirred up in the past, Mainstream gave a lead in opening up positive discussion of the issues; this contributed to the positive atmosphere and result at the Leicester Assembly, which debated the issue of Baptist membership and decided in favour by a considerable majority. My paper to the Mainstream conference urging our positive involvement had been well received. I had been appointed as the superintendent for the metropolitan area in 1989. With Derek Tidball coming to the presidency in 1990, and appealing for a fresh vision for Baptists to become a people of the future, and with the appointment of David Coffey to the major post of general secretary in 1991, it was plain that the functions defined at an earlier stage of Mainstream as a forum and a workshop for creative influence within the Baptist Union were fulfilled.

In some respects it has become plain that, in another sense, Mainstream has served as a nursery in which leaders have received valuable early training for their new roles within the

Baptist Union, as the four newest area superintendents demonstrated: Peter Grange, Iain Collins, David Taylor and Brian
Nicholls. None the less, its capacity to serve as a gadfly to the
establishment was still important. In the past it had been fulfilled
by its charismatics provoking fresh thought, shifting ground and
coming at things from new and unusual angles. I take the view
that since all religious groupings inevitably share the tendency
to take themselves too seriously and thus forget the pro-
visionality of all present church structures, including their own,
religious gadflies have a vital function to fulfil. There are not
many in establishment situations who are likely to appreciate
their contributions.

Further renewal experiments

With the appointment of David Coffey the Baptist Union
became committed to a rigorous process of self-examination
and exploration of possible change, which at the time of writing
still goes on. It may be that all this will diminish the need for
reforming groups within its structures. However, allowing
for the depth of the self-preservation tendencies within all
religious institutions and which are certainly to be found within
the wider life of the denomination, especially in its different
Associations, I doubt that. Two further groupings emerged with
Mainstream connections, of which the second has so far had a
greater and longer impact.

The first, Wellspring, emerged in September 1989 with a
consultation at Gold Hill, Chalfont St Peter. It was attended by
Jim Graham, Bob Allen of the host church, Mike Wood of
Streatham, Brian Tibbert and Peter Ledger of Brickhill,
Bedford, Keith Roberts of Mitcham Lane, Streatham, Alan Pain
of Sutton Coldfield and Nigel Wright from Spurgeon's College.
This was designed to examine the possibility of a network of
co-operating autonomous churches and ministries open to the
impact of others similarly motivated both at home and overseas,
and seeking to develop practical support and envisioning
through supportive relationships. It was a development of the
discussions begun in July 1981 at Lytham St Anne's, from which
one of the factors was the establishment of Manna Ministries
Trust. For the Wellspring consultants, Manna Ministries was

regarded as being at best only a partial fulfilment of those original hopes, and now it had closed, leaving some churches and ministers without the kind of help for which they have still looked.[23]

Although this provoked lively discussion among the inner core the problems raised were the obvious ones of finding the time, the money, the personnel and above all the energy to organise the network they desired. Some had already moved into closer relationships with other new church streams. Others were inclined to stay with Mainstream and contribute more effort to the various official levels of Baptist life. By the autumn of 1990 it was obvious that there was not going to be much progress with this, and a six-month moratorium was proposed before any further action. This has never been breached, and the initiative was largely overtaken by the second new development in the form of the Mainstream 'Word and Spirit' network.

This emerged in 1992 with Rob Warner advocating a further experiment, which is still in operation, through proposing a further consultation on this subject to take place in May 1993 in Sutton Coldfield. The basis was defined with the affiliation of Word and Spirit to the Evangelical Alliance and its desire to operate within the Baptist Union with positive and open relationships with all concerned there. At first sight it appeared that it was to be committed to an impressive not to say daunting agenda for action, including evangelism, renewal and church planting at all levels, with those involved agreeing to and declaring explicit goals for church growth. No doubt this was a reflection of the fact that the Baptist Union had not been able to define numerical targets for church planting following the production of its own national mission strategy in 1993. It would also be open to non-Baptist Union churches and people, and would encourage greater mutual accountability. These possibilities were discussed at the Mainstream conference in January 1993. By June 1994 Mainstream declared itself ready for a significant change of emphasis from the renewal of local church life to the renewal of Association life by challenging its present expression and exposing its inadequacy, and modelling new structures to replace what is there at present. In order to facilitate this a new network has been organised covering most of England and Wales.

At present there are 12 focal points for the network, with two national Mainstream chairmen in Rob Warner of Wimbledon for the south and Glenn Marshall of Wakefield for the north. These developments are still in their early stages, and personal experience confirms that it is one thing to launch new initiatives of this sort among independent churches like the Baptists, but it is quite another to sustain, service and finance the work that they demand to retain a credible sense of momentum.[24]

In this process there are the positive signs of the inner vibrancy the Spirit creates in his renewing work within us. In recent years there have been a series of consultations on such subjects as the Gospel and culture, apologetics in evangelism, issues raised by the task of leadership in large churches, preaching, and the debate over human sexuality and homosexuality. All of this confirms the appropriateness of a broad coalition like Mainstream serving in a key way as a forum for new ideas, a workshop and a gadfly, as Alastair Campbell had described it in April 1982. Can the new Word and Spirit network do more than the Mainstream from which it has emerged, or is it a return to the gathering of local clusters of ministers for their own fellowship and mutual support, much in the way that Manna Ministries gathered such groupings in the 1980s'? How can it encourage accountability without the service of several full-time and nationally recognised staff in a way that complements the work fulfilled by the Baptist Union with the aid of several full-time staff? Can Leading Edge, a camping week organised by two enterprising young ministers, Clive Jarvis and Ron Overton, build on its positive start in August 1996 to meet a major need for the encouragement, fellowship and teaching of a wider family of Baptists who have both renewal interests and evangelical convictions? All these issues are open questions at this stage.

As we draw this section to a close perhaps it is appropriate to raise some of the questions that Word and Spirit may well face. Having affirmed the need for gadflies for religious institutions, the point that needs to be gently made is that they too face a real danger, unknown in the strict world of scientific etymology, but real in its religious equivalent. For in the world of faith and conviction the gadfly that stings a larger body may

metamorphose into another kind of insect if it loses its sense
of direction and purpose. The species to which it may
degenerate is the male of the honey bee which lacks enough
work to keep itself occupied and which is incapable of self-
reproduction – the drone bee. I think I have heard an unimagin-
ative hum from just a few whose achievements are few, whose
work rate is slow, but who would regard their charismatic
credentials as impeccable. This is an unlikely future for a
reformist group which is well led, which keeps a broad agenda
of interest, which works out relevant strategies for change and
is prepared to apply them, and which learns the well-demon-
strated lessons of the history of the renewal.

For instance, it is plain that the renewal experience can
initiate fresh spiritual experience but that in itself it lacks the
ability to mature character. We thus need to remember that
the renewal which can provide the energy to discover new
forms for the fellowship of the renewed may not be able to
offer the strategies that such bodies always need to preserve a
sense of purpose for them. We must all beware lest visions for
change become merely frustrating day-dreams, absorbing time
and energy but achieving nothing. In the real world the life of
the Baptist is expressed in its larger body of the Union. It may
be said that the changes Mainstream first wished to stimulate
have taken place and are being fulfilled at this present time
because it retained an agenda that was sufficiently inclusive to
affect a broad coalition within the main family. This would not
have happened if Mainstream had chosen to become but one
exclusive charismatic element in the ongoing flow. Equally, it
would never have happened if the charismatics had lost their
zeal and had forsaken their appetite for more of the Spirit's
refreshing power. There were other factors involved in the
substantial progress that was made. Now it is time to examine
some of the other causes for change both within the formal
life of the Baptist Union and further afield.

The Dawning of a New Era

9

Ripe for Harvest

(John 4:35)

The story of the developments in the renewal movement and their impact on the Baptists must include an account of the three further distinctive elements of the 1980s. The first is the recovery of the work of the Evangelical Alliance after the débâcle already described in 1966. The second is the development of the largest Christian conference in Europe, Spring Harvest. This began in 1979 but was enormously influential throughout the 1980s and is still so in the 1990s. The last concerns the contribution to the future of the Baptist Union through the leadership of a new and personally modest general secretary, Bernard Green. He entered office in 1982 and continued to 1991, when he handed over to his present successor David Coffey.

It has to be admitted that these developments were unexpected. The Evangelical Alliance has had a long and honourable history but there were several who doubted whether it could survive the division over ecumenism, the strengthening of the British Evangelical Council which was then being advocated, and the developments that were taking place in the renewal.[1] A vast burgeoning new conference was not expected either and, as we shall see, Spring Harvest has enjoyed meteoric growth. Bernard Green emerged from his years as a skilful pastor into the high responsibilities of the well-established ecclesiastical office of a general secretary. He had a more immediate awareness of the grass roots developments in the churches, but no one expected the degree of shift that occurred there in favour of the conservative evangelicals and also the charismatic evangelicals.

Yet, as I shall attempt to indicate, in spite of these surprises, there is a rhythm between the contributions that come from these different sources. Change was in the wind and the denominational maps were changing. As the renewal permeated the evangelical movement which Spring Harvest served, so the effects spread beyond the interdenominational evangelical world and into the heart of the life of the Baptist denomination. Clearly this became the period in which the Baptist Union was prepared for many significant changes introduced by Bernard Green but effected by David Coffey, his successor. In Bernard Green we would be hard put to it to discover a Christian leader who gave himself more conscientiously to the goal of faithfulness in service, whether or not that service was rewarded by the popular approval of great numbers of those who benefited from his efforts. Many soon had cause to revise their initially negative opinions about him. We shall begin by summarising the story of the changes in the Evangelical Alliance from the unpromising scenario of the mid-60s.

The Alliance restored

Morgan Derham had become the general secretary of the Evangelical Alliance in 1966 just in time to inherit the explosive agenda of the National Assembly of that year. When he left in January 1969, he did not feel that he could remain as a representative of a constituency that was now so profoundly and probably irretrievably divided.[2]

Nevertheless, during his period at the helm there were a series of positive developments changing the face of the evangelical world. In 1967 the evangelical Anglicans had held their first National Evangelical Anglican conference at Keele University, and this marked a major growth in the resurgence of their confidence. This simultaneously reduced their commitment to the wider evangelical world.[3] Then in 1968, under Morgan Derham's leadership, Tear Fund was born and has grown into one of the largest relief and development organisations in Britain today.

George Hoffman, profoundly influenced by the Keele conference, took on the work of this fund which soon needed to become an independent though related operation of the Evangelical Alliance. The Arts Centre Group was another initiative started at this time, providing a network for hundreds of Christian artists to meet and to encourage one another in their specialist work. In the same year a report was published from the Evangelical Alliance Commission on Evangelism entitled *On the Other Side*. The chairman for this incisive diagnosis of the spiritual state of the nation was David Pawson. It contained some far-reaching assessments of the long-term value of crusade-type evangelism, some criticisms of the tendency to rely on the ministry of the specialist evangelists, and some penetrating comments on the smug, self-assured complacency of many evangelicals. It urged individual Christians to engage in the task on a personal one-to-one basis. In support of this, it quoted with approval the basic theorem of Kenneth Strachan with his Evangelism in Depth Programme: 'The growth of any movement is in direct proportion to the success of the movement in mobilising its total membership for the propagation of its beliefs.'[4] Yet, as Morgan Derham later commented: 'It never got the attention it deserved.'[5]

He was succeeded by an Anglican layman, Gordon Landreth, who initiated the Evangelist's Conference and was closely involved with European and world evangelical concerns. When it came to replacing him, there was no doubt as to the kind of person they wanted to appoint. It would need to be an outgoing preacher and teacher. The candidate would need to be gifted as a diplomat who could work with both the traditional denominations and the new churches that had developed out of restorationism. It would be a great advantage if the new secretary was skilled in broadcasting and television techniques. There was one young candidate who possessed these qualities and added to them enormous quantities of energy: Clive Calver. He was appointed to office in 1983.[6]

Since then, the work and the membership of the Alliance has grown significantly. Annual growth in membership has reached 25 per cent. This has mirrored the overall increase in evangelicals to 2.6 per cent of the population statistics and growing. Of this figure, 25 per cent are Anglican, 18 per cent are Baptist and 17 per cent Methodist. Baptist leaders like Derek Tidball, David Coffey and Steve Gaukroger have been closely associated with the Evangelical Alliance. Raymond Brown was president while principal at Spurgeon's College. Paul Beasley-

Murray was a keen supporter while in the same post, as is
Michael Quicke, his successor.[7]

By the 1990s they had adopted a target for 100 000 individual
members. In 1995 there were no less than 2778 individual
churches in membership, 707 other organisations, and 14 whole
denominations, making a sizeable constituency of 5000 member
churches.[8]

Another success story

Spring Harvest began in 1979. As with many new developments
there were established precedents from which their leaders drew
their inspiration. The Keswick Convention began in 1875 as a
means of drawing evangelical believers together for the development of the spiritual life and in the quest for greater personal
holiness. In 1956 the Filey Christian Holiday Crusade began,
targeting the younger generation. Through the earlier years of
the 1970s, the renewal movement had seen many developments
through conference weeks and the like, and these became a
particular feature for the restoration movement with Bible conferences in the Yorkshire Dales, the Sussex Downs and in
numerous conferences elsewhere.

The two main sponsors who have retained a major hold on
all Spring Harvest's developments are Clive Calver, and Peter
Meadows, most recently renowned for pioneering another bold
evangelical initiative with Premier, the Christian broadcasting
station for London, although others are now continuing to
develop the work that Meadows began. As they tell the story
of Spring Harvest, it began with a conversation together in an
old Ford Cortina car on the M1 motorway. Meadows had just
returned from a Methodist youth event at the Prestatyn holiday
camp in North Wales, and was full of enthusiasm for it and for
the potential that it represented. They decided that they would
attempt something similar for the wider evangelical youth constituency and, with the support of the two organisations with
whom they were then working, the magazine *Buzz* for
Meadows and *British Youth for Christ* for Calver, Spring Harvest
was born at Prestatyn and 2700 people came to its first week.
The main speaker was the Argentinian-born evangelist Luis
Palau. Ian Barclay gave the Bible readings. A thousand late

bookers were turned away because the accommodation was all taken.[9]

By 1983 the numbers attending had grown to 15 000. By 1988 this had increased to 50 000, meeting over three weeks on two separate sites at Minehead and Skegness. By 1990, 60 000 were anticipated on three sites. Since then the total of those attending has settled to a regular 70 000 over a period of three weeks on two or three sites.[10] The records show that those who attend come from a wide range of Churches of all descriptions, not just evangelical Churches. They divide into approximately 33 per cent Anglican, 33 per cent other denominations and 33 per cent from Baptistic churches, of whom the greater proportion, about 25 per cent of the total Spring Harvest attendees, are from Baptist churches associated with the Baptist Union.[11]

By this standard alone it is plain that these conferences have a greater impact on the lives of ordinary members of Baptist churches than any similar conferences, including the annual Baptist Assembly. It is possibly the case that Spring Harvest has the greatest single influence on the church life of all evangelical Churches of any translocal body, whatever their affiliation. With such a consistently high level of support there cannot be many obvious mistakes being made by those who carry responsibility for it.

How do they do it?

There must be many reasons for the growth and support of this organisation, which is unparalleled in modern church life. Firstly, we have to take note of its high level of organisational efficiency. There is a professionalism about the way the weeks are organised which is the fruit of much hard work by the unsung heroes behind the scenes who look after the administration, prepare the brochures, work on the site preparation, attend to all the mass of detail and somehow conspire not only to keep the guests satisfied, but also attend to the many and various eccentricities of the speakers, many of whom lay claim to specialist treatment normally reserved for the few genuine prima donnas – who probably would never demand it anyway. It is an amazing performance. While the speakers are required to affirm their evangelical theological credentials by signing statements to that effect, this does not apply to those who attend. Hence there is a unified speaking team available for what amounts to as varied and different a gathering of listeners as are likely to be gathered for any Christian event sponsored by evangelicals.

Those responsible for the recruitment and the running of the machine that makes it all happen are very talented servants of God. Nothing is left to chance in the advance planning. There can be no doubt about the level of commitment of those who serve on the advisory boards, the planning conferences, the editorial sessions, and all the other behind the scenes activities unseen by the general public. Preparations for each year's events begin 18 months beforehand, according to Hilary Saunders. For six months each year, two Spring Harvests are in view.[12]

There is also the attractiveness of those invited to teach and preach, both regularly and from time to time. The list includes many who have become household names in the evangelical world. In earlier years David Pawson was there. Jim Graham, Derek Tidball, David Coffey, Ian Coffey, Steve Chalke, Nigel Wright, Michael Quicke and Steve Gaukroger are still regularly present among a grand total of some 350 preachers each year. It is no surprise to see that many of these speakers have been closely connected with Mainstream. Several of them have moved into significant denominational positions. David Coffey recorded his own gratitude for the way in which he was prayed for in a spontaneous act at Spring Harvest as he entered his presidential year in 1986.[13] It is no surprise to find that aspiring Christian authors add to the advance publicity of their written offerings the phrase: 'Has spoken at Spring Harvest.' As far as their potential readers are concerned, this is the cachet for attractive orthodoxy combined with dynamic relevance. It says it all. As the great desire of an earlier generation of evangelical preachers was for being known as a preacher on the unofficial lists of approved convention speakers, today it is the desire to be known in this connection. Clearly, on the whole, the choices made have been good.

The meetings are always characterised by an explosive mix of informal humour, vibrant praise, and personal informality by those who lead them. Much of the music is new, with a high proportion provided by the best-known worship leaders in the land, under the overall leadership of Graham Kendrick who is himself in the front rank of the present generation of Christian musicians and hymnologists. Given the skills of wonderful orchestras, great instrumentalists, gifted lead singers and exhilarating words, worship in a Spring Harvest evening celebration is a high point in the week. It is a major event. There is no over-religious stuffiness about it. The theme is chosen with a great sense of purpose, and the plan of the meeting carries the worshippers through to the necessary climax in their personal response to the call of Christ to repentance, or faith, or commitment, or service, or sacrifice, or to a fresh reception of the power of God's Holy Spirit. There will have been much prayer before the event, in the event, and subsequently. Hence there will be a strong expectation for things to happen at this time. The evidence is that this is what does occur. If it is true that in its earlier years many pastors felt threatened by its growth in popularity, one of the reasons for a change of attitude among ministers is because they know that this is a time when the lives of some of their most needy members have been positively transformed. Certainly, some who go to a week may well come home at its end with unreal expectations for the improved quality of the pastor's preaching if he or she has been present too. They may be dissatisfied with the contributions from those who play an elderly church organ or even, as may be the case in the quiet backwaters, the positively geriatric harmonium due its honourable discharge from sacred service at least a generation ago. Nevertheless, they come back with fresh vibrancy which spells hope for the future.

Nor can it be said that their week away has only been a time of high-spirited praise with little biblical content and with no social application. The syllabus of workshops, seminars, study groups and varied activities for all the family is vast. People go in large numbers because they are at ease with the teaching given, and they are happy with the provision made for all age groups over the whole spectrum. An example of the breadth and depth of the programme can be seen in the seminar notes available to all who attend.[14]

Yet there is a further reason for the success of this enterprise that reflects the interest of our particular theme. Not only does Spring Harvest raise and attempt to deal with major themes of wide Christian concern, and apply the lessons learned by others in earlier conference activities, it specifically seeks to bridge the divide between those involved in the renewal movement and those who are still satisfied with a spirituality that owes most to their own more traditional evangelical background. It was not long before even restorationists were finding that attendances at their Bible weeks was declining while it was increasing among those of their own number going to the Easter event. With great foresight and wisdom, the Spring Harvest organisers made sure that the leaders of the former Bible weeks were invited to join their panels of speakers. Given the popularity of the evening celebrations, the net result has been a two-way benefit. Evangelicalism has been brought into a much greater awareness and sympathy for renewal, and the general ethos of renewal, its worship and teaching, have become more sympathetic to evangelicalism. As Peter Meadows put it:

> From the beginning Spring Harvest took a committed charismatic stance but worked hard to help people keep within their own comfort zone. By including both charismatics and non-charismatics on the speaking team together, friendships were formed and frag-mentation resisted.[15]

Throughout its first decade most, if not all, of the best-known charismatic preachers from around the world have been on the team of speakers. John Wimber, Paul Cain, Arthur Blessitt and many others have come from North America. Their message has been balanced by the approach of other speakers who would not necessarily subscribe to the particular doctrines for which these speakers have gained a particular reputation. Consequently, if there have been particular crises arising from a special emphasis they have brought, Spring Harvest has found a healthy way of containing it without losing the attract-iveness the speaker has to offer. A good example of this balance was in the response to the potential divisiveness of the so-called 'Toronto blessing' issue in which they built on the consultative work already undertaken by the Evangelical Alliance.[16] We shall refer to this again in the next chapter, but note here that the Spring Harvest executive made it clear to all invited speakers that there was to be no undue pressure to induct people, especially children, into manifestations of whatever kind. By this leadership some of the more flamboyant elements in the renewal movement have been drawn back from the isolation in which extremism can flourish. There is generally a greater recognition of the sensitivities of those for whom they may have had little sympathy before they served with them in this unifying event.

In addition, there is the well-organised programme for children and teenagers to which they look forward with anticipation not dread. A vast amount of counselling ministry is available, and the timetable for those who can provide it is regularly oversubscribed. Doubtless there are still some yawning gaps in the programmes that have been devised so far. David Tomlinson strikes a critical note when he points out that, while it is known that the conference attracts a wide ecumenical cross-section of support from the Churches, including Roman Catholics, with the exception of David Alton, the member of parliament whose views on the issue of abortion and related subjects are in accordance with those of many evangelical Christians, the organisers have not so far had the courage to invite other evangelically minded Catholic speakers. This is a serious omission: 'In a day when terrorists are laying aside their guns and bombs in Ulster, evangelicals should be prepared to upset some of their own applecarts.'[17]

Together with this I link a certain atmosphere of commercialisation which threatens to become rampant, and in my opinion both these factors impose an unnecessary threat to its future. To be fair, the present policy of Catholic exclusion is scarcely surprising in the light of the huge and unresolved divisions in evangelicalism caused by the ecumenical debate of the mid-1960s, and behind the unwillingness to face this issue is a lack of confidence about the unity of evangelicalism. But I do not want to make too much of these points. They are minor criticisms in the light of the enormously positive impact Spring Harvest makes on all churches. It is surely the fruit of much simple, humble and obedient prayer combined with much business acumen on the part of those who are responsible for it all. In this they provide the wider Church with a striking example of positive planning combined with an unpretentious dependence on God which represents what is best in the heart of the evangelical tradition. Peter Meadows confesses:

> My greatest fear is that one year God won't turn up. . . . God's presence is felt at Spring Harvest each year, invariably in a new way, and I would hate it to be trivialised. Each year I look for something special – and I see it.[18]

Perhaps the more recent growth of the Stoneleigh Bible Week organised by the New Frontiers network of churches indicates changes ahead. Although this group comprises some 200 churches, they are achieving an attendance of about 20 000 each year. This may well indicate a high level of support from Baptist Churches as well as those in their network. The New Wine Week organised by St Andrew's, Chorleywood, is also growing. If those who aspire to offer senior leadership to today's British Churches, whatever their theological predilections, attended a Spring Harvest week and gained inspiration from this source I think the life of our denomination would greatly benefit. In the story of the growing impact of renewal, there are also many other factors to remember. It is time now to return to the much less spectacular denominational story which none the less balances the advances we have briefly catalogued.

Renewing Baptist basics

Baptist Christians have a long history in which they have defended the freedom of individual judgement in matters of religion and the unique authority of the Scriptures in determining our understanding of the Christian faith. In our churches we believe that it is right that the government of the church should be locally exercised, without external interference, and insist that each member of a church has an inalienable right to take part in the decision-making processes of the church in the church meeting. This does not mean that each Christian should ignore the views of other believers or that each church should go it alone without regard to the need for good relationships with other churches. The balancing factors to our commitment to individualism are our understanding of the functions of leadership and our historic stress on the need for an ordained and properly trained ministry. In our ecclesiology, moreover, we insist on the need for interdependence to balance our independence. From the start we have known local church life and Association church life, which in turn has led on to Union church life as we have sought to develop our influence nationwide.

Out of this non-hierarchical view of the Church it follows that those who are called to special leadership functions require special gifts and qualities if they are not going to be driven to and fro by the strength of the opinions of those to whom they are bound to listen even while they attempt to lead them. In common with all Christian Churches, Baptists share the need for the highest standards of character, the most robust qualities of intellectual integrity, and the clearest evidences for spiritual perception from their leaders, especially their ordained leaders. A Baptist leader does not have special Church powers that only the ordained possess. Any church member can perform any and all of the ministry functions normally associated with ordained leadership, if so approved by the church meeting. It follows that the kind of leadership abilities Baptist ministers require are unique. The capacity to inspire the confidence of their colleagues to a common course of action, the spiritual skill to stimulate the growth of faith in the positive outcome of the endeavour, the ability to both model and create caring systems of mutual support, and to build up loyal teams of committed fellow workers – are all necessary. At the very least, Baptist ministers must believe themselves to be the Saviour's ambassadors who are entrusted with a holy mission to which they been called by God.

In order to enter into their ministry they need to convince their sending church, the ministry committees, the college faculties where they wish to do their training, and finally the churches that might receive their ministry once the training period has been successfully negotiated. Baptist ministry only begins at the end of this arduous process. It follows that they must also be able to communicate all this effectively in their preaching even though none of this is the subject of their preaching. That must be the Gospel and the message of the Scriptures. As a consequence, at their best, Baptist ministers have been renowned for their evangelistic ministry, their expository skills, and their campaigning zeal for social reforms. They tend to be exceptionally rugged individualists, possessing a wide range of skills and gifted with winsomeness. In a word, taking account of a range of personality traits and temperaments, in a non-technical sense, effective Baptist ministers are often strongly charismatic.

If all this is true for normal pastoral ministry it is also normally the case for those called to particular denominational leadership. Bernard Green became general secretary for the Baptist Union in 1982 after significant pastorates in Birmingham, Nottingham and Bristol. He had considerably more experience in local church ministry than either of his immediate predecessors, Ernest Payne and David Russell. While in Bristol he encountered some expressions of the charismatic interest in healing ministry in which he had been involved from his Nottingham days. There he had been in touch with the work of Frank Lake and his teaching on clinical theology. Lake was to play a significant role in the work of the Fountain Trust for a period. He had also developed his own prayer ministry for healing, though without any presumption that he possessed a gift for healing.

At the beginning of his period of service Bernard Green was aware of the tensions felt by the conservative evangelicals in the denomination. As he assessed the situation he understood that they felt they had not received even-handed treatment within the denomination, and that this sense of grievance went back many years. They felt themselves to be isolated and excluded from the structures of denominational life which had assumed a life of their own, separate from the life of the churches they were designed to serve. In this period it was the commonly accepted wisdom that the denomination was essentially a mildly liberal, Broad Church body theologically, with two small and ineffectual extreme wings of liberalism and fundamentalism. Bernard appreciated the lesson from the Christology debates of the earlier decade. The reality was then, as it has probably always been and is to this day, that the Baptists could best be described as inconsistently orthodox theologically. By this I mean that they hold to the essentials of the Christian faith summarised in the historic Christian creeds. They have a voracious appetite for the study of the Scriptures. Their inconsistency is no admission of weakness but a witness to their constant confession of the provisionalness of all Church structures in the light of the supremacy of the Kingdom which is yet to come, and also to the view in the oft-quoted lines of John Robinson from whose Church came the nucleus for the Pilgrim Fathers: 'The Lord had more truth and light to break forth out of his Holy Word.'[19] Bernard was determined to redress the balance here and to encourage the participation of those who felt themselves to be excluded.

He thus addressed his first council meeting in November 1982 on the theme of 'Some Signposts for the Future Strategy for the Union'. He saw their context in an understanding of the fellowship we share in Christ and in his mission, in the work of the different Associations called to the work of mission and ministry, and in the work of the individual churches. The current climate he described as being affected by charismatic developments, some of which he regarded as being positive while others, such as the tendency to authoritarianism to which the Fiddes report alluded, were not so.[20] He perceived the need to remain committed to ecumenical sharing in spite of the failure of the discussions about a covenanted Church in England. He believed that there was an open door of opportunity for our witness to society as a whole, but confessed that our structures often prompt a sense of frustration in our midst rather than encourage a due sense of partnership. His signposts represented a sevenfold call to a new strategy in the light of this. They were a call to:

1. Specific evangelism: with the aim that by AD 2000 we might win a whole generation of young people for Christ.
2. Special ministries: to city centres, rural areas and new estates through bold experimental pilot ministries.
3. Fresh community orientation: with a resurrected Nonconformist conscience.
4. Ecumenical commitment.
5. Forward budgeting.
6. Denominational renewal of deacons and church meetings, Association meetings, Union councils and National Assemblies.
7. Better, closer and more personal links between the national

office and the local situations, with much improved standards of communication between them all.

Bernard declared: 'We are here to grow as churches, to spread the Gospel, and to be agents for the Kingdom of God.'[21]

The Bugbrooke controversy

Among the charismatic developments with which an increasing number of churches were unhappy was the initiative in communitarian living associated with the Bugbrooke Baptist Church in Northampton. Eventually this led to the expulsion of the church from the Baptist Union and the local Association by the Baptist Union council, with the support of Bernard Green. There were several reasons behind this decision. There had been numerous complaints from neighbouring Baptist churches regarding their exclusive claims, typified by the rebaptism of those they received into their midst. In addition, it appeared as if they had formed a highly authoritarian leadership structure, to which the members had to acquiesce, which involved forms of physical punishment for the children of members of their community which many regarded as being both degrading and brutal. There were reports of financial manipulation which appeared to be unsavoury. Since it also appeared that they did not operate a form of congregational government that was consistent with their claim to be Baptist, the Union took the almost unprecedented step of expulsion. Likewise, the Evangelical Alliance had decided to suspend their membership of that body, prior to the decision of the Baptist Union council.

This was not a unanimous decision, and there were those who felt that at the least the Bugbrooke pastor and his elders ought to have been given the chance to speak for themselves to the Baptist council. At an earlier point the *Baptist Times* had produced a very positive report on the unique nature of the work of this fellowship, likening its work to that of a Catholic Order like the Franciscans. They were challenging our individualism, denying the clerical–lay divide, endeavouring to reveal the revolutionary demands of the Gospel, and reaching out to the drug-addicted drop-outs of our society.[22] None the less, in spite of their protestations that they were an orthodox church fellowship with reformed theological views as well as their charismatic experience, Bugbrooke represented the point beyond which the Baptist Union would not go in their tolerance of one extremist edge of the renewal movement.

Other Union developments

If Bugbrooke was at one extreme, it was the ecumenical debate that was at the other, with a major decision being taken in the Assembly at Leicester in 1989 to become full participating members of the newly formed ecumenical bodies Churches Together in England and the Council of Churches in Great Britain and Ireland, having formerly been members of the British Council of Churches. As we have already seen, central to that decision was the activity of some of the leadership of Mainstream in successfully decoupling what had appeared to many evangelicals as a necessary link between evangelical conviction and ecumenical hostility. This issue had been part and parcel of the broader evangelical scene since the mid-1960s. It had been tackled at a Mainstream conference prior to the Leicester Assembly, and a less apprehensive and more co-operative spirit had been engendered that subsequent events have confirmed as being much more appropriate for Baptists.

If the instincts of the more broadly based charismatics were supportive of the Evangelical Alliance, happy with the growth of Spring Harvest, and positively in favour of good ecumenical relationships, it must be supposed that those charismatics who oppose this development are more probably from the reformed background associated, as we have seen, with D.M. Lloyd Jones. The fact that such a divisive issue could be faced decisively and dealt with without great rancour must be seen as being due in no small measure to the patiently courteous and thorough way in which the general secretary had worked to make sure that the greatest consultation had taken place among the churches, and that the issue of the differing viewpoints had been thoroughly explored. Whatever lingering suspicions he had felt, arising from his stark introduction to some Mainstreamers in 1982 in Heywood, were now thoroughly discharged.

The other major issue he handled with great skill was the decision to move the denominational offices from Southampton

Row, London, to the fine new premises in the Broadway, Didcot, to be shared with the Baptist Missionary Society. These offices and their staff are sometimes miscalled the denominational headquarters, as if Baptists were corporately organised or directed by a group of seniors in a command structure, but that notion is a misleading myth. It damages the service of the dedicated team who work in Didcot and the churches which represent the real heart of the life of the denomination. There have also been some considerable losses in moving from the national capital (not least for some of us located in the metropolis, where there are more Baptists than anywhere else in Western Europe), but the new premises have obvious advantages in the upgrading of equipment and the improvements of the working conditions for the staff of Baptist House. Carrying through the operation required particular skills of advocacy and organisation, and it is to Bernard Green and his associates Douglas Sparkes, David Nixon and David Lovegrove that chief credit must go for its success.

All these achievements are the more remarkable when we recall that Bernard Green never regarded himself as a party man or a member of any pressure group in his service. Perhaps it is because of his intrinsic sense of justice and fair play that a more positive climate has flourished within the life of the Baptist denomination, allowing the best of the insights of the renewal movement to come through its structures. Perhaps it is that spiritual quality of inner stillness which is close to the centre of his life that explains his considerable effectiveness. It is not seen often in the lives of those who exercise considerable authority, and it always betrays the confidence of one who knows that his strength does not come from his own resources but from the Lord, his Maker. However we interpret the secrets of the inner strengths of another it is certain that, as a good workman, he prepared the way for his successor David Coffey, with his stronger renewal interests, to enjoy the benefits of these developments.

During the decade of the 1980s the two most significant renewal developments for Baptists outside the movement itself were the large expansion of the Evangelical Alliance and the evangelically based conference Spring Harvest. In addition, we have noted the quiet diplomacy of a leader committed faithfully

to representing the diverse views of the whole of his denominational family, which was becoming increasingly influenced
by conservative evangelicalism and charismatic renewal. The
reason for his success was in the degree of trust that he won
from all parties. At the end of this decade it might have been
supposed that the renewal would have been more or less sub-
merged within a greater and more lively conservative
evangelicalism. This has not happened, however, largely because
of the emergence of yet another example of the capacity for
charismatic renewal to renew itself once more by a new variant
of the same message. This latest development originated in a
Vineyard community church located just about at the end of
the main runway of the airport in Toronto. This is the new
story for us to attempt to interpret next.

Times of Refreshing

(Acts 3:19)

We have already seen that, from the early 1980s, the chief architect determining the shape of the renewal movement was the Californian teacher John Wimber. He had made the renewal message acceptable to a wide evangelical audience, much attracted by his achievements in the fast growth of his own church, his lecturing at Fuller Theological Seminary, his church growth expertise and his charismatic insights. I have already indicated some of the areas where, in my opinion, his teaching is seriously deficient theologically. His concentration on a religion of power was well suited to the spirit of the age, but I do not believe that it measures up to the core of the New Testament focus based on the message of the cross.

His ministry peaked before his involvement with Paul Cain and his companions from Kansas City. It has never recovered from the fallout from that period, for it was through this involvement that he made his most significant public pronouncements on the immediate proximity of vast worldwide revival. He expected this to begin in his meetings at the Docklands Arena in London in October 1990. When this did not happen he was at first at a loss to explain the mistake. By the following year, in September 1991, he was frankly admitting that he was wrong in his understanding and that he or Paul Cain or both of them had made a mistake. At the same time, however, he went on record in statements soon to be taken up in the vocabulary of the Toronto saga that we now examine. First, he believed that the time of his Docklands ministry had been particularly significant and that revival was now very near. Second, he described an important stage in revival in terms of what had been seen in part at Docklands in 'the return of the prodigals', that is, backslidden believers returning to faith. Third, he declared that in fact the effects of the meetings in October 1990 were considerable. He put it like this:

Last October the Holy Spirit lit a fire of revival in England. It touched families. It touched congregations. And it surely touched me – and I've been running like a scalded dog ever since, intent as never before on seeking 'times of refreshing from the presence of the Lord'.[1]

The phrases about the return of the prodigals, the times of refreshing and the nearness of the outbreak of revival within a charismatic meeting, spilling out on to the streets of the town, were key terms soon to be in common coinage to explain what was happening in Toronto. By December 1993 Wimber believed that God had urged him to tell his followers to stir up the gifts of the Spirit in their own lives and declared that God had spoken to him no less than 17 times, telling him that this was to be a time for new beginnings. In his own parent Vineyard in Anaheim, California, he started protracted Sunday evening meetings to provide an environment for the new beginnings that were now expected and looked for.[2] The dates become significant at this point. According to the interview with him reported in the *Sunday Telegraph* of 2 October 1994, on 16 January 'the Holy Spirit fell powerfully and sovereignly upon our church in Anaheim'.[3] Since he is still the best-known charismatic teacher on the subject of revival, there was no surprise in the news of a fresh movement beginning to break out in one his Vineyard churches. But this did not attract the attention of the world in the same way as the events that then followed in another Vineyard, not in California but in the Canadian city of Toronto. The date was 20 January 1994.

The Toronto blessing did not arise directly out of Wimber's own ministry although plainly it owed much to his teaching. The setting was a Vineyard fellowship, but the trigger was a visit there from Randy Clark, the founding pastor of the Vineyard Christian Fellowship in St Louis who in turn had been powerfully affected by the ministry of Rodney Howard-Browne, a South African-born evangelist now resident in the USA.

Howard-Browne comes from a Pentecostal background. He had been an associate of Ray McCauley of Johannesburg, and had also been associated with the work of Kenneth Hagin, Benny Hinn and Kenneth Copeland. Their teaching has been characterised by the proposition that the key to the mastery of ill health, poverty and many human disorders is through the exercise of unquestioning faith on the part of the sufferer in God's willingness to heal or provide with immediate abundance in response to their prayers.[4] This was never one of Wimber's doctrines – indeed, he reacted strongly against these ideas.

Not to put too fine a point on it, most evangelical Christians consider that such teaching is dishonest. Sad to say, it is also associated with forms of unscrupulous financial extortion on the part of its promoters, many of whom have gained the unsavoury reputation of being bogus preachers with dishonourable records. Their victims are often among those who can least afford to be exploited in this way. Howard-Browne scarcely inspires confidence when he defends the view that since Jesus was a wealthy man, so he too can be a wealthy man. Among his more bizarre claims is the view that he has a ministry in releasing holy laughter among the people of God. He has been engaging in this activity since an incident occurred during his ministry in Albany, New York. At first it disturbed him that outbreaks of raucous laughter were the response to his preaching. In due course he became persuaded that this was what God wanted to happen through him and indeed to him. There is a well-known video available that demonstrates the beneficial effects of this through scenes showing him and his colleague Copeland engaging in a merry platform scene in which the two of them exchange spiritual jokes while supposedly exercising the gift of tongues to each other.[5]

In so far as the Toronto blessing arises from the ministry of this teacher, we should not be surprised if many dismiss it because of its lack of serious credibility. This appears to be the view of a number of charismatic leaders. None the less, there are those, like the well-loved and kindly R.T. Kendall of Westminster Chapel, who remain convinced that he possesses unusual spiritual gifts and that Howard-Browne has a singularly significant Christian ministry as a prophet for the revival which is even closer to hand than it was in 1990.[6] Others would say that this view does indeed represent a triumph of hope over experience. Colin Dye, pastor of Britain's largest church, Kensington Temple, happily endorses Howard-Browne's ministry too. His supporters are evidently prepared to forgive him the astonishingly offensive personal statements that it is alleged he sometimes makes as only the signs of a youthful enthusiasm that is both understandable and allowable among the young.[7] In spite of the fact that Howard-Browne had not ministered in Toronto, he is widely credited as being one of the primary sources for the movement there.

Rapid advance

Although this phase only began in January 1994, news of the events taking place in Toronto soon spread worldwide, mainly through reports in the press, on radio broadcasts and through television. In fact, this feature of the friendliness of the media is what uniquely marked out the Toronto blessing. In the story of the current renewal, never before has a new development been given such a favourable press or such widespread publicity. Much of this was due to the repercussions of the January meetings as they affected British churches. By the summer of 1994 several British charismatics had travelled to Toronto and entered a new phase in their experience through the ministry there. In the London area, three Baptist churches were among the earliest wave of visitors: Wimbledon, Herne Hill and Bookham. The best-known church to become involved was the Anglican church of Holy Trinity, Brompton (HTB), long established as one of the leading charismatic congregations in London. The message of Toronto was first introduced there by Eleanor Mumford, the wife of the pastor of the South-west London Vineyard Church, John Mumford. Both of them have had many years in charismatic ministry. At Toronto, she had been dramatically overwhelmed by the Spirit on numerous occasions. She was invited to HTB to give her testimony before a crowded meeting on 29 May 1994, which made a major impact. 'Scenes reminiscent of the second chapter of Acts followed Eleanor Mumford's report to HTB on 29 May after her visit there,' claimed *Renewal* magazine in an excited piece of reporting headed 'Stop Press – Spreading like Wildfire'.[8]

When the *Sunday Telegraph* newspaper carried pictures of scenes of unusual activities at Holy Trinity television companies picked up the story, made visits to Holy Trinity and Queen's Road, Wimbledon, and then included some film of this in their news broadcasts. The information of what was happening in Toronto thus swiftly travelled the globe, much to the surprise of many people, including the original participants back in the Toronto Airport Vineyard. Strange as it may seem, it is a fact that Toronto scarcely knew what was happening in its midst until London told them, courtesy of the British television news-reels that were relayed across the Atlantic with the news of what was happening in London because of what was going on mainly in Toronto!

All this heralded an enormous outburst of meetings, dis-cussions, magazine articles, interviews, and books on both sides of the Atlantic. Many of the new church streams committed themselves wholeheartedly to the fresh charismatic move. Min-ister's meetings were called, prayer meetings organised, and people travelled far and wide to hear, discuss and enter into the blessing of fresh experiences of a different and more intense quality. By the early summer of 1994 *Alpha* magazine was proposing the notion that what we were beginning to witness was 'Rumours of Revival'.[9] Proponents and opponents were scanning the appropriate Scriptures on revival and also the writings of Lloyd Jones and John Wesley. Jonathan Edwards and especially the late Mrs Sarah Edwards were pressed into play in order to justify their own particular viewpoints on the legit-imacy of the phenomena that were sweeping through the churches at this time.

> It was impossible to do justice to Sarah's experiences that night [of the presence and power of the Saviour], which she described as the sweetest she had ever had in her life, without quoting her at length. Her description contains the phrase that captures the heart of her personal revival – *his nearness to me and my dearness to him*. These telling words also capture with great exactness the experiences of many believers in the present time of refreshing.[10]

For the deep heart of the new blessing was in this renewal of the love relationship between the believer and Christ, and Christ and the believer.

Distinctive new elements

Apart from this new sense of the intimacy of the Saviour's love, there was nothing new to emerge at this time for those who had been involved in renewal activities during the previous decades. In the 1960s I recall that this sense of God's surprising presence was combined with a radically different element which had entered into our lives when we had suddenly entered into the strange new world of charismatic gifts, often in the first place through the first halting exercise of the gift of tongues in our private devotions. But all that had been put into a deep shadow when Wimber first began with his power ministry in the 1980s. The claim about the new period of blessing was not of a fresh discovery about God's activities with us by the Spirit, but more to do with the intensity of it all. Perhaps the surprise was not to discover the extent to which those who were blessed had been blessed again, but just how bereft and barren many had felt at this point prior to their fresh infilling of the Spirit.

I do not think we should enter into criticism at all of the testimonies we have listened to about these happenings in our midst. After all, there has scarcely been a new emphasis brought to this country from North America that those of us involved in renewal have not initially wholeheartedly embraced before we ever engaged our minds to think through what was being proposed. In their time, healing ministries, words of knowledge, inner healing ministries, healing of memories, ministries of words of faith, being slain in the Spirit (that is, praying that people will collapse under the power of our praying or through the presence of the Spirit) and communitarian living have all been enthusiastically embraced and defended before being somewhat surreptitiously abandoned as the next emphasis came in view. It ill behoves older charismatics to approach Toronto with an attitude of superior disdain, for that would only show how short and selective our memories have become.

Where there is the evidence in the lives of many of a fresh awareness of the wonderful awesomeness of God's holy love for us, then that is self-authenticating evidence of the work of the Spirit. Of this it must be true that few of us can claim to know enough, and I for one would urge others to seek to enter into this holy place again and again, and always welcome personally any opportunities for the prayers of others who manifest these qualities. I need prayer and can soak up the ministrations of others in prayer with great gratitude. Yet it remains the case that, after a period of months to assess it all, the main characteristics to emerge at this time have been the renewed emphasis on the place for laughter, falling and physical trembling, which phenomena may mark our fresh dealings with God but may as easily mark our naïve suggestibility to the ministrations of others. The burden of the teaching from Toronto has been to expound the scriptural texts that justify experiences of holy laughter, or tears, bodily writhings, collapses, trances, shakings or trancelike movements. The prophet Ezekiel has become a singularly popular subject for many addresses of late because of his penchant for unusual activities, though, truth to tell, it has often been forgotten that the Lord found his capacity to fall down more of a disadvantage than a help when it came to Ezekiel's capacity to hear from God and respond to Him: 'Son of man, stand up on your feet and I will speak to you' (Ezekiel 2:1).

As I have listened to the stories being told I have discovered that most of them have carried the overtones of the conviction that all this was indeed the beginning of the long-awaited big moment of mighty revival, the hope of which has characterised the renewal from its earliest days, as we have seen. On the negative side, once more it has seemed as if the enthusiasts have been finding another standard by which they can decide whether to enter into accepting fellowship with others or whether to continue to hold them at a suspicious distance because of the questions they have insisted upon asking. This has not been a helpful aspect of their experience. It has always seemed right to me that we should neither promote strange behavioural reactions nor should we necessarily immediately forbid them. If they are a legitimate sign of the presence of the Spirit, however, there will be many more mighty transformations at the level of our inner attitudes of love for Christ, his Word and his people than we have ever known before. The real proof of spiritual blessing is in the realm of our characters, our morality and our approachability, not our occasional posture in prayer. If God has been doing something significant I suggest that we shall probably be less piously religious about it all, and

more human. We shall be more caring and less slipshod. Our
prayer life in the secret place of our lives will have a new
dynamic. We shall show the evidence of our dealings with God
by our response to the most needy, careworn, and disadvantaged
of all his people. These are the qualities that I search for,
together with a new gentleness of spirit. In their absence I
remain highly sceptical about the motives of the free-falling
demonstrants. Like those in the Gospels who loved to be seen
busy on the street corners with their prayers and their phylac-
teries, they already have their reward – in full (Matthew 6:5).
And we have the highest authority for saying that this reward
amounts to nothing compared with the blessings known to
those whose religious practices are less showy and much more
private.

The Toronto liturgy

A Toronto-type service will usually begin with a period of
prolonged praise and worship. This has been the case in all the
services of this kind I have been able to attend in London. I
managed one night at the Toronto Airport Vineyard in November 1994, and it appeared that the pattern on both sides of
the Atlantic was the same. This is then followed by the testimony of those who have recently manifested such experiences.
They are then encouraged to receive some more of what they
have already known and may normally be expected to receive
again. This practice follows the advice given by the Vineyard
teachers, who produced a simple brochure which was widely
circulated among those who were keen to help others into the
blessing.[11]

In order to establish a scriptural basis for all of this, a piece
of teaching follows that will encourage our thirst for such
experiences. The meeting will finally conclude with the opportunity for others to receive ministry to this end. Often this
entails the removing of the chairs, the use of prayer teams and
a general encouragement to enjoy an atmosphere of what might
be described as spiritualised pandemonium that was initially
described as being 'party time for the church'. By this time
those who first testified to the spiritual benefits of the exercise
will have recovered from their swoon or twitch and will be

ready to pass on the evidence of their blessing to others. It is generally the case that those who are praying for others expect and encourage physical collapses and are not pleased if they do not occur. As people are prayed for, many although not all manifest similar phenomena. I believe that falling is of no particular spiritual significance. Being seated has the merit of being more comfortable and more seemly for God's people. They should never be made to feel demeaned and foolish through the ministries that they receive.

All this is reminiscent of the scenes we have already described in Wimber's earlier ministry, although there is less restraint about them and, in my experience, the quality of the teaching that is given seems to be far less significant. If it is the case that it is the Holy Spirit who is responsible for all that follows, and that this is how he now wants his people to behave in times of worship and prayer, then it has to be confessed that many of us have many problems in store. However, it is incredible to assume that these scenes are through the direct action of the Spirit alone without some element of the theatrical about them. As we shall see, the Scriptures give us clear guidance to enable us to distinguish between what is inspired by God and what is ordered by enthusiasts on his behalf.

To redress the balance of my argument, however, I would register a positive point in favour of expecting the element of the unusual when we seek the presence of God for ourselves. I shall return to this again in my last chapter. The Scriptures surely do not permit us to retreat into a view of God that reduces his awesome numinosity to the limits of propriety prescribed by reserved Englishmen. Jesus knew experiences when He was 'full of joy through the Holy Spirit' (Luke 10:21). Peter knew unusual trance-like states in which he received visions (Act 10:10). Paul can describe curious out-of-the-body experiences in which he entered into heaven and heard inexpressible things that he was not allowed to disclose (2 Corinthians 12:2). Surely, therefore, we may anticipate occasional spiritual excursions into ecstatic states from time to time. The exercise of spiritual gifts may be described as being like 'tasting the powers of the coming age' (Hebrews 6:5). The patriarchs and the prophets of ancient Israel could never be accused of encouraging tepidity among those who hunger for

God and his righteousness. There are many reasons for supporting the view that our spiritual life should be permeated with an expectancy for sudden encounters with the divine presence that will simultaneously shake us, comfort us, stimulate us and transform us.

The work of David Hay in his examination of the extent of the incidence of such encounters both among the religiously committed and also among those who have no clear Christian commitment advises us against a dismissive attitude of the experiences of others because we do not know them for ourselves. From his investigations it is evident that the majority of British people pray even though only a minority go to church.[12] These experiences may be like the charismata of the Corinthian church, which the apostle noted were popularly present even among the unspiritual and were not therefore to be taken as any kind of barometer indicating the great maturity of those believers. 'You do not lack any spiritual gift,' he declared (1 Corinthians 1:7) They may be spiritually neutral factors indicating the extent of our own human religiosity more than our profound Christian godliness.

One thing that is clear about a post-modern society in a post-Christian age is that it is certainly not post-experiential. All of this begs the question, however, as to whether or not meetings designed to foster a hunger for vivid experiences, because they may be associated with times of special encounter, thereby become the necessary conduits through which God chooses to work today in a special reviving way. Opinion among evangelicals and charismatics remains divided on this issue. It was folly to describe the Toronto meetings as being an outbreak of revival. Wimber's terminology of 'times of refreshing' was and is wiser and appears now to be the chosen terminology preferred by all, for good reasons. Before we attempt an assessment on a movement that has suddenly arisen and may be declining as swiftly as it arose, we should get up to date with what has happened to them since they began early in 1994. Toronto moved on very quickly.

By the end of 1996

A considerable volume of literature has been written about the Toronto happenings in the few short years since they began. The worldwide spread of the information has been enormous. On the occasion of my own visit it seemed as if the majority of those present were from Britain, other European countries, Australia, New Zealand and the United States. In response to the request for a show of hands about our national origins, those from Canada itself were in a minority on that occasion, and I understand that to be fairly typical.

In spite of this, it seems that the growth in actual local church involvement in these developments has proved to be surprisingly limited. There are a few well-known centres for Toronto-style ministry – Holy Trinity, Brompton, Queen's Road, Wimbledon, Pioneer churches, Kensington Temple, the Sunderland Christian Fellowship, several New Frontiers churches and a few others come to mind. The list spreads around the country at large, but it is by no means as long as the list for those churches which would be considered to be centres for renewal ministry. The stress on the visible and audible events has not been wise. It may be possible to justify these responses by the selective use of certain Scriptures, and even to indicate their possible therapeutic value, as Patrick Dixon does, but one is bound to ask, to what end do we pursue such abstruse discussions when there are far more important issues to occupy us?[13]

After a period, even the most persistently prostrated seekers after God have to get to their feet and attend to more pressing business and the laughing believer has to sober up. Having sought to discuss sympathetically these experiences with many who have enjoyed these moments, my deep impression with most is that, after a while, they find the actions less and less helpful until they abandon them altogether.

Undoubtedly, the major crisis that was faced was the decision of John Wimber to dissociate himself and the Vineyard movement from the Toronto events. This caused great difficulty for Toronto and great surprise to Wimber's own followers in Britain. For Wimber, the issues were to do with the interpretations being put on the Toronto phenomena by John Arnott and others from Toronto. The reasons given were by John Wimber and on behalf of the Board for the Association of Vineyard Churches, and their message was clear:

> We cannot at any time endorse, encourage, offer theological justification or biblical proof texting for any exotic practices that are extra-biblical – whether in Toronto or elsewhere. Neither can these practices be presented as criteria for true spirituality or as a mark of true renewal. Our position is that the renewing works of the Spirit are authenticated by that which is clearly stated in Scripture as works of the kingdom of God. Though we understand that when the kingdom is manifest among us there may be phenomena that we do not understand, it is our conviction that these manifestations should not be promoted, placed on stage, nor used as the basis for theologising that leads to new teaching.

The Board goes on to identify

> hype, the featuring of manifestations in testimonies, the use of tape on the floor and assigning catchers to each person being prayed for, conveying the strong impression and suggestion that if ministry is successful the recipient will fall down or manifest in some way . . . and the acceptance of prophecies which set up an élitist mentality among churches, that incite a division between the have's and the have-nots. . . .
>
> We are concerned that among some of the TAV [Toronto Airport Vineyard] leadership there is an emerging prophetic theology centered on the rise of a new kind of ecstatic prophecy which could herald the advent of a second Pentecost, a second book of Acts, and the last days revival. We feel that there are significant problems with this understanding of the nature of prophecy and the role of prophecy in the church.[14]

John Arnott responded to these decisions by expressing gratitude to Wimber for his personal kindnesses and a desire to continue in an attitude of loving respect for the Vineyard ways of working. Others had earlier made pejorative comment, likening Wimber to King Saul to be followed by the more anointed David. Arnott made it clear that he held Wimber in high regard and apologised for the stress and hurt that the disagreement between them was causing. The parting was evidently on reasonably good terms all round.

The repercussions of this division are likely to be profound, not only in the official Vineyard network but even more among those churches in Britain and around the world that are loosely attached to it while remaining within other official allegiances. Will they follow Wimber at this point, and disown the practices they thought he had sponsored in the first place? Will they take the opposite course and continue with their new-found friends in Toronto with whom they have now forged numerous new links? Will they do neither, expressing bewilderment and pinning their colours firmly to the fence on these issues, declaring that they are grateful to God for both sets of leaders and with all their viewpoints, even though the one now disowns the other? Or will they bide their time and then choose to move off to another new allegiance when the next extremist edge of the renewal movement surfaces, as it undoubtedly will in due course?

We need to notice a common feature of the renewal movement at this point which may well emerge more strongly in the future. It is that the energies of the renewed – which are considerable – are easily drawn towards a fresh emphasis or a dynamic new leader as they begin to emerge. It takes time for the renewed to settle down to more tenable viewpoints. Rodney Howard-Browne may be the heir apparent to the Wimber dynasty. He is a much more aggressively minded apostle of the spectacular, who certainly demonstrates the capacity for younger disciples to go much further than their master in their specialist teaching. Without wishing to enter into too much speculation on the likelihood of these different responses, I do not think that it is difficult to predict how many who have seized hold of the opportunity to give national charismatic leadership through the Toronto blessing will react. They will have thoroughly enjoyed their moments in the spotlight, and if they are far-sighted and somewhat professional they may even now be scanning the horizons for the next new wave that will surely come. This has only been the latest in a long line of new emphases. It is a surprise that Wimber of all people should take issue with it in the way that he has. After all, his ministry worldwide has been characterised by such events. He has scarcely been a stranger to the cause of religious hype, as we have seen. But to be generous about it, perhaps it is a case of wisdom being proved right by her children!

It has to be said that much of the commentary has been

little more than the trivial repetition of anecdotal testimony, similar in kind to the excited reporting of renewal in earlier days. Stories have grown with the telling. A typical tale was the one reported in the first instance by Eleanor Mumford on her visit to the exuberant congregation at Holy Trinity, Brompton. It was to do with another visitor to the Airport Vineyard who travelled there by car and was pulled off the freeway on their return home on suspicion of drunken driving. On being cross-questioned by the police officers, the Holy Spirit who was supposed to be the cause for the erratic driving moved from the driver to the officer, so that in the end the driver and the officer were rolling around on the edge of the motorway incapable of further actions. He was subsequently converted in his local church and a whole family was saved. Indeed, a whole community was remarkably blessed. This tale bears all the marks of being on the ever-growing list of highly unlikely apocryphal stories. When given at Holy Trinity there were gales of appreciative glee. Patrick Dixon records a version of it as recounted by two expertly humorous speakers, John Wimber and Gerald Coates.[15]

Nevertheless, the interesting aspect of Eleanor Mumford's use of the tale is not so much the precision of her timing, but much more the way she introduced it and then the way in which she summed it up. Her opening phrase went: 'I heard a story this afternoon about Toronto . . .' With the delighted laughter of a large congregation ringing in her ears she went on to say: 'Honest to God – it's true. . . . Evangelism is a breeze, people!'[16]

This serves to illustrate the point that, as far as the preachers are concerned, good charismatic stories scarcely need to have any verification, providing they can be told sufficiently convincingly so that even the reporter who is using the tale begins to believe it. They also illustrate the need for much higher standards of accuracy in reporting these stories, and the need for the discovery of a better theological grid by which to assess their probability. I do not think they serve much of a purpose in helping the Church confront the ever-growing scepticism of an unbelieving world.

Negative reactions

In contrast to the element of hype to which Wimber has drawn
attention, there have also been several attempts at a more critical
approach from others, some of whom have come down on
the side of vigorous criticism even if they have been basically
sympathetic to the charismatic movement as a whole. Clifford
Hill is one such. Although he is committed to the ministry of
prophecy in the modern Church his dissatisfaction with
Toronto arises from his rejection of the earlier era when the
Kansas City prophets were in vogue. He had become convinced
that much of their ministry was bogus, and in particular he
took exception to the way in which Wimber was ready to
allow one of them, Bob Jones, to continue in public ministry
after it had been discovered that his personal life was morally
compromised. He was deeply distressed at what he regarded as
the culpable naïvety of a group of English charismatic leaders
who issued a statement in support of the American prophets
which was publicised in *Renewal* magazine:

> We believe they are true servants of God, men of sound character,
> humility, and evident integrity. . . . We observed their radical com-
> mitment to the word of God. . . . We have no doubt about the
> validity of their ministry . . . and encourage as many as possible to
> attend their conferences.[17]

As far as Hill is concerned, his discernment of the inadequacy
of this episode was vindicated through the non-arrival of the
promised revival. He went further than this. Not only was
this an example of misplaced trust on the part of the English
supporters, it was further evidence not of the close proximity
of national revival but of a period of awesome national judgement the like of which we have not known before. Hill
organised a series of consultations on the matter from which
he gathered the support of a group of leaders who went into
print on the issue with their rebuttals and their stark warnings
to the wider Christian community:

> From the summer and autumn of 1990 I believe that the charis-
> matic movement actually became a stumbling block to the Gospel.
> The glory departed, the blessing was withdrawn. The charismatic
> movement, which the pioneers in the early years had seen as

restoring New Testament ministries and gifts to the church to enable her to fulfil her true prophetic function and save the nation, now became a hindrance to the fulfilment of these aims.[18]

Hill and his colleagues regard Toronto as an example of the deceiving power of the enemy, as it were, rubbing his hands with glee at the capacity of the British Church to bring the certainty of judgement to come in the future on itself today.

I hold no brief for what I regard as the extra-biblical inanities to which most of us in the renewal movement have been attracted from time to time, but I find myself much more drawn to an eschatology which does have some hope in it for the life of the British Church, the European Church and the world Church than I do for promises of its share in imminent judgement. As I have already indicated, I came to the conclusion that John Wimber's ministry contained an unusual mixture of valuable insights and major flaws a number of years ago. I can scarcely believe that the ministries of the various signatories of the supporting statement regarding Kansas City visitors are of such huge national significance that, wrong as they may have been, their mistake should warrant Hill's proposal concerning God having run out of patience with us all. No, all this is a good example of the kind of in-house rhetoric into which renewal can so easily run when it adopts an exaggerated view of its own significance because its sponsors do not listen to the insights of other believers.

Yet negative views are not confined to the British. Taking matters much further is Nader Mikhaiel in his book *The Toronto Blessing: Slaying in the Spirit – The Telling Wonder*. He comes to the following uncompromising conclusion:

> This is not a time for God's people to sit on the fence, afraid to throw the baby with the bathwater. In fact, it is not a baby in the bathwater, but a python. It is time for us to stand for Christ who was not ashamed to die for our sin and shame. This is not a time for laughter, it is a time for weeping.[19]

The evangelical authors of various other small booklets are of the same opinion that, at best, the production of the phenomena is a matter of hypnotism, and at worst an example of the power of Satan to deceive in the last days.[20] It is no surprise that the Evangelical Alliance needed to call together the consultation to which we have already alluded. There have been many differing reactions around that are broadly against the recent move. Not all the sober reactions to Toronto lead to negative conclusions.

Careful advocates

For a measured, positive view there are the writings of Mark Stibbe and Rob Warner. Both of these authors have been personally involved in these developments and record their sense of indebtedness for the blessings they have received. Stibbe is in parish ministry in Sheffield which he combines with work in the Department for Biblical Studies at Sheffield University. While he does not advocate an exaggerated view of the significance of odd phenomenal behaviour, he does ask the question as to why it is that such things are currently happening and he also comes up with an intriguing answer that has at least the merit of making sense for us. It is because God always operates in a way that is suitable to the culture in which we find ourselves, which he then characterises as one committed to ecstasy and addiction. Taking the view that the Church as a whole is an irrelevance in this culture, he perceives some place for a limited experience of its own Christianised ecstasy which then becomes a means by which the Church can begin to communicate to those whose whole world is dominated by such powers.[21]

There is room for thought for all of us in Stibbe's ideas if we are persuaded that most normal forms of Christian worship, testimony and experience are almost totally unhelpful in our attempts to communicate the Gospel in an existential age. This was the positive intention behind the ill-fated Nine O'clock Service in Sheffield. Certainly he is right to go on to insist on the need for an articulate presentation of the Gospel, but I remain unconvinced that this adequately explains or justifies the appeal to irrationality that accompanied much of the Toronto episode. There has been too much manipulation around leading to whipped-up hysteria in some cases.

Warner's defence of Toronto is not as robust as this, but is none the less helpful as he summarises no less than 36 biblical indicators of a significant new wave of the Spirit. Given that not all of them will necessarily be present all the time, they present a helpful check-list by which we can measure the extent to which the excited claims of revival have been justified. In large measure it would seem that they have not.[22]

This, then, is the point to which our examination of this most recent charismatic surge has brought us. The phenomena to which so much attention was drawn in the first place may be hypnotically inducted, as Nigel Copsey indicated although writing from a sympathetic viewpoint. They could be the human response to a sense of God's presence, and Nigel Wright has suggested that we should not make too much of them.[23] But at a time when what suddenly swept through the land is just as swiftly retreating out of our midst, it is important to note that the wider world has remained largely unaffected. The task of mission to a secularised society remains to be done and is still as daunting as ever. In my article in the same series I concluded my description of a visit to a Holy Trinity, Brompton, service where a large number of worshippers finished the service either on the floor or in various unattractive physical postures which they adopted with great noise and with few restraints. My writing then remains my conviction still:

> As I left I wondered what on earth a less sympathetic enquirer would make of it all. Especially if they understood the clearly presented word, how would they relate the response of the mainly Christian members of the congregation to the world outside to which they would return, when it seems as if God's providential care is often suspended and awful mindless tragedies occur.

The Christian Church cannot afford to indulge itself in foolish carnivals declaring that this is their party time. We are called to discharge the sacred commission to communicate by word and live out by act God's saving good news without which the multitudes perish.

Post-Toronto renewal

Since this last episode brings us up to date with the story of the impact of the renewal over the past 35 years, we conclude this chapter by summarising the relative worth of our renewal experiences over the past three decades.

I hope that my readers will see that I have not attempted to gloss over what I regard as the unacceptable face of the modern renewal movement. Surely Toronto has demonstrated for us once more the lengths to which some charismatic Christians are prepared to go in pursuit of special new experiences, and the great dangers facing a movement in search of one singular cure-all intervention through which the illusive goal of the great transforming revival is suddenly achieved. The deception to which most aspects of the renewal movement have fallen has been to pursue the revival goal as if it is the quarry that can be snatched by the most skilful spiritual huntsman, whatever their innermost motives. Our understanding of Church history should have told us otherwise. Revivals have never come through the powers of those who seek them but through the sovereign action of a gracious God and by his Spirit in answer to the humble prayers of those who have continued to seek his face.

If this has been the cause of much disappointment leading to deep disenchantment for many, the blame for this precedes the advent of Toronto and, indeed, the Wimber ministry that lies behind it. Alastair Campbell has been a trusted friend for many years, with whom I have not always agreed, but whose integrity I greatly respect. His pungent comments have often helped to bring what is hazy into sharp focus. At the beginning of my investigations I circulated a questionnaire to London Baptist ministers to find out some details of their own involvement in renewal. By way of response Alastair has offered the following criticisms of the broader movement in comprehensive terms. They could scarcely be improved on as a summary of the many failures and excesses of which our experience of charismatic renewal has made us aware and to which many of us have on occasions contributed. I comment further on these responses, but they carry weight in that they reflect the perceptions of one who was strongly committed to many aspects of the renewal but from which he now distances himself:

> I think those who were heavily into this movement need to be more honest about the negative side. In personal terms I think my years in the charismatic movement were a wasted time. It encouraged a tendency in me to sectarian arrogance. It discouraged the

development of my intellectual gifts, and allowed me to become lazy. I observe that this is not uncommon. The effect on local churches has been pretty mixed. While I would not want to go back to the tepid decorum that characterised many churches before it . . . back in pastoral charge I find I want to pursue a well-ordered, intelligent, professional ministry. The worship needs to be lively but not crass, well prepared but not pompous. . . . I preach the Christian faith of the historic creeds. I belong to no movements. I peddle no gimmicks. The secret of church government/management lies in the overseer, as it has done since the NT days.[24]

Alastair is surely right in insisting that the negative side of the story must be faithfully recorded, but as I survey the ups and downs, the minor almost incidental triumphs and the deep sadnesses, I am certain that his account majors on the negative side that its wiser leaders have not attempted to hide. The renewal years have coincided with those of the deepest decline in faith in the western world, and the fact remains that in this general climate of spiritual despondency it has been those Churches which have enjoyed some measure of renewal, for all its faults, that have coped best, while many Churches which have resisted its message have faced greater difficulties. In particular, it has been the charismatics that have led the way in seeking to discover more relevant forms of worship and a greater practice of the ministry of prayer. Miracles of healing have indeed been few and far between, and the evidence for special interventions without full medical participation virtually non-existent. Yet there have been numerous occasions when slender medical hopes have been surprisingly enhanced, and we should not rule out the proper place for the value of intercessory prayer in these responses. Even if it is the case that those who have pursued a ministry with only a single charismatic string to their bow have sometimes been shipwrecked in one way or another, the growth of the influence of a much broader renewal including the charismatic but not excluding sound scholarship, the exercise of the mind in balanced worship, and a policy of integrated mission has certainly advanced. The results of my questionnaire produced many stimulating endorsements, but also gave strong evidence of the offensiveness of the approach of those bent on avoiding the processes of rational thought. Graham Nind, minister at Sudbury, Wembley, wrote:

I see this as an error equal and opposite to the cessationalist view which needs to be countered by a brand of charismatic Christianity which is solidly biblical and scholarly. I find the trio Walker, Smail and Wright to be a wonderful breath of fresh air to the church.

Roger Standing of West Croydon had this to say:

> On the whole I am very positive towards the experience that flows for the activity of the Holy Spirit. Indeed, I am happy to own the fact that both my Christian experience and my ministry are products of charismatic renewal. However, in its 'classic' incarnation I have serious reservations about the renewal movement. I guess that these are based on too many experiences of manipulation and human manufacture which have led to situations that have been destructive of people and congregations. I believe that this is in part due an overemphasis on emotionalism and a tendency to equate the sensational as requiring and demonstrating more faith than in a commitment to read, digest and act on the Word. Missing completely is the Pentecostal 'devotion to the apostle's teaching'.

If the whole Church seeks the renewing Spirit it may yet be that the story of this movement, that betrays all the signs of the human weaknesses of those who have been involved in it, may still become a source for the greater good of the whole. As I consider the tale that I have attempted to follow as it has worked out so far among the Baptists, I conclude that it is vital that churches do not confine their interests within self-limiting charismatic cloisters. The charismatic renewal needs the ministry of the whole Church of which it is a part to give it balance, just as the whole Church needs the fire and the release of the Spirit to which the charismatics at their best have given their testimony. Even in the midst of the turbulent cross-currents from Toronto there are the signs and evidences of lives made sweeter, more wholesome, and more like Jesus than they were before. Indeed, far from complaining about the move to greater moderation on the part of many who have been involved, I urge that this is a supreme sign of the activity of the Spirit of wisdom within renewal.

It is true that the call to arms for the support of a position of balance does not easily recruit support. None the less, long live the moderating tendency! It is the exclusivity of viewpoints that is always our weakest characteristic, whether it be exercised by liberal evangelicals, as was the case at one stage in the Baptist denomination, or charismatics, or conservative evangelicals today. Derek Tidball is surely right about charismatic renewal in what he declares about evangelicalism as a whole:

> Positions of strength carry with them the inherent seeds of decline. Perhaps the position of weakness is not such a bad location after all. Evangelicalism at the turn of the twenty-first century needs to read its history with care and take note.[25]

The problems of renewal have been accentuated by the way in which we have foolishly yielded territory to a vast number of itinerant experts, mainly from North America but also from Africa and Asia, whose claims for expertise have depended on the greater numerical success attending their ministries in utterly different cultures to our own. Such naïvety on our part has been deeply misleading, and we could all have heeded the advice Frank Maguire gave to Michael Harper at the beginning, when he counselled caution regarding the sort of speakers to invite, with greater profit.

We have much to learn from others, but how much has our credulity been based on our ungodly desire for quick results, and increased influence, at any price? In the end the spiritual power merchants go on their way, claiming far more from their encounters with the British Church than their true credentials have ever warranted. All too often we have been left the poorer from the exchange. Having attempted a broad survey of our past experience we must conclude our study with one final chapter. It will take us forward from the renewal we now know, with its strengths and its faults, to the renewal we now need. The future health of all our churches depends on our finding the secrets of this renewal and employing all our best efforts in living them out.

From the Known to the Needed

11

Washing by the Spirit

(Titus 3:4)

We have traced the effects of the renewal movement among the Baptists and seen the evidence for God's gracious activity through the Spirit mediated by the Church composed of normal, sinful believers. It has proved to be the case that the advent of the Spirit has not necessarily eradicated human arrogance, dishonesty, or our ceaseless lust for power. Rather, on occasions our human weaknesses have threatened to neutralise God's intentions. This final exercise is more difficult to pursue, taking us from a reflection on historical events to an area in which speculation dominates and the facts may turn out differently. I do not claim any special prophetic insights in describing some necessary developments if renewal is to be a source of health for the Church of the third millennium. This is a subtle task to undertake, and my comments on them are brief.

We begin by reminding ourselves that the business of religion is all to do with the issue of meaning. Dean Kelley rightly observes that it is because conservative churches attend to this more effectively than others that they are the growing section of the Church today.[1] We may add that charismatic churches which are even more strongly convinced about the significance of their being are for that reason more likely to prosper, as in fact they are doing. Moreover, they possess enormous reserves of will-power buttressed by enhanced levels of experience, and these factors combine to the upbuilding of their convictions. Hence they have a confidence about the success of their task of mission which is both strong and resilient.

I want to expound now an outline of some of the necessary elements for a growing movement of the future if it is to combat the causes of its own decadence and become even more healthy and useful in the purposes of God. Its greatest danger is not in further developments towards the extremist tendencies we have already described but in one single factor which is much more mundane. Together with the rest of our evangelical family, many renewal churches attract and hold a greater proportion of the young than other churches, but our age profile is still distressingly high. For this reason alone, our present numerical strength is fragile. If we are to continue to grow we need more effective programmes to reach and integrate our children and youth.[2] Written into the suggestions I offer, therefore, must be an awareness of the hugely significant strategic task that must be attempted in giving full rein to the energies of our present youth leaders. Natural law will see to it that those who rely mainly on the insights of their seniors will fail. We have not yet addressed this crucial issues in all our church structures.

The renewal that we need explains the meaning of life in terms of the historic message of Christ as contained in the Scriptures. Renewal also needs to return to its own roots for the growth of a healthy inner spirituality. Too often the causes for the collapses of charismatic Christians have been indicated by early warning signs that have been ignored. So we begin our visions and dreams for more healthy developments in the future at this point of inward vitality.

A renewal of personal devotion

We may observe that Christians who come from the Churches with a strong liturgical tradition are often in a much stronger place in their personal walk with God than those whose background has been exclusively evangelical and in the Free Church tradition. The aid of a different religious tradition, built around the framework of the Daily Office for prayer and meditation, supported by the rich heritage of the prayers of the great saints throughout the centuries, and the regular Sunday diet of worship attuned to the events of the Christian year, offers great resources to us, still known by relatively few.

I was helped to see this at the beginning of my renewal journey, which started with a move from a pastorate in Stoke Newington, north London, to a church in Wishaw in central

Scotland. At the time that seemed like madness. In London we had known great progress, but in Wishaw, in spite of the love of a warm-hearted people, it was a different story. I felt inwardly desolate. Then the words of the Anglican Prayer Book came to my rescue, especially with the collect for the sixth Sunday after Pentecost for the presence of the Spirit:

Almighty God, without you we are not able to please you,
Mercifully grant that your Holy Spirit may in all things direct and rule our hearts;
Through Jesus Christ our Lord. Amen.

For about a month God heard that prayer faithfully prayed daily. It taught me a lesson about the need for replenishing the resources of my inner life from the deep wells of the Spirit and also through the prayer lives of others. That was the point that marked the beginnings of my personal pilgrimage in the life of the Spirit. In north London we had learned something of the riches awaiting our spiritual plunder through the ministry of a senior pastor, Stephen Winward, who was at the time a leading liturgist among Baptists. The lessons learned in London were a great help in Scotland.

Since those days many more writings have become available. Richard Foster has put us all in his debt with his plea for a return to disciplined spirituality, including the classical spiritual disciplines of prayer, meditation, fasting, study, simplicity, solitude and others, in two of his best sellers.[3] He has pointed out the need for habits of prayer, and for keeping a note of our prayers. He urges the use of our powers of imagination in our prayer life but also points out what he describes as 'the scandal of Christianity in our day . . . the heresy of 5 per cent spirituality'. He offers ways to overcome this by learning to pray the ordinary prayer within the context of all the normal parts of everyday life. 'Everything that we turn in the direction of God is prayer.' I find it helpful to make up my own prayer book and write down some of my own intercessions in addition to the regular topics associated with my ministry responsibilities. Stephen Winward kept set periods for prayer during the day. Perhaps we need to analyse the reasons for our own reluctance to engage in the practice of the presence of God in our prayers.

I owe a debt of gratitude to the friend who suggested to me

Celebrating the Daily Office, a version of the Daily Office used by the Franciscans.[4] I find the Taizé book of common prayer a great help.[5] Recently I discovered the marvellous writings of Henri Nouwen. A friend presented me with a copy of his wonderful book *The Return of the Prodigal Son*, containing his meditations on the Rembrandt picture of the same name.[6] I have commended that book all over London because it has such marvellous riches in it for all. There is a huge variety available to help us in our prayer life, and even more guides to the study of the book of books. We need to follow the ambition of John Wesley regarding the Scriptures. His desire was to be a man of one book, the Bible.

If we would know a fresh spiritual quality in our lives we need to become better people for God. It was the hunger for this that brought many of us into direct and surprising encounters with the Holy One, and we need to return to the same quest again and again.

Not long ago a young minister who was a former acquaintance came to see me in great distress. His ministry was over, he was necessarily out of any church responsibilities, and he was weighing up the prospect of the painful process of discipline through which it might be possible for a return to the privileges and responsibilities in due course. After we had talked and prayed together his world crashed in again, as far as I was concerned, in his explanation for his own pastoral débâcle. It was all due to the devil's attack on him. There were unrecognised demonic powers at work in the place where he had served. It was not a case of fault on his part, he was the victim of the dirty tricks of our spiritual foe. Although my heart went out to the man in his need, I could not accept this facile explanation. The reality was that he had long since abandoned the necessary practices of seeking God for himself and carrying God's word in his heart. The downward spiral had begun when he had become consumed with a lust for easy ministerial success. What he really wanted was to become a widely known leader. In truth, he was a victim of the ploys of the marketing men who have jumped on to the bandwagon of charismatic spirituality because there is money to be had out of it They had persuaded him that in the end it is all down to good methodologies.

That is a lie that needs to be nailed before others lower their spiritual defences, give up their earnest practices, spend their hard-earned cash, and go for the false gods of cheapened religion. We need to uncage God out of the folly of the demand mentality and let the Holy One speak to us again. Charismatic renewal has produced far too many instances of avoidable moral error and frequent demonstrations of church-hopping by the religiously dissatisfied. Perhaps another denomination will do the trick for us. But there is no trick that anyone can do on our behalf. I comment on this tendency later. As Augustine discovered many centuries ago, only God can satisfy our religious longings. If we would know him better, we must revive our commitment to seek his face and hear his voice and walk in his ways. In short, we need a revival of the kind of personal spirituality with which renewal began and that has been there intermittently at every stage in the renewal journey.

Awesome worship

Worship today has become exceedingly sloppy in many churches. The diet on offer is entirely predictable, irrespective of the denominational background, and is often almost entirely self-centred. In place of the order of a call to worship, the praise of God and opening prayers of praise and adoration, all of which carry us into his presence, today we start with the height of informality bordering on the banal: 'Good morning and welcome. Has anyone had a birthday?' I do not object to gentle fun in worship, nor do I find informality of dress or language a necessary barrier. But the first question to be asked is to whom we are seeking to come and what we are wanting to do in his presence. The purpose of worship is that together we meet with God. There is a current mood of worship that is essentially anthropocentric because it focuses in on us, our moods, our longings and our personal needs. This is an irrelevance when compared with the true worship of the Christian Church which surely must be Christo-, Pneumato- and Theo-centric to our one God in community, who nevertheless wishes to join us in our praise.

Leaving aside issues of liturgy, I would like us to drastically change our buildings. In London the supposedly poor Baptists have spent out millions of pounds on their buildings during the years of my service in their midst. Most of the new structures are outwardly attractive and inwardly comfortable. The rooms are light and airy. The floors are carpeted. The seats are luxurious. But the buildings are empty of art. Evidently it can be assumed that we are so spiritual that we are fully satisfied aesthetically by a simple reading desk, a bank of microphones, miles of electric cable, a smiling minister and perhaps some tastefully arranged flowers. That is all I see in most buildings – perhaps with the addition of a cross somewhere on a table, or in the woodwork. I would like to change this because it is so barren, so out of touch with a world where visual impressions are stronger than the verbal, and such a poor witness to our wonderful God. I do not advocate the wasteful spending of unlimited money on buildings rather than people for ministry. If it is a matter of choice, it must always be people who are the priority. But we can recruit our buildings to make them into our allies in the quest for greater renewal by releasing the captive artistic skills of our members. Let us adorn the walls with original and imaginative art that promotes spiritual reflection. Buy good furniture made of beautiful wood for the table and the preaching desk. Let there be beautiful glasswork in the windows and in the building, as there is in Baptist churches in Denmark and Germany.

Our buildings should be full of light of all kinds – half-light, bright light, reflected light, coloured light and beautiful candlelight. How interesting to discover that the reason why the Baptists in Denmark use the light of magnificent candles in their services goes back to the days of their occupation in the Second World War. They found that no service would ever be interrupted if the occupying forces saw lit candles inside.

And why do Baptists of all people have to hide the water for baptism? Are we ashamed of the quantity that we use? We ought to be proud of our baptismal practices for good scriptural reasons and insist that the rest of Christendom which uses only a minute amount has misunderstood the New Testament norms. But our buildings scarcely support us in this. The irony is that by far the most beautiful baptistry in London is in a Roman Catholic church, not a Baptist church. It is in the Mile End Road, and the pool is always open and lit. The water is silently pumped so that it gently swells and silently flows over the top steps and into the depths of the pool and is then recycled.

Of course, I hear the objection that an open pool would be very unwise for us. Children would push each other in and practise total immersion on a regular basis in many fellowships. So why not change the mentality with which we approach our sanctuaries, not by attributing mystic powers to wood and stone, but by designating them as Houses of Prayer for all nations, open to all and welcoming all as often as we can manage to staff them with those who will give them care?

These days we are learning the possibilities of creating beautiful banners without words to celebrate Scripture truth or significant events in recent experiences. The Baptist and United Reformed Church in Leytonstone keeps a magnificent store of banners which are regularly added to for special occasions. We should drop the philistine approach that imagines that somehow we promote our spirituality even while we do battle with our finer feelings and consecrate ugliness in our surroundings. Nothing could be further from the truth. If, as the dieticians tell us, we become what we eat, it may also be true that we become like what we look at most.

It may be that we need to use our buildings in a multi-functional way, but we can still set aside a prayer room. Many have discovered the beauty of that secluded little prayer chapel at the John Bunyan Church in Kingston, the home of the Kaleidoscope Project. It speaks volumes to us of the need to harness our corporate devotional resources before we take up demanding and down-to-earth servant ministries such as the great drug rehabilitation work in which they engage. When I am on holiday and want to find a quiet spot to pray, I will often find a little Anglican country church building designed for the purpose. I would search in vain for a Free Church alternative. Places of quietness are at a premium in today's hectic world. During the working week we should be able to provide havens of solitude for all who want to escape from the triumph of noise.

To return to the issue of the pattern for our worship, for me it is 'Yes' to the informality that is the current vogue, but in its proper place of a framework of healthy order. The Scriptures demand intercessory prayer, and the reality or the sad absence of such a ministry speaks volumes about our true spiritual temperature. We are told to give attention to the public reading of Scripture. The only service which carries the direct mandate of Christ is the Lord's Supper or the Eucharist. It is the great act of thanksgiving when through bread, wine and word Christ draws near to us to preside in our midst. So let it be the best home-baked bread and the finest wine, not home-brewed vinegar! Why an oversweet Ribena substitute without body and without bouquet? Let the Eucharist be celebrated weekly and let it be the time for corporate absolution and mutual reconciliation. If there is the need of prayer for healing, then it can best be fulfilled after receiving the bread and the wine but in an inconspicuous way.

Why do we need always to receive the elements seated in rows? Would it not release more opportunities for ministry if we changed the pattern at least from time to time to allow the physical movement of going to the table in order to receive? Let communion be the focal point for healing ministries, not exercised for the trivial benefit of the reputations of those who minister but for the genuine care of those who suffer. We need to free the service from the heritage we have sometimes received of a sense of dismal nostalgia for a long-absent Lord, or from the equally disturbing trite flippancy into which it has sadly declined in places where man-centred worship is the fashion. Through the Spirit it can become the great time of celebration for His joyful presence in the midst, signified by simple elements. Eleanor Kreider makes a powerful case for the greater use of symbolic actions in our worship, especially in communion:

> Through the symbolic [sacramental] bread and wine, we can lay hold on the promises of God. We can reach out to grasp in faith what God offers to us in pure gift. We can 'drink' the draught of undeserved forgiveness. We can 'chew up' that assurance that we are God's chosen loved children. The whole work of redemption lies behind this bread and wine made sacrament – God's promise, gracious gifts and our receiving it.[7]

We must be grateful for the remarkable musical outburst that has characterised the renewal. Although it has been fashionable to denigrate much that has appeared, by common consent there is much for which all sections of the church can give thanks. Graham Kendrick has brought us pieces like 'Meekness and Majesty' and 'The Servant King' which have found their way into most new collections of songs. The type of music that is available has been categorised accurately in an article on the subject by Jeremy Begbie.[8] He offers a critique of the whole scene in the conviction that it is weaker in what it lacks than in what it has grasped in its rightful stress on joy, intimacy, praise and reverence. More music of greater variety is needed, together with the best of the traditional too.

Let us recover an approach to worship which expresses all this, and also attends to the greatest single need in our worship today, for a recovery of scholarship on fire and expository preaching of the Word. The preaching ministry needs to inform our minds and stimulate our wills and encourage our faith. We need good preaching not man-pleasing verbal titillations. We need to distinguish between the ministry of the teacher and that of the preacher.

Of course, humour is allowable, but it is sad when those who are called to share the world's greatest message imagine that their function is not to preach but to entertain. Put the comedians on the stage or on television, but keep the preachers at the preaching desk for this is a ministry which is to be exalted not derisively dismissed. A healthy renewal needs much better preaching than the thin fare that is commonly available in many renewal churches. No wonder that the renewed are swift to chase after the latest charismatic fashion when their souls are desperately undernourished through the sparse food they regularly receive. The problem is that after a while we lose our taste for food, and the days foretold by the prophet Amos come upon us:

> When I will send a famine through the land – not a famine of food or thirst for water, but a famine for hearing the words of the Lord. Men will stagger from sea to sea and wander from north to east, searching for the word of the Lord, but they will not find it. (Amos 8:11–12)

My pastor is a young preacher and my son is just starting out on the task. I treasure their efforts whenever I am fortunate enough to hear them. I trust that they will be encouraged in their ministry. Healthy renewal needs good worship supported by excellent preaching. In a day when we have been told again and again that nobody wants to listen to anyone, good preachers are a precious asset to be highly valued and frequently endorsed.

Social action

It is all to the good that churches in renewal have realised the need to flesh out their faith by the good works of compassionate care. Among those that have led the way have been the churches of the Ichthus Christian Fellowship, inspired by their dynamic leaders Roger and Faith Forster. Roger's initial calling has been to do the work of the evangelist. He has given himself to this unstintingly, and has also taken a lead in finding the church planting strategies for his work throughout the south London area where he is based, around the country and across the seas. His fellowships are not particularly large, but the work has grown significantly from the original gathering of 14 in their own home. At the present time there are in the region of 2000 meeting regularly in the 45 Ichthus congregations in south London. Some use Baptist buildings that could otherwise have fallen out of use altogether in an earlier day. Relationships between the mainstream Baptists and Ichthus independents, who so closely resemble the continental Anabaptists, are cordial and mutually beneficial.

What is of particular note is the passionate commitment Roger has shown over many years to the good works of the Gospel. Not surprisingly, he supports the proposals to celebrate the new millennium advanced by the Jubilee 2000 group.[9] This is part of the Debt Crisis Network, and we are invited to urge our government and our banks and our financial controllers to celebrate the new millennium by cancelling the unpayable debts of the world's poorest countries on a case by case basis. They plan to build up a membership base of concerned and informed members, and to develop a huge media campaign in 1998 and 1999 to bring pressure to bear on world leaders to put the necessary change into action.[10]

The programme adopted by Pope John Paul II for the millennium is also built on the Old Testament notion of Jubilee and the Sabbatical year, including the dimensions of the release from captivity, the cancellation of debts, the proclamation of freedom, and the protection of the weak.[11]

Christian Aid are already involved in a vigorous campaign entitled 'Who Runs the World?', and are adding to that another aimed at British supermarkets entitled 'The Global Supermarket'.[12] This is an imaginative attempt to recruit the sympathies and support of the affluent countries of the north for the poorer countries of the south, especially in monitoring the working conditions of those whose produce is sold by our major retailers. These bold schemes deal not only with questions of world economics but also with the spirit of greed and power that rob our Churches of their integrity on many occasions. When we find that similar initiatives are being proposed in anticipation of the new millennium, the thought must cross our minds that this is the working of God's renewing Spirit in our midst calling us to vigorous prophetic action. It is good to know of the dozens of new social initiatives that are being sponsored by individual churches in caring for the young, the disabled, the mentally retarded, the elderly and the dispossessed.

All evangelical Christians owe a great debt to John Stott not only for the excellence of his expository preaching ministry over many years but particularly for the lead he has given in urging the Church to face up to the issues of work and unemployment, industrial relations, racism, poverty and wealth, marriage and divorce, issues of the gender divide, abortion and homosexuality, the global issues of the divide between the wealthy north of the world and the poor south, and all the tangled knot of problems around matters of human rights.[13] We rejoice in the work of Against the Stream, a pump-priming operation of the Baptist Union to help start local works for the good of the communities among whom local churches are called to serve as both salt and light. The Anglicans have been generous in their support through the Church Urban Fund.

The point to which all this bears witness is that a healthy form of renewal for the future will remain in close touch with the local communities that they serve and will stimulate a strong conscience response to the issues of social justice and international righteousness. The energies of the renewed will not just be fulfilled in acts of worship and conferences about renewal. They will be directed towards filling the many vacancies in local school governorships, in serving their trade union, in local government, or in national politics as parliamentary candidates. Renewed churches will regard this service as of front-line significance. This broad commitment will inevitably discourage the simplistic proposition that all we need to do to win our communities for Christ is to set up our new church plants anywhere that it is geographically possible for our congregations to reach, without regard for the practical needs of the people where they are planted. Recently I visited a new church that currently draws its congregation from a wide area of London, but that runs its house groups in Southampton, Winchester, and other locations many miles away. Hence the members of the congregation owe no allegiance to the townships where they live nor the one in which they worship, and probably not to the places where they work. Such disjunctive religion in fact often specialises in exotic forms of experience. But it does not demonstrate the spiritual health of the renewal that is down to earth in the midst of the lives of real people who need the compassionate touch of Jesus and respond warmly when they receive it.

Servant leadership

The spiritual level of our churches is determined by the standards set by those who lead them. If we are to enjoy strong renewal we shall need the ministry of effective leadership that can be given by both women and men, a few over the age of 55 but the majority well below that mark, full time and part time and with varied skills to offer.

My ideal leadership team for a church in renewal will be composed only of those whose sense of call to this work is authenticated by the support of those whom they lead. They will not be the chosen few of whom the pastor approves, but they will be people of trust, who are strong in prayer, and able to make far-sighted decisions with courage and with faith. They will all be good pastors, for the dominant motif of the original apostolic team is that of the shepherd. Every church leader will be capable of leading others to put their trust in the Saviour.

All of them must be able to pray for others to be filled with the Spirit and released from life's sickening bondages. They will know the Scriptures well. They will not stand on ceremony but will be willing to turn their hand to any task, however trivial, if this is the work that most needs doing at any particular time. No leader worth their salt will ever expect others to do what they are not prepared to do themselves.

In my youth I used to serve as padre to a camp for boys who were thought to come from one of London's poorer areas. This was probably only one of a number of social illusions perpetuated by the actions of the evangelical world in those days. But the leader of the camp was gifted with wonderful skills which he generously spent for the benefit of his lads. He also taught me some lessons I have not forgotten. Our shared task at the end of each day was to clean out the loos – which were decidedly primitive. Nor have I forgotten the method of coping with this unpleasant duty that someone had to do, and on the rare occasions we meet I can expect him to steal up on me and whisper the magic words in my ear, before he disappears once more into the relative anonymity of his retirement. 'Breathe through your teeth, so that you don't swallow any of it!' I recall this amusing but rather disgusting incident because it left a marked impression on my understanding of service. My leadership today is of no value unless I emulate my Master in his. He who stripped off his clothing to do the most humble task for his disciples charges us to do likewise (John 13:1–17). How tragic it is for the Church if those who serve as leaders imagine that this bestows unusual status upon them and claim the titles, the styles, and the salaries that express all this.

At one stage in the history of renewal a major mistake was made by confusing the role of leaders with ideas of human domination in the name of spiritual authority. It was assumed that the Church should work on élitist principles, and that every Christian community needed a group of macho-style male elders gifted with the authority that only belongs to the Omniscient Lord. Jesus expressly warned against this (Mark 10:42). There is something seriously wrong about forms of leadership that concentrate on matters of authority. In my travels in New Zealand some years ago I once visited a fellowship which was locked into these pyramid structures. Elders ruled and they in turn were 'in submission to' a great charismatic apostle living at that time in Vancouver some 9000 miles away. They had to consult him on all major issues, like the leadership for their house groups. They were to pay him lavishly for the love relationship which they shared. In short, they were tricked by the fraudulent boasting of a preacher sadly convinced by his own bombast. We need none of that. In a free society the limits of authority are determined by the extent to which others are prepared to trust them. But the call of Jesus is to a form of leadership that is strong on the compassionate service that builds trust. It is the very weakness of this proposition that demonstrates its greatest strength. A truly renewed Church will be excited by the joyful discoveries that this will bring, and its leaders will be people of moral nerve whose word is truth.

Church commitment

I have already observed the practice of too many who show scant loyalty to the churchmanship in which they were reared and, in their quest for the perfect Church here on earth, leave their parent body to join another that is supposedly nearer to their scriptural ideals. There are exceptions to the rules as I perceive them, though they are not many. When believers do this because there is no church of their own tradition in the vicinity, then it is a case of needs must. If they have moved from one nation to another or if they have become convinced of the error of the practice of infant baptism and seek believers' baptism, with all that this entails in our understanding of the nature of the Church, then they have good grounds for making changes. The commitment I urge is for those who have no such reasons for changing Church to remain where they are and do their best to make the imperfect system work where they are. Nor is it just a case of making the local church as effective as possible for the tasks of the Kingdom. Baptist churches are independent, and this is one of their deepest strengths. But from their earliest origins, they have also held to the necessity of profoundly strong commitments to and strong relationships with their Baptist neighbours with whom they share in what are historically called our 'Associations'. These days, happily, many do so with their ecumenical neighbours

too. It is not just a shame when local churches choose not to
fulfil this part of their Church commitment, it is a sin against
the understanding expressed in the great New Testament word
for fellowship, *koinonia*.

Certainly this responsibility demands a rigorous programme
of reform from those who serve the parent body for the wider
links, in the case of the Baptists either in the national Union
or the local Association, to make these bodies worthy of the
support they seek. Above all, they need the strong agenda for
mission that fits them for their role not as units for administration but as agencies for the mission, for the fellowship, and
for the ministry of the Gospel. Over these last few years in
London we have enjoyed an exhilarating period of change and
service as we have seen our local Association, well served by
its secretary, my colleague Peter Wortley, strip down for action
and gear up for service.

But church-hopping charismatics miss this point because
they just like to go where they think the action is to be found.
They are living without a commitment to the Church that in
New Testament terms is impossible for a believer to avoid.
The crux of the denominational question turns on matters of
principle concerning our understanding of the nature of the
Church which have bothered Christians for hundreds of years.
It is a poor response to their struggles and their sufferings just
to ignore the issue. The financial facts are that the major sources
for the funding of ongoing mission are denominational, so I
urge a stronger Church commitment in the renewal we need.
All our denominational structures are marked by their pro-
visionality, and one day will die when the Kingdom comes.
Until then, we need to love them to their death, and thus
thoroughly earth our renewal convictions in the soil of their
down-to-earth experience.

Theological reflection

The dictum that I first heard expounded by Tom Smail was
that the charismatic renewal was urgently in need of an adequate
theological framework if it was to make a lasting contribution
to the life of the Church. In his days as director of the Fountain
Trust, it was to this need that he gave his energies through the

production of a supplement to the *Renewal* magazine entitled 'Theological Renewal'.[14] Sadly that supplement survived only briefly after Tom departed to St John's College, Nottingham, and the number of those who wanted the opportunity for serious thought on the profound issues it dealt with was too small.

Tom's insight was entirely right, however. The endless diet of mindless testimony has never been capable of satisfying the hunger caused by searching minds. Left unsatisfied, the hungry soon despair of finding the nourishment they need and often give up their new-found spiritual resource. Happily, the scene has now changed. A new team of renewed thinkers is emerging to study the Scriptures, to examine the theology and teach the Church afresh. This is another aspect to the renewal that needs a higher profile than many of its current leaders appreciate if they neglect the common factor behind the tendencies to exaggerations that lead on inevitably to a sense of disappointment. That common factor is conceptual. A faulty theological framework always produces a flawed message.

A first area of reflection must be to come to grips theologically with the initial nature of the renewal experience itself, often described as the baptism in the Spirit. This has been helpfully tackled in a number of ways by charismatic thinkers who are far from satisfied by the Pentecostal framework that has often been attributed to them. David Pawson suggests that its proper place is in the constellation of events associated with the normal beginnings of faith in the life of a believer who will not be effectively 'birthed' without the conscious reception of the Spirit.[15]

However, the coming of the Spirit needs to be perceived in the pattern made clear by the account of the ministry of the Spirit according to the Gospel of John as well as the writings of Luke. In the Johannine account it is equally plain that the gift of the Spirit is made available through the Spirit anointed Saviour. But the gift is tied more to his work on the cross for the forgiveness of our sins than it is to the post-Pentecost accession of power to which Luke draws attention. This is the point developed by Tom Smail as he draws together the need for both a paschal approach to the Spirit and a Pentecostal approach.[16] In the light of this we can see the application that must follow – not to engage in the pursuit of power for itself, but to follow the path of the Saviour that even leads to sacrifice, in the strength of the Spirit. A more biblically comprehensive understanding transforms our approach to mission away from the flamboyant and towards the servant ministry approach.

There is then the crucial area of understanding the nature of Christian fellowship as a reflection of the relationships within the persons of the Godhead. Nigel Wright wrote about this in an article on *koinonia* and Baptist ecclesiology in which he paid tribute to the insights of the Pentecostal scholar Miroslav Volf, who is in agreement with the Orthodox claim that the Church exists as a reflection and representation of the Trinity.[17] In the light of this it is a recovery of an understanding of the given relationships of the persons of the Godhead which provides a much more rewarding basis for understanding the work of the Spirit than the notion that the activity of the Spirit is a detached post-Calvary extension to the Gospel.

At the heart of our faith we relate to God who is Trinity, who himself embodies all that we understand by community, and in whom in Christ there is already the glory of humanity fully expressed. The inner relationships of the Trinity maintain a perfect non-hierarchical balance and distinctive salvation functions towards the world and creation. All our attempts at finding a wholesome spirituality are better based, with more explorations into all that this leads us, rather than the proposals for becoming easily successful by which renewal has frequently become consumed. For the work of the Spirit in us is never beyond the work of the Spirit in the Son. This was the distinctive truth that Edward Irving, with his profound grasp of reformed theology, had perceived and to which I referred in Chapter 1. It is so different from the notions that begin to flow once it is supposed that the Spirit works in a subsequent way in the Church beyond all that he achieved in Jesus.

Tom Smail expounds the significance of this in some detail in his examination of Trinitarian theology from both a reformed and an Orthodox perspective, which insights he then applies to a sound renewal theology. The danger of the Orthodox understanding of the gift of the Spirit who comes from the Father is that this can lead to a breakdown in the perceived relationship between the Spirit and the Son which may give rise to two-blessing Pentecostalism in which the Spirit and the Son preside over two distinct areas of Christian experience. The problem with the reformed and indeed the Roman position was classically stated by the great Augustine and encapsulated in the Nicene Creed, where it is declared that the Spirit comes forth from the Father and the Son (the celebrated *filioque* clause), is that it can lead to a downgrading of the work of the Spirit to the primacy of the work of the Son. As Tom Smail indicates, ancient Christian controversy has an unfortunate habit of resurrecting into modern Church practice. We need to understand the tangle that led to the great schism of the Church of the East and the Church of the West. We can do so by examining the teaching of the Scriptures, revisiting the teaching of the theologians, and then exploring some fresh explanations for ourselves.[18] There could scarcely be a more absorbing subject for these exercises than to understand the nature of the relationships between the Father, the Son and the Spirit. How challenging for Christians in renewal to apply their fresh insights in pursuit of a mighty theological agenda like this.

In healthy renewal there has always been a hunger for the Scriptures and a realisation of the great theological riches to be mined through a return to their serious study. Take Gordon Fee, who shows us an example of the magnificent material available in his powerful exposition of the work of the Spirit in the writings of the apostle Paul, *God's Empowering Presence.*[19] In it, Fee not only analyses the text and expounds the meaning but also insists that the Holy Spirit must be experienced as a living person in the Church today. He is an outstanding Pentecostal scholar.

The point that I make is simple. It is that the first need for a healthy renewal is conceptual. Ideas have the force to carry us into consequential actions. The joy of the theological recovery that is now taking place in the renewal is the way in which the span of our attention is spreading beyond the immediate areas of the Spirit and ecclesiology, and into broader channels. Nigel Wright has provided us with good evidence for this in his most recent work, in which he applies his insights to a range of issues including our understanding of grace, judgement, the final truths of heaven and hell, the authority of Scripture and the defence of a more generous religion.[20] We must not despise the offerings of the past, but we do not need to be necessarily confined to their conclusions.

Evangelistic strategy

The whole Church needs to see itself not so much as a social institution but as a unit for God's mission. This is not to deny the institutional elements in the life of the Church but to keep them in their rightful place, secondary to the greater task of evangelism that still awaits. The renewal has produced some signs of fresh strategy, but as yet the main task facing us in our increasingly secularised society remains untouched. The advent of the millennium gives us an unparalleled opportunity for fresh evangelism.

This must be the task of the whole Christian community, not just a part of it; in other words, the Church must commit itself to evangelistic mission in every part of its life. Our worship, prayer, fellowship, study and service must take up this agenda and so reform themselves that they become the mission agency. In its local expression, this means that the church will define the group of people or the geographical area they occupy, that it wishes to reach. They will audit all the facts that they can concerning their 'parish': their age, gender, status, work, schooling, social background, ethnic origins, religious commitments and so on. Moreover, they will have studied the Gospel afresh and prayed much for those whom they would serve. As far as is possible, they will share with other churches in ecumenical partnership for the task belongs to us all. Some of my best experiences in evangelism were in Manna Ministries days, when we ran ecumenical missions in a variety of churches ranging from Roman Catholics to black Pentecostals, stopping off at all stations in between! We found that our ecumenical appeal was unrefusable when a Catholic priest and a Baptist minister worked in tandem, perhaps because the sympathetic unchurched naturally support ecumenism and oppose sectarianism in all its forms. When we both offered prayer with appropriate practical help for their sick relative, their out-of-work offspring or the husband in prison, the barriers came down and the Good News was shared.

The task of evangelism demands the specialist gifts of the

ministry of the evangelist as well. I fear that some of our most gifted preacher–evangelists have forgotten the need to live within the area of their primary gifting and have been led away from their calling to the lesser works of setting up new networks of churches. I have listened on occasion to some of these most gifted preachers and felt convinced that given the faith, the self-control and the sound advice that Billy Graham has manifestly received, they could be his British successor. We owe Billy Graham an enormous debt of gratitude for his self-effacing commitment to the task. Would that we could see those emerging who could not only speak as he has spoken to thousands in great national stadiums, but also put the message on the front page of our newspapers as this man has consistently done.

There are numerous other forms of the ministry that are more accessible. The Willowcreek pattern pioneered by Bill Hybels for reforming the worship patterns of the church so that there are regular 'seeker-sensitive' occasions attuned to the expectations and interests of the seekers, not the members, offers fresh definitions of the ministry of the specialist evangelist. Their task remains the same, of communicating the truth of the Gospel in understandable thought forms for the secular world in which we serve Christ.[21] None the less, we should not despair of the ordinary. Most people are won to Christ through the caring witness of their friends and in the context of the normal weekly services of a church determined to win others for Christ.[22] David Hay gives us the evidence for the God-consciousness of the vast majority of the unchurched of our own generation. We need to devise strategies that will build on this, so that those who share an experiential awareness of God understand and believe the Gospel message of Christ.[23]

As we have already indicated, music is always a great resource, with the style and kind being determined by the outreach that is planned. There is a positive lesson to learn from the Nine O'clock Service approach in Sheffield, which failed not because of mistakes at this level but for other reasons reflecting common human faults. There is still a deeply ingrained folk memory that can be tapped by the traditional hymns of our common Christian culture. For some years in Streatham we toured our district with a good choir supported by some Guards bandsmen to sing the traditional Easter hymns. It was effective in stirring up the memories of those who once went to church, and the size of our services grew as a consequence.

We must seize the millennial opportunity that is ours. Among London's 284 Baptist churches we have recently run a successful month of simultaneous mission. For many months of my early years as general superintendent, I travelled the metropolis for Saturday morning meetings with leaders from our churches to share the vision I believe God had given. On these occasions we began with a substantial breakfast, and brief devotions. Then I attempted to get across my convictions in my own way, before we split into working groups to consider some of their implications. We then spent time in prayer before we convened again for morning coffee. The moment of release came just after 11 a.m. to allow the leaders to enjoy the precious time of the rest of their Saturday at home. This was followed on the Sunday with a regional celebration, as we called it, in which we filled the largest church available and I preached on the need to move out of a maintenance mode and into mission in the power of the Spirit.

Could we adopt a similar strategy nationally for the millennium and beyond? There was immense strength in working simultaneously. We were well served by our evangelist trainer Geoff Shattock, whose expertise is in enabling the Church to become a mission agency. We did not, however, prescribe how individual churches should organise their programme.

If we add to this a commitment to the worldwide task through the imaginative schemes of many societies like the Baptist Missionary Society, and encourage the widest exposure of the greatest number to the varieties of opportunity, we shall be renewed for the mission task. Every young minister and church leader should be encouraged to spend at least three months during their early years of ministry in an overseas church in the developing world. Perhaps this should even be a requirement for their early years. It would transform their attitude to their task and enrich their service in Britain as well as their understanding of God and His present activity in the world today.

Fresh expectations for the Spirit

For all that we have known of the movement of the Spirit over the past 35 years, I am convinced that God still has much more to show us. The present renewal depends too much on human enthusiasm and too little on the Holy Spirit. At the start we made far too much of the minor matters of tongues, prophecies and the like. Now we have almost lost sight of them altogether. There are still a few occasions when one hears what could be described as a song in the Spirit that cannot be rationally understood but which communicates a fresh moment of worship by the beauty of its sound, and then quietly subsides into a profound silence. We should stir up these little gifts in our midst to enjoy their lightly mystical qualities.

More than this, however, as we have followed the story of the impact of the Spirit on the Baptist family we have observed the flow of two cross-currents that ultimately conflict. The most obvious has been the individualistic stream focused on the ministry of one dominant leader with whatever contribution they have offered. Although the Spirit has occasionally hovered over these waters, they have usually been dangerous in attracting attention, energy and finance to the wrong centre. They have often been destructive, even of the person instigating the flow, in the grip of what seems to me to be a Messiah complex. Through their own muddled ideas or the erroneous dreams of their supporters or sometimes their spouse, they have come to believe that theirs is the unique work to initiate the great revival preceding the returning Lord. This promise always flatters only to deceive, and the future does not lie with greater individualism or even in ever more exotic personal spiritual experiences for many people.

The other current is the integrational flow, which regards the desire to encapsulate our understanding of the activities of the Spirit within the limits of our own experience as something of a spiritual cul-de-sac. The ultimate ambition of the Spirit is to do more than this through revealing to us the potential of greater union with God in Trinity. 'For through Christ we both have access to the Father by one Spirit' (Ephesians 2:18).

Where this is pursued the renewal becomes a major synthesising force, bringing fresh vigour and inspiring new life wherever it moves. These are the deep waters in which the Spirit is most frequently found, and many Churches rejoice in all the fresh discoveries the Spirit brings. The setting for this is not the whole story of the renewal among Baptists in recent days. It is a major motivating factor for a large number in the context of the history, traditions, structures and doctrines of the whole. The Spirit knows nothing of narrow sectarianism. Whenever the Spirit shows us others under the imprint of Christ, there he renews our grace, our love, and our fellowship. Here he has other surprises for us. Being blessed by the Spirit, we grow in graciousness and in the God of all grace. Thus we may begin to discover what it means for the whole Church to be really renewed, fully charismatic, and truly Christian.

Notes

Chapter 1 Roots by the Stream

1. F.A. Sullivan, 'Catholic Church Renewal', in S.M. Burgess and G. McGee (eds), *Dictionary of Pentecostal and Charismatic Movements*, Zondervan Publishing House, Grand Rapids, Michigan, 1993, p. 111.
2. D.B. Barrett, 'A Survey of the Twentieth-century Pentecostal Charismatic Renewal in the Holy Spirit with its Goal of World Evangelisation', ibid., p. 812.
3. P. Hocken, *Streams of Renewal*, Paternoster Press, Exeter, 1986, p. 184.
4. Ibid., pp. 79 and 117.
5. Michael C. Harper, *None can Guess*, Hodder & Stoughton, London, 1971, p. 60.
6. Paul Beasley-Murray and Alan Wilkinson, *Turning the Tide: An Assessment of Baptist Church Growth*, Bible Society, London, 1981, and Peter Brierley, *Christian England: What the English Church Survey Reveals*, Marc Europe, London, 1991.
7. H. Leon McBeth, *The Baptist Heritage: Four Centuries of Baptist Witness*, Broadman Press, Nashville, Tennessee, 1987, p. 520.
8. Report of the Panel on Doctrine, *The Charismatic Movement within the Church of Scotland*, Edinburgh, 1974.
9. Ibid., p. 4.
10. Paul Fiddes, *Charismatic Renewal – A Baptist View Commentary*, Baptist Publications, London, 1980, p. 8.
11. *The Charismatic Movement in the Church of England*, Church Information Office, London, 1981, p. 2.
12. Robert Gordon, *What is Renewal?*, Gear Monograph no. 2, 1979.
13. Kilian McDonnell, *Presence, Power and Praise*, Liturgical Press, Collegeville, Minn., 1980.
14. Michael Eaton, *Baptism with the Spirit: The Teaching of Dr Martyn Lloyd Jones*, IVP, Leicester, 1989, p. 125.
15. T.A. Smail, *Reflected Glory*, Hodder & Stoughton, London, 1975, p. 37.
16. Ibid., p. 142.
17. Ibid., p. 141.

18. M.T. Kelsey, *Speaking with Tongues: An Experiment in Spiritual Experience*, Epworth Press, London, p. 6. 'They believe that the same life and vitality which was found in the apostolic church can be experienced now, and that speaking in tongues is the outward and visible sign of this new life.'

19. C. Gordon Strachan, *The Pentecostal Theology of Edward Irving*, Darton, Longman & Todd, London, 1974, p. 21.

20. H.C. Whitley, *Blinded Eagle*, SCM, London, 1955, pp. 28ff.

21. Arnold Dallimore, *The Life of Edward Irving, Forerunner of the Charismatic Movement*, Banner of Truth, London, 1983.

22. Columba Graham Flegg, *Gathered under the Apostles: A Study of the Catholic Apostolic Church*, Clarendon Press, Oxford, 1992, pp. 62ff.

23. W. Hollenweger, *The Pentecostals*, SCM, London, 1972, p. 26.

24. Ibid., p. 26.

25. W.Y. Fullerton, *F.B. Meyer: A Biography*, Marshall, Morgan & Scott, London, 1929.

26. W. Graham Scroggie, 'What is the Baptism in the Spirit?' *Bethesda Record*, July 1912.

Chapter 2 Roots Below – Fruits Above

1. William Martin, *The Billy Graham Story – Prophet with Honour*, Hutchinson, London, 1991 p. 178. 'On the second evening snow and rain kept the crowd a bit below capacity, but on not more than two or three nights of the remaining twelve weeks did a single spot in the twelve-thousand-seat arena go unfilled. On weekends, extra services were scheduled to accommodate the overflow.'

2. Douglas Johnson, *Contending for the Faith: A History of the Evangelical Movement in the Universities and Colleges*, IVP, Leicester, 1979.

3. Martin, op. cit., p. 185.

4. D. Martyn Lloyd Jones, *Preaching and Preachers*, Hodder & Stoughton, London, 1971, p. 525.

5. A. Hastings, *A History of English Christianity, 1920–1990*, SCM, London, 1991, p. 456.

6. I. Murray, *D.M. Lloyd Jones: The Fight of Faith*, Banner of Truth, London, 1990, p. 369.

7. J.E. Orr, *The Second Evangelical Awakening*, Marshall, Morgan & Scott, London, popular edition, 1955, p. 142.

8. Hocken, *Streams of Renewal*, p. 119.

9. Ibid., p. 87.

10. I. Murray, op. cit., p. 475.

11. D.C.K. Watson, *You are my God*, Hodder & Stoughton, 1983, p. 58.

12. J.R.W. Stott, *The Baptism and Fullness of the Holy Spirit*, IVP, London, 1964.

13. I am indebted to Henry Tyler for this information.

14. R.W. Thomson, *The Story of the TerJubilee of the Baptist Union*, BUGBI, 1964.

15. W.M.S. West, *To be a Pilgrim: A Memoir of Ernest A. Payne*, Lutterworth Press, Guildford, 1983.

16. E.A. Payne and Stephen Winward, *Orders and Prayers for Christian Worship*, Carey Kingsgate Press, London, 1960.

17. Ibid.

18. S.F. Winward, *The Reformation of our Worship*, Carey Kingsgate Press, London, 1964.

19. Payne and Winward, op. cit., p. xii.

20. Lesslie Newbigin, *The Household of God*, SCM, London, 1953, p. 96.

21. Henry P. Van Dusen, *Life*, 44, 9 June 1958, 'The Third Force in Christendom'.

22. Nils Bloch-Hoell, *The Pentecostal Movement*, Allen & Unwin, 1964. For Dr Payne's perceptions it is interesting to see his book review in the *Baptist Times*, 12 November 1964: 'Some 12 years ago in the Kerr Lectures, Bishop Lesslie Newbigin urged that the Catholic–Protestant debate needed to be supplemented from the standpoint of those Christians whose emphasis is on the experienced power and presence of the Holy Spirit. He called this the "Pentecostal angle" and, while admitting the errors and distortions that have sometimes characterised those whose churchmanship is of this type, argued that it must be taken seriously in any adequate doctrine of the Church.'

    Noting that two Pentecostal churches had now joined the WCC, Payne goes on to affirm that 'Nils Bloch-Hoell is a distinguished theological lecturer and editor'. He concludes his favourable review thus: 'The Pentecostal denominations are developing into free churches. A better knowledge of them is desirable, and to that end this book will make an important contribution.'

23. P. Rowntree Clifford, 'The Place of Feeling in Religious Awareness', *Canadian Journal of Theology*, xiv, 4, 1968.

24. The booklet *Liberty in the Lord* was published by the BRF in 1964, having been approved by their conference in 1963. It was subtitled 'Comments on Trends in Baptist Thought', and was co-

authored by Theo M. Bamber, B. Hugh Butt, A. Morgan Derham, John Eaton, R. Michael Frost, Philip Jones, Geoffrey R. King, David Kingdon, Edward Kirk, Leslie Larwood, Ronald Luland, Samuel Nash, I.J.W. Oakley, Harold Owen, T.A. Steen and Herbert Ward. At the time of their writing, they were all accredited Baptist ministers (BRF Trade Agents CK Press, London, 1964).

25. I am indebted to George Beasley-Murray for this information.
26. Conversations with Harold Owen and Henry Tyler.
27. J. Robinson, *Honest to God*, SCM, London, 1964.
28. David Wilkerson, *The Cross and the Switchblade*, Bernard Geiss Associates, New York, 1963.

Chapter 3 Like a Tree Planted by the Streams

1. P. Hocken, *Streams of Renewal*, pp. 62–4.
2. M.C. Harper, *None can Guess*, Hodder & Stoughton, London, 1971, p. 22.
3. Hocken, op. cit., p. 86.
4. Ibid., p. 116.
5. Harper, op. cit., p. 57.
6. M.C. Harper, *Prophecy – A Gift for the Body of Christ*, privately published by Michael Harper, 1964.
7. Hocken, op. cit., p. 122.
8. Murray, op. cit., p. 480.
9. Hocken, op. cit., p. 122. J.D. Pawson also confirms the details concerning his own contact with Harry Greenwood.
10. Michael Harper's *Newsletter* no. 4, July 1964.
11. *Renewal* 21, June/July 1969.
12. Hocken, op. cit., p. 96.
13. These ministers' meetings were a veritable lifeline at the time for those who came. They grew in size from time to time to include Richard Leighton, an Elim minister from Coatbridge, Keith Edwards of the Church of Scotland and Iona Community, Glasgow, and others less frequently. The same group were responsible for organising the Motherwell meetings for David du Plessis, Arthur Wallis, Dennis Bennett and James Brown, as well as the Jean Stone meeting. They also formed a singing group, and found that the Scottish churches that were resistant to a new teaching enjoyed a new song.
14. Clason Memorial Church, Motherwell, magazine, vol 1, no. 9, May 1964.

15. Gilbert Kirby, '300 Years after – The Pentecostal Churches', *Crusade*, September 1962.
16. J. Hywel Davies, 'The New Pentecostalism', *Crusade*, January 1964.
17. J.R.W. Stott, *The Baptist and Fulness of the Holy Spirit – An Explanation and an Exhortation*, IVF, London, 1964.
18. Godfrey Robinson, 'The Power of the Spirit', *Baptist Times*, 11 June 1964.
19. Archbishop Coggan, 'Don't neglect the Pentecostals', *Baptist Times*, 5 November 1964.
20. *Renewal*, 1 January 1966. Also *Voice*, January 1966.
21. *Baptist Times*, January 1965.
22. Hocken, op. cit., p. 40.
23. *The Christian Newspaper*, 3 December 1965.
24. M. Harper, *Newsletter* 4, July 1964: 'We feel called to serve every section of the church without fear or favour'. Contrast the BRF *Bulletin* 87, April/June 1966: 'Baptist and Church merger in Ceylon'. The editorial comment declares: 'The above article indicates some of the issues we ourselves would have to face if our denomination decided to enter negotiations with others towards some kind of union scheme.'
25. E.A. Payne, *The Baptist Union – A Short History*, Carey Kingsgate Press, London, 1959. The *Baptist Times*, 3 November 1960, on the unveiling of the plaque commemorating the calling of the council of the British Council of Churches for the first time: 'This chamber is the home of the BCC – Dr Geoffrey Fisher.'
26. *Baptists and Unity* (Baptist Union Report), March 1967.
27. *Baptists and Unity*, p. 30.
28. Murray, op. cit., p. 531.
29. Murray, op. cit., p. 522.
30. *The Christian and Christianity Today*, no. 5040, 21 October 1966.
31. Baptist Union Annual Report, 1966.
32. The Minutes Book of the General Purposes Committee of the Baptist Union, 1967.

Chapter 4 A Day of Good News?

1. *Renewal*, 1. For the details regarding the Baptist ministers, I am indebted to the Revd W. Gordon Thomas.
2. *Renewal*, 9, June/July 1967.
3. I retained a complete list of all attenders at this conference.
4. Arnold Bittlinger, *Gifts and Graces – A Commentary on 1 Corinthians 12–14*, Hodder & Stoughton, London, 1967.

5. A. Morgan Derham, 'Talking Point' in *The Christian*, 10 December 1965.

6. Douglas Ross, 'A Movement of the Holy Spirit?', *Scottish Baptist*, August 1968. He comments that the speakers were Arthur Wallis, Dennis Bennett, David du Plessis, 'a Pentecostalist minister who roams the world sharing his faith and hope with the older denominations and leaders of the World Council of Churches'.

7. *Baptists for Unity*, Reynolds Press, Coventry, 1968. Prepared by Michael Taylor with Robert Brown, Peter Coleman, Roger Nunn and Donald Smith.

8. Walter Bottom's review of *Baptists at the Crossroads* by David Kingdon, *Baptist Times*, 29 February 1968. The review brought forth further correspondence in subsequent editions showing the sharpness of the issues, including letters from S. Voke, R.S. Luland, J.C. Beyer, K.L. Savage and S.L. Henderson Smith.

9. *The Christian and Christianity Today*, 21 June 1968.

10. See the Baptist Union Annual Report for 1969.

11. *Baptist Times*, 27 November 1969 and also 15 January 1970 for the letter from T.M. Bamber, chairman of the BRF. It should be remembered that when Bamber was questioned about the BRF at its start in 1938, he affirmed that this organisation was for all, not just for fundamentalists: 'All are wanting revival, not just fundamentalists.' I am indebted to Dr G.R. Beasley-Murray for this recollection.

12. This judgement is that of the author alone, but based upon such statements as are found in the 'To Be a Pilgrim' memoir by W.M.S. West, p. 203.

13. These findings are from the notes supplied by Dr D.S. Russell, who became general secretary of the Baptist Union in 1967.

14. *Baptist Times* report, 22 January 1970, under the title 'Wanted – A Strategy for Mission' by Dr G.R. Beasley-Murray.

15. *Ministry Tomorrow – Report of the Commission on Ministry 1969*, Baptist Union of Great Britain and Ireland, 1969. The chairman was the Revd N.B. Jones, and L.W.J. Angell, N.D. McLeod and the Revds W.G. Channon, N. Clark, G.C. Robinson and Dr W.M.S. West also served.

16. London Baptist Association Annual Report for 1970.

17. This information is from Dr D.S. Russell, who invited J.D. Pawson to the denominational conference.

18. In the full text of the address given by Michael H. Taylor, there is little doubt that his understanding of the humanity of Jesus leaves no room for an understanding of his deity that the Christian Church has always regarded as being essential Christian

doctrine, e.g. 'God then is transcendent, he is different, but he is in this world, always active and active everywhere – and there is nothing special about this Jesus in this respect. God is present in this human life as he is present in all human life. God was there in Palestine 2000 years ago, and he is present in the western world of the twentieth century.' It is one of the great ironies of Baptist life that this address, which more than any other single event was to polarise and divide the denomination as never before in this generation, was heard with rapt attention, and when it was completed was given a standing ovation by the congregation.

19. See notes from Dr D.S. Russell.
20. Baptist Union Annual Report 1971. Godfrey C. Robinson died on 16 June 1971, aged 57.
21. *Renewal*, 34, September 1971.
22. Fountain Trust archives for 1971.
23. *Renewal*, September 1971, and Fountain Trust archives, 1971.
24. The minute book of the Advisory Committee on Church Relations for September 1971.

Chapter 5 *Contending for the Faith*

1. *Signs of Hope – An Examination of the Numerical and Spiritual State of the Churches in Membership with the Baptist Union of GB*, received by the council in March 1979, Baptist Union, London, 1979. The members of the working group were J.H.Y. Briggs, P.N. Clark, Mrs C.C. Morgan, Dr D.F.G. Pusey, Mrs M. Warwick, Revd D. Cranefield, F. Goodwin, W.C.R. Hancock, W.V. Thompson, Mrs N. Alexander, Dr E.A. Payne, Dr D.S. Russell and Dr W.M.S. West.
2. *Renewal*, 34. The quote about the coming of age of the movement was attributed to Dr James Dunn.
3. *Renewal*, 89. The executive committee with the trustees announced on 1 September that all the activities of the trust would cease at the end of the year.
4. The Yorkshire Baptist Association issued an undated report entitled *The House Church Movement*, which makes this point clear. With the focus in Yorkshire being on the church associated with the work of Bryn Jones and his Bradford fellowship, the YBA would have been affected by their strong restorationist teaching. The report wrongly states that the house church movement is a product of the current charismatic renewal, but this is not an accurate assessment.

5. A.M. Ramsey and L.J. Suenans, *The Future of the Christian Church*, SCM, London, 1970.

6. The minute book of the council of the Baptist Union for this period, 1971, 1972, 1973.

7. The unpublished script of the address by Michael Taylor entitled 'The Incarnate Presence: How much of a man was Jesus Christ.'

8. I am grateful to Dr W.M.S. West for this recollection.

9. The minutes of the council of the Baptist Union.

10. Report in the *Baptist Times*, October 1971, on the meeting in Bloomsbury Chapel on 2 October 1971.

11. The paper was entitled *The Christological controversy in the Baptist Union*. It was privately published by Dr G.R. Beasley-Murray and sent to all accredited ministers. In sending this, Dr Beasley-Murray included a letter of explanation. He had intended the paper to be an article in the *Baptist Times* but the editor had closed discussion on the matter. He declined to re-open it. Shortly afterwards, Beasley-Murray was ill and in hospital, but felt nevertheless that the article should be available to others, his reason being that he was being constantly asked about the matter. He also felt that those who held a similar position to his own were being seriously misunderstood as if they were the holders of an outdated right-wing theology, whereas a progressive theology took account of the realities of our time.

12. The addendum to the council statement reads: 'This Council declares that, whilst asserting and cherishing its special affinities with those of the evangelical tradition, our denomination has always claimed a place in the one holy universal Church and desires the closest possible fellowship with all who love and trust our Lord Jesus Christ. Not only is it characterised by evangelistic and missionary zeal; it possesses a treasured heritage of liberty of opinion and utterance, and since the seventeenth century has shared in the struggle for religious toleration and the freeing of men's minds and consciences from intellectual and civil fetters. Accordingly, the Union has always contained in its fellowship those of different theological opinions and emphases, believing that its claims for toleration involves toleration and mutual respect within its own ranks.'

13. This statement is contained in a letter to the general secretary of the Baptist Union.

14. Council report for 1971, Appendix 9.

15. Report in *The Times* by Clifford Longley.

16. Cardinal Leon Joseph Suenens, *A New Pentecost* (Darton, Longman & Todd, London, 1975).

17. L.J. Suenans, *A New Pentecost*, xii: 'Why are you a man of hope? I am an optimist because I believe that the Holy Spirit is the Spirit of creation. . . . I believe in the surprises of the Holy Spirit.'

18. *Renewal*, 94: 'Renewal welcomed into the heart of the Church'. A report relating to the Catholic charismatic leaders' conference held in the Vatican in the presence of the Pope John Paul II, a cardinal, 15 bishops, 180 priests and 330 lay people. 'Now is the time to move from the periphery to the centre.'

19. Michael Harper, *A New Way of Living – How the Church of the Redeemer found a New Lifestyle*, Hodder & Stoughton, London, 1973.

20. Michael Harper wrote in the foreword of *Gathered for Power* that the story of what was happening in Houston was a miracle of the highest order. In 1972 the magazine *Guideposts* awarded the Church of the Redeemer their annual award, 'To a Church reborn'. CBS gave the church an hour-long documentary which was subsequently on hire as a film from the Fountain Trust. It was called *Following the Spirit*.

21. *A New Way of Living*, p. 12.

22. *Renewal*, 45.

23. Letter from J.D. Pawson to Michael Harper, 29 July 1971: 'As I sat in the conference I found myself thinking how appropriate a series of Bible studies in depth of Galatians would have been. . . . So there's a suggestion for a future conference.'

24. E. Sullivan, SA, *Can the Pentecostal Movement renew the Churches?*, British Council of Churches, SE/35, vol. viii, no. 4, 1972. In giving a cautious affirmative to the question, Sullivan quotes from an article by Paul Rowntree Clifford that first appeared in the *Canadian Journal of Theology*, vol. XIV, 1968: 'Whatever the theological deficiencies and uncontrolled enthusiasms, it does seem to have rung a bell in the hearts of a host of people to whom traditional churchmanship has made no appeal. . . . It constitutes a challenge of the first importance to any Christian thinking about renewal.'

25. *Renewal*, 46, report by Emmanuel Sullivan.

26. Pagaard's itinerary as printed in the first Baptist Church Chula Vista newsletter entitled 'Our Life Together'. May 1975 included visits to Kingfield, Woking (Philip Greenslade); Woking (Harold Owen); Thrapstone (K. Humphries); Guildford (J.D. Pawson); Dunstable (S. Jebb) and Brandhall (J. Bedford).

27. *Renewal*, 64.

Chapter 6 Teaching and Integrity

1. T.A. Smail, *The Forgotten Father*, Hodder & Stoughton, London, 1979, p. 15.

2. T.A. Smail, *Reflected Glory*, Hodder & Stoughton, London, 1975, p. 22.

3. An early example of Smail's approach is found in the report on his first visit to America, after his appointment as general secretary to the Fountain Trust, as contained in *Renewal*, 46. He records his experience of the 'emerging breed of Pentecostal personalities followed by adulating crowds and tempted into eccentric exhibitionalism and sensational miracle mongering'.

4. *Theological Renewal*, 1, October 1975 editorial entitled 'The Theology of Renewal and the Renewal of Theology': 'We need to think hard about what God has done for us so that we can see it scripturally and to see it whole.'

5. The night school courses opened in the autumn of 1975. They began with a leadership training course which was held at Millmead, Guildford.

6. *Renewal*, 53.

7. *Renewal*, 64: 'Are we Downhearted?'

8. *Gospel and Spirit*, a joint statement prepared and agreed by a group nominated by the Fountain Trust and the Church of England Evangelical Council. The group comprised J. Baker, C. Buchanan, J. Collins, I. Cunday, M. Harper, R. Johnston, B. Kayes, G. Landreth, R. Nixon, J. Packer, H. Parks, G. Reid, T. Smail, J. Stott, T. Walker, R. Turvey and D. Watson (The Fountain Trust and the Church of England Evangelical Council, Esher, 1977).

9. *Renewal*, 82.

10. Andrew Walker, *Restoring the Kingdom – The Radical Christianity of the House Church Movement*, Hodder & Stoughton, London, 1985, p. 50.

11. *Renewal*, 52. In this copy there are two articles, the first written by David Watson urging a policy of patience and staying within the historic Churches, the second by Arthur Wallis urging a willingness to explore new Church structures and a total disbelief about historic Churches.

12. *Renewal*, 52, p. 16.

13. Arthur Wallis, *The Radical Christian*, Kingsway, Eastbourne, 1981, p. 8.

14. A. Walker, *Restoring the Kingdom*, pp. 50ff.

15. Nigel Wright, *The Radical Kingdom – Restoration in Theory and Practice*, Kingsway, Eastbourne, 1986. Nigel Wright argues that

restoration is another development of the same movement that has produced the continental Anabaptists, the Moravians, the Puritans, the English Baptists, the early Quakers, the Brethren in Christ, the Disciples of Christ, the Plymouth Brethren and the Pentecostals. In a similar vein, we also note Adrian Hastings in his *History of English Christianity 1920–1990*, SCM, London, p 520: 'Through the development of House Churches, the Charismatic Movement has become a major source for a new sectarianism. A "born-again" Congregationalism which was long part of English religion but had, prior to this new arrival, seemed outside of the black community, to be not far off its last legs.'

16. J. Steven, *Worship in Restoration Churches*, Grove Worship Series Booklets no. 110, Grove Books Ltd, Bramcote.

17. J.D. Pawson so described the restorationists in personal conversation with me. His view is born out by Andrew Walker in *Restoring the Kingdom*, p. 128: 'The Church is the cutting edge of the Kingdom or the hardened tip of the arrow. The Church leads and the Kingdom follows.'

18. Letter to Michael Harper from Harold Owen, 29 December 1970: 'Men like myself seeking to witness to the Pentecostal experience in an evangelical church are constantly accused of being "unsound". When one's critics learn of the FT conference and its public rallies in Guildford, they will delight in making mincemeat of us once again. Really, brother, you have landed some of us in great difficulty.' In reply, Harper rebutted the claim that Leslie Davison had rejected the substitutionary doctrine of the atonement.

19. Derek Tidball, 'The Challenge of Restorationism – A Critical Reflection', an unpublished paper. He quotes with approval the more conservative estimates of the total membership of Andrew Walker at 34,000.

20. This is a personal judgement made on the grounds of my experience as general superintendent of the metropolitan area of the Baptist Union. The remedy to this is in a theological clarification of the meaning of accreditation. See my *Baptist Times* article, 'Making the Most of Accreditation', *Baptist Times*, 17 January 1991.

21. The mission kits referred to were available from the Mission Department of the Baptist Union.

22. The Baptist Union Annual report for 1976, presented to the Assembly in 1977, recorded that the council had agreed to support the initiative that came as the fruit of a coalition between the Billy Graham Evangelistic Association, the Evangelical

Alliance, the British Council of Churches and the Baptist Union. They agreed together that 'the time is ripe for a concerted national effort', and representatives of these bodies met together at Lambeth Palace at the invitation of the archbishop of Canterbury, Dr Donald Coggan.

23. BU annual report, 1980. See also, Roger Whitehead and Amy Sneddon, *An Unwanted Child?*, BCC/CCBI, London, 1990. Note the presence of the Revds T. Houston, D.S. Russell, J.D. Pawson, L. Misselbrook and D. McBain at various stages of discussion.

24. *Baptist Times*, 25 November 1971.

25. *Baptist Times*, 23 November 1972.

26. *The Times*, 5 March 1973.

27. For examples, see *The Charismatic Movement within the Church of Scotland*, report of the Panel of Doctrine, May 1974; 'The Charismatic Renewal – Impressions from a World Survey Study', *Encounter*, vol. XI, no. 4, WCC 1975; The Scottish Baptist Union statement of the Inter-Church Relations Committee on the charismatic movement for May 1973; the report on the charismatic movement by the Faith and Order Committee at the Methodists' Conference, 1974. The Church of England report entitled 'The Charismatic Movement in the Church of England' was first published in 1981.

28. *Baptist Times*, June/July 1975. A series of four articles was written by me on the disputed theme of baptism in the Spirit and published in June/July 1975. The fifth article was added by request. My understanding was that baptism in the Spirit is part of normal Christian initiation, enriched by a deeper understanding and expectation of the coming of the Spirit, and best located in believers' baptism but not totally identified with that sacrament. The fifth article argued against a new group of churches that restorationist were advocating, and urged a positive attitude within the denomination.

29. Paul Fiddes, *Charismatic Renewal – A Baptist View*. The working group that produced the report comprised D. Mackenzie, E. Heddle, G. Ruling, J. Briggs, D.D. Black, H. Logan, and Dr D.S. Russell.

30. *Renewal*, 82, 'Where the Shoe Pinches', by Dr D.S. Russell. This article was written from Dr Russell's observations on charismatic renewal at a consultation called by the British Council of Churches and the Fountain Trust. As a senior denominational leader, Dr Russell was asked to respond and gave what he describes as five blunt guidelines to charismatics: 1, not to be

odd, a race apart; 2, not to be a new denomination; 3, to work within church frameworks; 4, to thank God for the gifts they have but take care in their use; 5, to show the difference between authority and authoritarianism. He particularly warned against intolerance, loss of denominational loyalty and authoritarianism.

31. See Baptist Union annual report 1976.
32. *Signs of Hope* report.
33. See letter from Dr D. Tidball: 'I am so glad you have challenged both the form of the Assembly and the direction of the denomination. I write to thank you and to assure you of my prayers and backing at this time,' 19 April 1977.
34. At least one representative was invited to this meeting from each denominational area by a letter from Dr R. Brown: 'I have long felt that an immense amount could be achieved in the light of the denomination, if Baptist evangelicals could come to a similar experience to that of their Anglican evangelical friends in 1967 when they committed themselves to serve in the life of their denominations. The main purpose being of an exploratory nature to discern whether other evangelicals in the denomination share our main vision.'
35. The introductory leaflet said that Mainstream was composed of 'people who see themselves standing in the mainstream of Christian life in general and Baptist life in particular. Believing that our denomination is on the verge of one of the most exciting periods of its life, the aim of Mainstream is to encourage, co-ordinate, publicise and support every venture that will lead to further life and growth within the Baptist Union of Great Britain and Ireland and to give wholehearted commitment to the Gospel as expressed in the Union's declaration of principle and also to the life and work of the denomination.'
36. *Baptist Times*, 3 May 1979.
37. *Crusade*, June 1979.
38. Dr W.M.S. West in a letter written as incoming Baptist Union president to Patrick Goodland, 4 April 1979.
39. *Baptist Times*, 7 February 1980. Story written by M. Caddick.
40. *The Call to Commitment – Baptist Christians through the 1980s.* Prepared by Dr D.S. Russell for presentation to the Baptist Union council and the Annual Assembly in the spring of 1980. The commitment was to be to worship and prayer evangelism, learning, caring, serving and releasing for leadership
41. Donald McGavran, *Understanding Church Growth*, Eerdmans, Grand Rapids, Mich., 1970.
42. T. Houston was the chairman of the Evangelical Alliance working

group called 'Let my People Grow'. They declared that their goal was to treble the number of convinced Christians in the country by 1980, and to have at least 5 per cent active and informed Christians in every segment of society. Houston gained the support of the Bible Society for his thoughts, and the Bible Society thus opened up a department dealing with church growth matters.

Chapter 7 *Christ's Power in Weakness*

1. *Crusade*, January 1982. A report on a controversial address by J.D. Pawson given at Leeds Town Hall on the opening night of a tour by BYFC, 'Let God Speak'. He also referred to the need for baptism in this address: 'It's not a matter of choosing dogmatically between infant and adult baptism. What we are to do is to ask God if we are baptised in his sight.'
2. J. Wimber, 'Signs and Wonders Today: "Zip to 3,000 in 5 years"', *Signs and Wonders Today: a Christian Life Compilation*, *Christian Life*, Wheaton, Illinois, 1982, p. 20.
3. *Renewal*, 162. J. Noble, 'Revival on the Way'; C. Urquhart, 'The 90s will be a decade of revival'.
4. P. Brierley, *Christian England*, Marc Europe, London, 1991, p. 60.
5. Martyn Percy, 'Fundamentalism and Wimber: Signs, Wonders and Church Growth', an unpublished PhD thesis, 1993. Also, J. Gunstone, *Signs and Wonders: The Wimber Phenomenon*, Darton, Longman & Todd Daybreak, London, 1989, pp. 3–4.
6. J. Gunstone, *Signs and Wonders*, p. 8.
7. K. Springer (ed.), *Riding the Third Wave – What comes after Renewal?* Marshall-Pickering, Basingstoke, p. 46.
8. Springer, op. cit., p. 64.
9. Percy, op. cit.
10. *Renewal*, 152, N. Wright.
11. J. Wimber letter to R. Pointer, then of the Bible Society, September 1981, and copied to the author. The purpose of his tour: '1, to teach and to train; 2, to demonstrate; 3 to impart. Our aim is to teach and demonstrate the miraculous ministry of Jesus, to pray that this same ministry will be imparted to those who are hungry for it.'
12. A. Toffler, *Third Wave*, Pan, London, 1980.
13. D. McBain, *Discerning the Spirits*, Marshall-Pickering, Basingstoke, 1992, p. 181.

14. M. Percy, *Words, Works and Power – Understanding Contemporary Fundamentalism and Revivalism*, SPCK, London, 1996, pp. 14–15.
15. J. Wimber and K. Springer, *Power Healing*, Hodder & Stoughton, London, 1986, p. 15.
16. Springer, op. cit., p. 26.
17. J. Wimber, *Signs and Wonders and Church Growth*, Vineyard Ministries International, Placentia, Calif., 1984, section 5.8.
18. J.D. Douglas (ed.), *The New International Dictionary of the Christian Church*, article on 'The Enlightenment' by Wayne Detzhe, Paternoster, Exeter, 1974, p. 343.
19. Wimber and Springer, op. cit., p. 89.
20. Springer, op. cit., pp. 20ff.
21. S. Hunt, 'The Anglican Wimberites', *Pneuma: The Journal of the Society for Pentecostal Studies*, vol. 17, no. 1, spring 1995, p. 106.
22. *Power Evangelism*, p. 28.
23. Ibid., p. 18.
24. Ibid., p. 33.
25. Heard first uttered by Wimber in a pre-Third Wave conference in Holy Trinity, Brompton, June 1984. This conference was hastily arranged by me because the Anglicans who became involved in the Third Wave conference were uncertain as to the extent of Anglican support for it. Wimber and his team came over early for this purpose, but Wimber was unhappy to do so.
26. *Power Evangelism*, p. 142.
27. Ibid., p. 135.
28. Ibid., p. 146.
29. T.A. Smail, A. Walker, N. Wright, *Charismatic Renewal: The Search for a Theology*, SPCK, London, 1993, p. 72.
30. *Power Evangelism*, p. 55.
31. D. McBain, *Discerning the Spirits*, p. 181.
32. *Renewal*, 184, September 1991: J. Wimber on 'Revival Fire'.
33. Ibid.
34. *Renewal*, 234, 1995.
35. Ibid.
36. T.A. Smail et al., op. cit., is a cautious example.
37. D. McBain, *Discerning the Spirits*.
38. *Power Evangelism*, p. 55.
39. P. Jensen and T. Payne, *John Wimber, Friend or Foe? An Examination of the Current Teaching of the Vineyard Ministries Movement*, Reprint from *The Briefing*, St Matthias Press, London, April 1990, pp. 11ff.
40. Smail et al., op. cit., p. 76. The rhetoric exceeds the reality.
41. Ibid., p. 76.

42. J. Wimber, 'Prophetic Practice', *Alpha*, October 1990.
43. Ibid.
44. D. McBain, op. cit., p. 188.
45. *Renewal*, 234, November 1995.
46. Wimber and Springer, *Power Healing*, p. 221.
47. M. Percy, *Words, Wonders and Power*, p. 149.
48. *Baptist Times*, 8 September 1994: 'The Toronto Blessing'.
49. Wimber and Springer, op. cit., p. 147. See also M. Percy, op. cit., p. 88, 'Wimber's Christology is subordinational'.
50. A. Kinnear, *Against the Tide: The Story of Watchman Nee*, Victory Press, Eastbourne, 1974, pp. 134–5.
51. T.A. Smail, 'The Love of Power', *The Anvil*, vol. 4, no. 3, 1989.

Chapter 8 Fire, Water and Abundance

1. B.R. White, *Opening our Doors to God*, Mainstream Booklets 1, Morleys, Ilkestone, 1980, p. 16.
2. *Mainstream Newsletter*, 7, April 1981.
3. D.S. Russell, *Call to Commitment – Baptist Churches through the 80s*, presented to the Baptist Union Assembly, spring 1980.
4. Douglas McBain, *No Gentle Breeze – Baptist Churchmanship and the Winds of Change*, Mainstream Booklets, p. 17.
5. Mainstream executive notes, Swanwick postbag, 1982.
6. *Grassroots*, vol. 8, no. 1, Jan./Feb. 1982.
7. 'Charismatic Apostles and Baptist Superintendency Notes', an outline paper by the author, January 1982.
8. *Mainstream Newsletter*, 10 April 1982.
9. *Mainstream Newsletter*, 9 January 1982.
10. Keith Hodson (ed.), *The Believers' Church – An Introduction to Radical Discipleship Themes*. Articles by Douglas McBain, Nigel Wright, T.M. Huck, Geoff and Kate King, Mike Wood, Heywood Bible College Publications, 1983.
11. *Mainstream Newsletter*, 13 April 1983.
12. D. McBain, *Eyes that See – The Spiritual Gift of Discernment*, Marshall-Pickering, Basingstoke, 1986, subsequently published and extended as *Discerning the Spirits – Checking for Truth in Signs and Wonders*, HarperCollins, London, 1992.
13. *Mainstream Newsletter*, 19 April 1985.
14. *Mainstream Newsletter*, 19 April 1985.
15. *Mainstream Newsletter*, 21 January 1986.
16. *Mainstream Newsletter*, 26 September 1987.
17. *Baptist Times*, 27 January 1983.

18. David Coffey, *Build that Bridge*, Kingsway, Eastbourne, 1986, pp. 17, 103.
19. D.W. Bebbington, op. cit., p. 268.
20. B. Haymes, *A Question of Identity – Reflections on Baptist Principles and Practice*, Yorkshire Baptist Association, 1986.
21. *A Perspective on Baptist Identity*, Mainstream, 1987. The contributors were D. Tidball, B. White, A. Campbell, N. Wright, M. Nicholls, S. Ibbotson and G.R. Beasley-Murray.
22. *Mainstream Newsletter*, 23 April 1989.
23. Nigel Wright, 'Wellspring: A Proposal for a Network'. A discussion paper written for a team of co-operating ministers and a network of autonomous churches dedicated to the renewal of the Church, etc., 1990.
24. *Mainstream Newsletter*, 3 May 1995.

Chapter 9 Ripe for Harvest

1. S. Brady and H. Rowdon (eds), *For Such a Time as This – Perspectives on Evangelicalism, Past, Present and Future*, Scripture Union, London, 1996, p. 180.
2. Ibid.
3. I. Randall, an unpublished paper, 'New Directions in Spiritual Unity', p. 22.
4. J.D. Pawson, *On the Other Side: The Report of the Evangelical Alliance Commission on Evangelism*, Scripture Union, London, 1968, p. 169.
5. Brady and Rowdon, op. cit., p. 188.
6. Randall, op. cit., p. 26.
7. Ibid., p. 27.
8. Ibid., p. 31.
9. *Renewal*, 131, April 1987.
10. Statistics were provided by the Spring Harvest office, July 1996. The *Baptist Times*, 11 January 1996, included an article by John Capon on Clive Calver.
11. Spring Harvest records.
12. *Renewal*, 215, April 1992.
13. Spring Harvest seminar notes, 1988; Spring Harvest seminar notes, 1996.
14. Letter from Peter Meadows to the author, 11 June 1996.
15. The Spring Harvest response to the Toronto blessing endorsing the results of a consultation in December 1994 by the Evangelical Alliance.

16. David Tomlinson, *The Post-evangelical*, Triangle, SPCK, London, 1995, p. 26.
17. *Renewal*, 131, April 1987.
18. H. Leon McBeth, *The Baptist Heritage – Four Centuries of Baptist Witness*, Broadman, Nashville, Tenn., 1987, p. 30.
19. Paul Fiddes, *Charismatic Renewal – A Baptist View*, Baptist Publications, London, 1980, p. 24.
20. *Baptist Times*, 18 November 1982, 'About the Father's Business', a summary of Bernard Green's council address in November 1982.
21. *Baptist Times*, April 1980, 'Bugbrooke: its life, work and witness', by Lewis Misselbrook.

Chapter 10 Times of Refreshing

1. *Renewal*, 184, September 1991: John Wimber on 'Revival Fire'.
2. 'What in the world is happening to us? A Biblical perspective on Renewal'. Notes provided by Bill Jackson, July 1994, Champaign Vineyard.
3. *Sunday Telegraph* interview with John Wimber conducted by Paul Goodman, 2 October 1994.
4. Stanley Jebb, *No Laughing Matter – The Toronto Phenomena and its Implications*, Day One Publications, Bromley, 1995, p. 8.
5. Op. cit.
6. An example of this is R.T. Kendall's review of the book *The Touch of God* by Rodney Howard-Browne, *Renewal*, 244, September 1996.
7. I have heard this defence being offered in personal conversation with Mr Howard-Browne's supporters as they have sought to justify the indefensible.
8. *Renewal*, 218, July 1994: 'Spreading like Wildfire'.
9. *Alpha*, July 1994.
10. Patrick Dixon, *Signs of Revival*, Kingsway Publications, Eastbourne, 1994, p. 34.
11. Suggested ministry tips from Champaign Vineyard: 'It is usually helpful to begin each ministry time with worship followed by testimonies of people who have been touched. Immediately after the testimony, invite the Holy Spirit to come upon the individual again and do a further work. . . . They often begin to experience the same outward manifestations again.'
12. David Hay, 'The Everyday God – Transcendence Today', an address given at the National Retreat Association conference, 1996.

13. Dixon, op. cit., p. 234.
14. Association of Vineyard Churches statements issued 13 December 1995.
15. Dixon, op. cit., p. 57.
16. Tape of Eleanor Mumford's address at Holy Trinity, Brompton, 29 May 1994.
17. *Renewal*, 173, October 1990. Letter from G. Coates, Graham Grey, Roger Forster, Lynn Green, Brian Hayes David MacInnes, Sandy Miller, John Mumford, David Pytches, Brian Skinner, Teddy Saunders, Barry Kissell, Terry Kings, Anne Watson, Rick Williams.
18. Clifford Hill, Peter Fenwick, David Forbes and Peter Noakes, *Blessing the Church – A Review of the History and Direction of the Charismatic Movement and the Impact of the Toronto Blessing*, Eagle Press, Guildford, 1995.
19. Nader Mikhaiel, *The Toronto Blessing: Slaying in the Spirit – The Telling Wonder*, (Southwood Press, Marrickville, NSW, second edition 1995, p. 330.
20. *No Laughing Matter: Toronto – The Baby and the Bathwater*, Day One Publications *The Briefing*, St Matthias Press.
21. Mark Stibbe, *Times of Refreshing – A Practical Theology of Revival for Today*, Marshall-Pickering HarperCollins, London, 1995, p. 70.
22. Rob Warner, *Prepare for Revival*, p. 146.
23. A series of articles in the *Baptist Times*, September 1994, written by Nigel Copsey, Nigel Wright, Peter Nodding, Douglas McBain and Andrew Walker.
24. A letter from Dr Alastair Campbell in response to the ministers' questionnaire.
25. Derek Tidball, *Who are the Evangelicals – Tracing the Roots of Today's Movements*, Marshall-Pickering HarperCollins, London, 1994, p. 238.

Chapter 11 Washing by the Spirit

1. Dean M. Kelley, *Why Conservative Churches are growing – A Study in the Sociology of Religion*, Harper & Row, New York, 1977, p. xxiv.
2. P. Brierley, *Christian England: What the English Church Census reveals*, Marc Europe, London, 1991, p. 92.
3. Richard J. Foster, *Celebration of Discipline: The Path to Spiritual Growth*, Hodder & Stoughton, London, 1980, and *Prayer: Finding the Heart's True Home*, Hodder & Stoughton, London, 1992.

4. *Celebrating Common Prayer: A Version of the Daily Office*, SSF, Mowbray, London, 1992.

5. *Praise in all our Days: Common Prayer at Taizé*, Mowbray, Oxford, 1981.

6. Henri Nouwen, *The Return of the Prodigal Son*, Darton, Longman & Todd, London, 1992.

7. Eleanor Kreider, *Communion shapes Character*, Herald Press, Scotsdale, Pa. (due to be published 1997).

8. J. Begbie, 'The Spirituality of Renewal Music,' *The Anvil*, vol. 8, no. 3, 1991.

9. Roger Forster, *Renewal*, 245, October 1996, 'Set the Debtors Free'.

10. *Jubilee 2000: The Debt Cutters Handbook – A Debt-free Start for a Billion People*, Jubilee 2000, 1996.

11. *Tertio Millenio Adveniente*, apostolic letter, Pope John Paul II, Catholic Truth Society, London, 1994.

12. *Who Runs the World?*, Christian Aid, November 1994; *The Global Supermarket: Britain's Biggest Shops and Food from the Third World*, Christian Aid, 28 October 1996.

13. J.R.W. Stott, *Issues facing Christians Today: A Major Appraisal of Contempory Social and Moral Questions*, Marshall-Pickering, Basingstoke, 1977.

14. *Theological Renewal* 1. October/November 1975, T.A. Smail: 'We need to think hard about what God has done for us so that we can see it scripturally and see it whole, so that we may bring every thought captive to Christ and be renewed in our minds.'

15. J.D. Pawson, *The Normal Christian Birth*, Hodder & Stoughton, London, 1989, p. 11, 'The four spiritual doors.'

16. T.A. Smail, A. Walker, N.G. Wright, *Charismatic Renewal – The Search for a Theology*, SPCK, London, 1993.

17. N.G. Wright, *The Baptist Quarterly*, vol. xxxv, no. 8, October 1994: '*Koinonia* and Baptist ecclesiology'.

18. T.A. Smail, *The Giving Gift: The Holy Spirit in Person*, Hodder & Stoughton, London, 1988, pp. 128ff.

19. Gordon D. Fee, *God's Empowering Presence*, Hendriksen, Peabody, Mass., 1994.

20. N.G. Wright, *The Radical Evangelical*, SPCK, London, 1996.

21. Bill Hybels, *Creating a Church to reach the Unchurched* (audio tapes).

22. John Finney, *Finding Faith Today: How does it happen?* BFBS, Westlea, Swindon, 1992, p. 36, 'Factors leading to faith.' 'Ministers need to be confirmed in the importance of their personal ministry and may need further training in the skills involved in this form of spiritual direction. A minister's dialogue with those

who are coming to faith is clearly so important that much in-service training is needed.'

23. David Hay, 'Religion lacking Spirit', *The Tablet*, 2 March 1996, p. 292.

Index